RESEARCH IN LAW, DEVIANCE AND SOCIAL CONTROL

A Research Annual

Editor: STEVEN SPITZER
Chairperson
Department of Sociology
Suffolk University, Boston

VOLUME 5 • 1983

 JAI PRESS INC.

Greenwich, Connecticut   *London, England*

Copyright © 1983 JAI PRESS INC.
36 Sherwood Place
Greenwich, Connecticut

JAI PRESS INC.
3 Henrietta Street
London WC2E 8LU
England

ISBN: 0-89232-334-5

Manufactured in the United States of America

Volumes 1-3 Published as: RESEARCH IN LAW AND SOCIOLOGY

CONTENTS

LIST OF CONTRIBUTORS   vii

FOREWORD
Steven Spitzer   ix

PART I.   DEVIANCE, LAW AND SOCIAL CONTROL: INTERNATIONAL AND HISTORICAL PERSPECTIVES

LAW AND THE SOVIET SECOND ECONOMY
Louise I. Shelley   3

JUVENILE DELINQUENCY IN ISRAEL 1948-1977: PATTERNS AND TRENDS
Yael Hassin   25

THE ANTI-ALIEN CONTRACT LABOR LAW OF 1885 AND "EMPLOYER SANCTIONS" IN THE 1980s
Kitty Calavita   51

WOMEN'S BODIES AS DISEASED AND DEVIANT: HISTORICAL AND CONTEMPORARY ISSUES
Alexandra Dundas Todd   83

PART II.   LAW AND JUSTICE IN CONTEMPORARY AMERICA

IMPLEMENTING PUBLIC LAW 94-142: THE EDUCATION FOR ALL HANDICAPPED CHILDREN ACT, IN THE ILLINOIS SCHOOL DISTRICT
F. James Davis and Barbara Sherman Heyl   99

URBAN REDEVELOPMENT AND PUBLIC
DRUNKENNESS IN FRESNO: A CALIFORNIA MOVE
TOWARD RECRIMINALIZATION
Richard Speiglman and Friedner D. Wittman   141

PARENTS IN PRISON: A COMPARATIVE ANALYSIS OF
THE EFFECTS OF INCARCERATION ON THE FAMILIES
OF MEN AND WOMEN
Linda Abram Koban   171

PART III.   ISSUES IN LAW, DEVIANCE
AND SOCIAL THEORY

RETHINKING DEVIANCE: TOWARD A SOCIOLOGY
OF CENSURES
Colin Sumner   187

A POLITICS WITHOUT A STATE: THE CONCEPTS
OF "STATE" AND "SOCIAL CONTROL" FROM
EUROPEAN TO AMERICAN SOCIAL SCIENCE
Dario Melossi   205

LIST OF CONTRIBUTORS

Kitty Calavita

Department of Sociology
Middlebury College
Middlebury, Vermont

F. James Davis

Department of Sociology
Illinois State University
Normal, Illinois

Yael Hassin

Institute of Criminology
Hebrew University
Jerusalem

Barbara Sherman Heyl

Department of Sociology
Illinois State University
Normal, Illinois

Linda Abrams Kobran

Community Research Center
University of Illinois
Champaign-Urbana, Illinois

Dario Melossi

School of Law
University of Bologna
Italy

Louise I. Shelley

School of Justice
American University
Washington, D.C.

Richard Speiglman   Alcohol Research Group
                                   University of California
                                   Berkeley

Colin Sumner   Institute of Criminology
                                   University of Cambridge
                                   Cambridge, England

Alexandra Dundas Todd   Department of Sociology
                                   Suffolk University
                                   Boston

Friedner D. Wittman   Prevention Research Group
                                   Medical Research Institute
                                   San Francisco

FOREWORD

This is the fifth volume in the JAI series that began as *Research in Law and Sociology* and has become, in the last two volumes, *Research in Law, Deviance and Social Control*. In this volume, as in Volume 4, there are three major foci: comparative and historical explorations of law and deviance; investigations of legal and other forms of social control in contemporary America; and theoretical problems surrounding deviance and control. Although they frequently proceed from very different assumptions and methods, all of the papers attempt in one way or another to understand how rules and rule breaking are embedded in broader problems of social organization and social change. The research and concepts described herein are thus distinguished by their focus on the context, as well as the causes and consequences, of law, deviance and social control.

Another priority influenced the fashioning of this volume: the desire to continue the critical examination of law that had begun in Volumes 1 through 4. The major features of this examination are sensitive to (1) connections between law and the spheres of politics, economics and ideology; (2) the ways in which law both emerges from and is imposed upon social conflicts; (3) the significance of law and other forms social control in the struggles of a number of status and class groups (e.g., women, the handicapped, immigrants, and "public drunks") within contemporary societies; (4) the ways in which law-making and lawbreaking are tied to the structures of societies in which they take place; and (5) the social origins and critical significance of various attempts to explain law, deviance and social control—theories which are themselves a product of the changing social meaning surrounding order, conflict and change.

Part I of this volume contains four papers concerned with the shifting relationships between deviance, law and social control over time and across cultural contexts. Two of the studies examine deviance and control in societies which combine important elements of Western and non-Western legal traditions: the Soviet Union and Israel. The remaining two contributions are devoted to an exploration of the relationship between aspects of deviance and control over the last century: in the first case with respect to legal control over immigrant groups; in the second with regard to the development of medical control over women's bodies.

In the first paper, "Law and the Soviet Second Economy," Louise Shelley offers a fascinating glimpse into the operation of the second economy in the Soviet Union as seen through the eyes of a sample of émigré lawyers. These lawyers, many of whom were in positions to directly observe and participate in the workings of the second economy, provide a revealing portrait of the structural and institutional supports for the circumvention of bureaucratic directives in a command economy. Beginning with a comparison between the operation of hidden economies in Western and Soviet societies, Shelley explores the ways in which *iuriskonsulty* (legal advisers) function to lubricate the structural and organizational frictions produced in the relationships between the overall economic system, enterprises, managers and workers. She also develops a number of analytic insights to help us better understand the complex articulations between structural conditions, organizational operations and forms of bribery and corruption in modern industrialized societies. At the heart of her analysis is the desire to describe and unravel the dual-edged character of the second economy: the ways in which the conflicts between institutional responsibility and personal financial interest both promote and undermine the economic and political objectives of modern states.

In "Juvenile Delinquency in Israel 1948-1977: Patterns and Trends" Yael Hassin describes and attempts to explain some of the most important variations in indicators of juvenile delinquency in Israeli society. Basing her analysis on records provided by the Juvenile Probation Service, Hassin explores the relationship between changing rates of official delinquency and a number of background factors. Among her most significant findings are that: (1) unlike most other relatively industrialized and industrializing societies, the rates of juvenile delinquency seem to have declined over the last eight years of the period studied; (2) during the period of study the ratio of first offenders to recidivists and the distribution of offences against property and persons remained relatively stable;

and (3) there was a significant decrease in the crime rate of those African and Asian origin as compared to both native-born youth and other immigrant groups.

In order to account for these findings, Hassin draws on the rich heritage of sociological studies on cultural conflict, rising expectations, ethnic tensions and other approaches to the explanation of delinquency in "developed" societies. But none of these perspectives proved satisfactory because of the special circumstances faced by immigrants and youth in Israeli society. Among the most important of these circumstances are Israel's rather unique immigration policy, structural supports for assimilation in Israel and the peculiar interaction between intra- and interethnic relationships in the Jewish state. Overall, this analysis represents a very useful addition to the growing efforts to develop a comparative framework for investigating those age-specific forms of deviance we call deliquency—a phenomenon which is clearly rooted in but not entirely determined by the social and cultural organization of "modern" Western states.

The third paper, by Kitty Calavita, is "The Anti-Alien Contract Labor Law of 1885 and 'Employer Sanctions' in the 1980s." Calavita argues that despite the century separating them there are striking similarities between these two legislative intiatives—similarities which are based on the fact that both represent efforts to "resolve" the contradiction between the labor control and symbolic functions of immigration law in capitalist societies. Through a careful analysis of the social and legal context of the 1885 law, she demonstrates how the conflict between the new-found strength of organized labor and the need to expand the immigrant labor supply led to a legislative compromise supported by both labor and industry. Perhaps the most important features of the compromise was the fact that it represented a form of "symbolic legislation": a type of social intervention which addressed the concerns of protesting groups but did not significantly alter conditions nor threaten even the short-term interests of economic elites.

Comparing the 1885 law with recent recommendations of the Select Commission on Immigration and Refugee Policy (1981) and the Simpson-Mazzoli proposal, Calavita finds a number of important parallels. These proposals, which make it illegal for employers to knowingly hire undocumented workers, reflect the same kinds of contradictions which were apparent in the older legislation. More specifically, immigrant laborers—in this case Mexicans— are scapegoated for problems endemic within the economic order, and a "kind-of-worker" approach is taken in an effort to balance the immigrant's economic utility with political demands to limit the supply of cheap labor. And while there are important differences between the two legislative responses to political and economic conflict (the modern version being far less of a response to both the pressures of organized labor and the imperatives of conscious "tokenism"), the comparison produces a rich yield of insights on how national immigration policy and legal arrangements are deeply intertwined.

The final paper in the first section is "Women's Bodies as Diseased and

Deviant: Historical and Contemporary Issues" by Alexandra Todd. In this investigation Todd focuses on how childbearing was transformed from a natural and female-centered activity into a medicalized and male-dominated aspect of obstetric practice. The significance of this process for the "diseasing of reproduction" and the definitions of women's bodies as deviant is explored with attention to (1) the peculiar dynamics surrounding the professionalization of medicine; (2) the changing relationships between midwives and doctors; (3) the origins and consequences of the moral interpretations of female sexuality; and (4) the developing efforts of women to come to grips with their role as birthing mothers.

In her historical investigation Todd discovers that the subjection of birth to male definitions and prerogatives was part of a larger process: the colonization and domestication of female sexuality. Because of the link between this process and the rise of medicine, women became increasingly defined in terms of their (suspect) physiology and surgical intervention became commonplace in dealing with moral as well as physical transgressions.

In the last section of the paper Todd considers the implications of these historical developments for contemporary medical attitudes and practices and how they are reflected in the handling of birth control decisions, menopause, premenstrual behavior and other aspects of women's reproductive life.

In interpreting the significance of these developments, she explores the ways in which these issues are addressed by Marxists, radical feminists, socialist feminists and those who believe that the scientific world view supports a definition of women and the reproductive process as passive entities best dealt with through technical medical control. The paper ends with a consideration of the double bind that women face: "on the one hand, the very definition of being a woman is objectified into sexual and/or reproductive bodily parts; on the other hand those same parts are seen as unnecessary, often inconvenient and diseased, and can be lopped off or cut out without regard."

Part II of this volume comprises three studies which examine dimensions of law and justice in contemporary America. Each of the papers is concerned with the translation of legal principles into legal practice and the manner in which this translation reveals tensions between the "law on the books" and the "law in action." Focusing on the handicapped, "skid-row" alcoholics and incarcerated parents, these investigations attempt to understand the law from the perspectives of those who make it as well as those who have to live with its consequences. "Implementing Public Law 94-142, the Education for All Handicapped Children Act," by F. James Davis and Barbara Sherman Heyl, is a study of the impact of the federal law passed in 1975 to ensure that children not be discriminated against because of their handicaps. This paper reports and interprets the results of field research undertaken in one school district to assess the way in which the law influenced the lives of children representing all classifications of special education except the profoundly mentally retarded. Utilizing an "interest group" model, the authors explain how the effects of federal law are mediated by special and regular educators, parents of "special" and "normal" children, and administrators of local, state and federal educational agencies.

The first part of the article is devoted to a description of the interest groups involved in the passage of the act, its key provisions, as well as the intrinsic and extrinsic problems associated with its implementation. The controversies surrounding issues of "mainstreaming," "least restrictive environment" and "normalization" are explored to identify the context within which interest group struggles emerged.

Three specific questions guided the next stage of the analysis: (1) What impact has P.L. 94-142 had on the schools and families in a district that already had a relatively progressive system of special education? (2) How has application of the major provisions of P.L. 94-142 been influenced by interests groups within the district? (3) To what extent do the parents of handicapped children participate in procedures established by P.L. 94-142, either as partners in program planning or as adversaries when they feel it necessary to oppose professional educators? On the basis of 445 interview and observational reports and selected statistical and case data, Davis and Heyl conclude that even though there was considerable resistance to the implementation of the act school districts were able to address the rights of handicapped children by assigning them to existing programs rather than by trying each year to create the best settings for individual needs and by maintaining control over the number of referrals to special education. Finally, Davis and Heyl point out how the compromises already being made in implementation are likely to be even more damaging to the spirit of the acts as the decline of federal support for education becomes even more pronounced.

The second paper in this part is "Urban Redevelopment and Public Drunkenness in Fresno: A California Move Toward Recriminalization" by Richard Speiglman and Friedner D. Wittman. This analysis, like that of Public Law 94-142, examines the social origins and consequences of legislative action. The law investigated in this instance was a California statute providing convicted inebriates with a choice between punishment in county jails and longer stays in treatment facilities.

Focusing on the influence of both structural forces and triggering events, this paper reviews the development of public drunkenness laws generally, their pattern of implementation within California, the specific actions taken by policy-influentials and policy makers in Fresno, and the significance of the entire process for understanding legal change and recriminalization. While the bill appeared on the surface to protect the civil rights discussed and reflected in the *Sundance v. Municipal Court of Los Angeles* decision, the authors contend that the national and statewide movement toward decriminalization was mediated and distorted in this case by the specific objectives of interest groups in a single California city. Instead of representing an expansion of legal rights for the dispossessed, it is argued that the law was created primarily to remove inebriates from a downtown shopping area in Fresno.

Criticizing conventional accounts for their narrowness and reformism, Speiglman and Wittman argue that any analysis of the type they undertake must look beyond the "problems" of public drunks to the particularities of social policy and legalistic maneuvers. In this endeavor the authors stress the types of conflict that often take place in cities between the interests of business and those who traditionally use inner city areas—the socially marginal. As long as this conflict is misunderstood and redefined as an "alcohol problem," it is the authors' belief that land-use disputes over social and economic claims will continue to occur.

The last paper in Part II is "Parents in Prison: A Comparative Analysis of the Effects of Incarceration on the Families of Men and Women" by Linda Abram Koban. The author reports the results of a study on the effects of incarceration at a correctional facility for women in Kentucky. Basing her analysis on the assumption that disruption of contact between women and their children would negatively affect their chances for rehabilitation, the author goes on to investigate the relative impact of family separation on men and women in the Kentucky prison system.

Two conclusions are drawn from the findings reported. First, female offenders had closer relationships with their children prior to their incarceration, as evidenced by the following facts: most women were living with their children, and most men were not; most women retained legal custody; fewer women than men made the decision not to have their children visit; children were more likely to be visited by women at least once; and more women planned to be reunited with their children after release. Second, the impact on relationships with children and the family unit was greater for women than for men because men's children usually remained with their mothers; more men than women had frequent contact with their children; men's children were less often separated from their siblings; and men were usually not incarcerated as far from their home communities as women. Overall, Koban suggests that a greater amount of concern about the level of familial disruption for women in prison is justified and that, at least in Kentucky, movement in the direction of more liberal parenting programs is more apparent than real. As a result, she concludes that incarcerated women are as clearly discriminated against in their effort to maintain family contact while in prison as they are by inadequate vocational training, employment counseling and community reentry resources.

Part III of this is entitled "Issues in Law, Deviance and Social Theory." It contains two papers dealing with the theoretical problems confronting any attempt to extend our understanding of the relationship between deviance and control in modern capitalist states. While the papers differ substantially in their orienting assumptions and levels of analysis, they both try to offer an alternative starting point for studying the complex and dialectical relationships between the political problems of class societies, the crises of modern states and the behaviors that come to be defined as subject to sanctions.

In "Rethinking Deviance: Toward a Sociology of Censures," Colin Sumner begins by redefining the field of deviance as based upon "a series of flexible ideological terms of abuse or disapproval which are used with varying regularity and openness in the practical networks of domination." Taking issue with prevailing conceptions of deviance both within and without Marxist discourse, he attempts to go beyond the definitional problem and present a new point of departure for the consideration of what used to be called deviance. Sumner's critique begins with an attack on the Durkheimian and cybernetic roots of contemporary deviance theory. But his analysis leads him in other theoretical directions as well. Most important in the recasting of the study of deviance, according to Sumner, is an ability to understand that social censures are negative ideological categories with specific historical-material applications. Rejecting the notion that censures are "scientific" or behavioral categories, he argues that their general function is to denounce and control, not to explain. Moreover, he reasons that any effort to arrive at the theory of censures must recognize that whatever their ideological functions, censures are not *just* labels; they are "loaded with implied interpretations of real phenomena, models of human nature, and the weight of political self-interest." Taken together, these insights lead to the conclusion that a much more sophisticated theory of ideology must emerge before any further study of censures becomes possible.

In demonstrating the utility of this new conceptual approach, Sumner offers a number of fascinating examples of how power has been exercised through the "censuring" of prostitutes in Victorian England, landless peasants in colonized Africa and working class students in contemporary Britain. These examples make it clear that the concept of social censures moves theory and research away from the study of abnormal individual psychology and action toward "an emphasis on the social relationships which generate opposing ideas and interests, and the political conflicts which precipitate their condensation in censure and its subsequent implementation in practices of penalty and tutelage."

The ninth and final paper in this volume is "A Politics Without a State" by Dario Melossi. Two major hypotheses frame this inquiry: (1) that the principle of social and ethical cohesion shifted, in the transition of social science from nineteenth century Europe to twentieth century America, from a concept in which it was seen as embodied in "the state" to one in which it was seen as an outcome of process of "social control"; and (2) that such a change can be explained only in the context of a broader social change which deeply affected the cultural, political and economic representations of reality from one situation to the next.

Melossi develops his argument by examining the historically shifting relationship of state and society through the eyes of social thinkers such as Hegel,

Marx, Kelsen, Weber, Freud, Mead and Parsons. It is his contention that Hegel first developed the concept of the state in a way that revealed its antagonism to democracy and that this antagonism was understood and made explicit by Marx. Although Hegel tried to present the ethical as the very core of the state, after Marx's critique it became impossible to conceive of the state as a medium for social cohesion. According to Melossi, two theoretical directions were pursued by those who refused to accept Marx's formulation: (1) the idea of a superindividual ethical feeling which held the social fabric together (a view favored by Toennies and Durkheim), and (2) the notion that Marx was basically correct in his diagnosis of class conflict but that the state could only be conceived as isomorphic with the legal order. The major proponents of the latter view, Kelsen and Weber, argued that cohesion was the by-product of a process through which actors "orient" their behavior toward the legal order and call it "the state." In other words, the secret of social cohesion is to be found in the *perception* that society is held together by the state, not in the simple exercise of state power. The author goes on to indicate how this notion is further developed by Freud in his theory of "group psychology"—a theory which emphasizes the internal psychic bonds holding society together.

The theme that Melossi examines—the development of a conception of law *as* social control—is further explored through a critical review of the work of G. H. Mead, Roscoe Pound and Talcott Parsons. In general, according to Melossi, we have come to take for granted a conception of social control which avoids rather than resolves the contradictions in the relationship between morality and law. Much like Sumner in his critique of contemporary deviance theory, Melossi argues that we must carefully distinguish the ideological from other elements of law and that we need to develop a more skeptical attitude toward the concept of "the state" itself.

PART I

DEVIANCE, LAW AND SOCIAL CONTROL; INTERNATIONAL AND HISTORICAL PERSPECTIVES

LAW AND THE SOVIET
SECOND ECONOMY

Louise I. Shelley

I. INTRODUCTION

The second, or hidden, economy is difficult to research in any society; study of this problem is even more difficult in the USSR, where there is an ideological commitment to a centrally controlled economy. The initial opportunity to study the second economy systematically has been provided by the departure of significant numbers of former Soviet citizens to the West. Western economists have seized on this chance,[1] using émigré informants to analyze the extent, dynamics and impact of the Soviet second economy—yet this eagerness has not been matched by researchers in other social science disciplines. This is a major oversight because the second economy affects more than just economic relations in Soviet society. The existence of the second economy affects interpersonal relations, introduces flexibility into the system and undermines individual respect for the law and the overall effectiveness of the legal system. This paper focuses

Research in Law, Deviance and Social Control, Volume 5, pages 3-24
Copyright © 1983 by JAI Press, Inc.
All rights of reproduction in any form reserved
ISBN: 0-89232-334-5

on the legal effects—specifically, the legal problems created by the existence and operation of the second economy.

Interviews with lawyers formerly employed in diverse work environments provide the basis for the conclusions presented in this paper. Enterprise lawyers are particularly valuable informants because the Soviet workplace is the focal point of the Soviet citizen's existence as well as the source of much of the material diverted into the second economy.

II. THE INTERVIEWS

The lawyers interviewed had worked as *arbitry* (arbitrators in the system of economic boards used to resolve Soviet financial disputes) and *iuriskonsulty* (legal advisers) to individual enterprises. Twenty-five lawyers in Israel, Canada and the United States were interviewed between May 1980 and April 1981 to study the operation of Soviet work life. The informants were located through referrals and newspaper advertisements in émigré newspapers. The selection process ensured a geographic distribution—including lawyers from all the western republics, several Caucasian and Central Asian republics, and Siberia (even encompassing the remote areas of the Far East and Far North). Selections were also made using age and professional criteria. Male and female lawyers, ranging in age from 30 to the late 70s, formerly employed in diverse elements of light and heavy industry, trade, cultural and educational organizations were selected for interviews.

The in-depth interviews were conducted exclusively by the author. The interviews ranged from a couple hours to a full day and were held most frequently in the homes of friends or relations of the interviewer. Prior to the interview session, a biographical questionnaire was completed and the approximately 50 interview questions were mailed to the lawyers. The questions addressed the nature of their previous work environment, their most frequently encountered legal problems and the impact of the law on the operation of the first and second economies. The questions were sufficiently open-ended that it was possible for the lawyers to comment on individual cases of particular interest and the attitudes and reactions of their professional colleagues and the work force to the surrounding second economy.

The insights of the lawyers dating back to the early 1930s were remarkably consistent. The second economy, according to the informants, was more widespread earlier in the Soviet period in the Asian republics of the USSR, but in more recent decades the second economy has pervaded all Soviet republics. Adherence to legal norms was greater in social, cultural and educational organizations than in industrial enterprises because the caliber of personnel is higher and there are fewer tangible goods to be siphoned into the second economy.

III. THE NATURE OF THE SOVIET SECOND ECONOMY

As Stuart Henry points out in *The Hidden Economy* (1978:114-17); the socialist economies of Eastern Europe also share the illicit economic practices that he has so clearly documented in the case of Western capitalist economies. Henry separates the hidden economy into two parts (1978:112-13)—one concerned with production and consumption, while the other is concerned with taxation and welfare. In the USSR, the opportunities and benefits of engaging in illicit activity on the redistributive side of the economy are much fewer than the opportunities and benefits of engaging in illegal market activities. This is true because there is a shortage of available goods and ample access by numerous citizens to state property, whereas the taxation and welfare functions of the Soviet economy are much less extensive than in most capitalist societies. Direct taxes are small and standardized, and the welfare system is confined almost entirely to pensions, disability and family assistance payments. The focus of this paper will, therefore, be on illicit economic activity within the production and market sectors of the Soviet economy.

Extensive research has been done by Western scholars on the diverse sectors of capitalist economies from which goods are diverted and stages of the marketing process at which the goods are diverted and stages of the marketing process at which the goods are channeled from the first to the second economies. Western research focuses on diversion from roads and docks, whereas in the Soviet Union the emphasis should be on diversion from railroad transport.[2] Service industries have been the focus of much study by British researchers (Henry, 1978:113) examining the second economy, and the same locations (railway dining cars, bread sales and food stores) were cited by Soviet lawyers as areas of extensive illicit activity. Whereas Western researchers have focused on the extensive illegal activity of professionals (Geis, 1968:Clinard, 1968), Soviet lawyers have chosen to minimize or excuse the participation of their colleagues and such trained specialists as doctors and dentists in the illicit economy. Paralleling the Western experience, Soviet lawyers have chosen to emphasize the participation of supervisory personnel, workers and particularly management in the pervasive illegal economic conduct. But in the USSR, unlike in Western research, little mention has been made of the illicit activity of consumers, i.e., switching of price tags in stores.[3]

The participants in the second economy and the foci of their activities are similar in Western and socialist economies, but the reasons for their involvement may differ. Personal enrichment and corporate or private advantage are reasons that individuals participate in the illicit economy in both economic systems. The Soviet émigré lawyers interviewed gave ample evidence that individual financial gain was responsible for much participation in the second economy. But in socialist societies, a prime reason that individuals engage in illicit economic activity is that they have no choice. Systematic constraints as well as inflexibility make participation in the second economy in socialist societies a necessity. While in the West corporate executives may feel they are pressured into illegal economic practices by their corporate trading partners, goods are sufficiently available so that most Western organizations can resolve their supply problems without resorting to illegal methods. In socialist economies, however, the system of centralized planning often makes it difficult if not impossible for organizations to produce or grade according to their economic plans. Managers of socialist organizations are, therefore, forced to resort to illicit practices to accomplish state-mandated objectives. In this latter case, the second economy is providing the flexibility unavailable in the official planned economy.

The flexibility achieved by informal (and, in the Soviet context, illegal) economic relations is in many ways similar to that described by Sally Falk Moore in her analysis of the American garment industry (1978:59-60). She found that violations of the union contract were sometimes beneficial both to the union and the garment manufacturer ("the contractor"). Gifts are presented by the contractor to the union representative and other essential personnel, and favors are performed, all to ensure that operations continue smoothly:

> All these extralegal givings can be called 'bribery' if one chooses to emphasize their extralegal qualities....Despite the symbolic ambience of choice, there are strong pressures to conform to this system of exchange if one wants to stay in this branch of the garment industry....This complex, the operation of the social field, is to a significant extent self-regulating, self-enforcing, and self-propelling within a certain legal, political, economic and social environment....The penalty for not playing the game according to the rules—legal, non-legal, and illegal—in the dress industry is: economic loss, loss of reputation, loss of goodwill, ultimate exclusion from the avenues that lead to money-making (Moore, 1978:62-64).

The informal, semilegal and illegal relationships that Moore describes in the garment industry are pervasive in the USSR. These illegal and unofficial relationships that operate on all levels in Soviet trade and industry are as important elements of the second economy as illegal activities conducted for personal gain. While the American garment contractor engages in these informal exchanges to ensure benefits to his personal operation, in the USSR there are not such advantages to be gained in a centrally owned and managed economy. Soviet managers are motivated by the same forces as the American contractor, to ensure the smoothness of operations, but their gain from this may not be as direct because they are only the administrators and not the owners of the enterprise. But the need of Soviet managers to resort to illicit economic practices is even greater because the constraints of the planned economy and of continual shortages makes the achievement of their organization's economic objectives even more difficult than in the free-market economies.

Lawyers and the law are much more involved with second economy activities initiated for personal gain. Since illicit economic activity conducted for the benefit of the Soviet economy is perpetrated by high-level managerial personnel, i.e., individuals of significantly higher status than the enterprise lawyers, this illegal activity is rarely disciplined through legal channels. Only when an enterprise manager has offended the Communist Party hierarchy will his involvement in the second economy become the cause of his criminal prosecution. But the initiation of this legal activity will come from the Party apparatus rather than from the *iuriskonsulty*. Activities of the latter are confined either to combatting malfeasance of lowly participants in the second economy or addressing the financial damages caused to the Soviet economy by extensive illicit economic activity.

IV. THE SECOND ECONOMY
AND PERSONAL BENEFITS

All levels of employees are involved in the numerous manifestations of the Soviet second economy—managers, workers, supervisory personnel and sometimes the *iuriskonsulty*. These diverse individuals choose to violate the laws governing economic activity to promote their personal welfare: managers receive undeserved bonuses; supervisors divert materials for resale from warehouses under their control; and workers appropriate available commodities. Gifts are made and favors are provided to arbitrators (*arbitry*) to influence the decision-making process.

The role of the enterprise lawyer, the individuals interviewed for this study, in the second economy is more complex than that of Soviet management and workers. There are frequent conflicts between his interests and responsibilities; he is often at the same time a participant in the parallel economy as well as the individual responsible for upholding the law. His dual role limits the extent of his illegal activities and his success as a law enforcer. The *iuriskonsult* is seldom implicated in the second economy. Few *iuriskonsulty* appear to take advantage of available opportunities; they are observers rather than participants in the second economy. Supporting evidence is that none of the lawyers interviewed mentioned trials of *iuriskonsulty* on corruption charges while the majority of them were familiar with specific trials of former judicial and procuratorial employees as well as those of enterprise directors and other managerial personnel.

The legal advisers' detachment from the second economy is not explained by their virtue. Many *iuriskonsulty* who have the enterprising qualities needed to succeed financially turn their energies to the benefit of their organizations and use available legal weapons to enhance the economic indicators of their organizations. These lawyers benefit from the gratitude of their directors, who reward them in semilegal ways, providing the valued *iuriskonsult* with good housing and sanctioning his employment at more than one enterprise (*sovmestitel' stvo*). Lawyers who refused to violate legal norms, however, might encourage or tolerate blatant criminal involvement of others in the parallel economy. Some lawyers served as unofficial legal advisers to the major beneficiaries of the second economy, their directors and enterprise management. More corrupt lawyers falsified reports to camouflage the diversion of funds or materials from authorized users: bought goods at reduced prices from the storerooms of state or cooperative stores under their jurisdiction: accepted payments from individuals threatened by criminal charges: and paid large bribes to individuals who could provide jobs which would enrich the jobholder.

V. *IURISKONSULTY*: BENEFICIARIES OF THE SECOND ECONOMY

The following biography of one of the most colorful lawyers interviewed refutes the claims made by some legal advisers that there was no way for a *iuriskonsult* in a factory to benefit from the surrounding corruption. This lawyer, practicing in one of the Baltic Soviet republics, had accumulated well over 100,000 rubles (approximately $130,000) at a time when his salary hardly exceeded 2,000 rubles a year, indicating the kind of profits achievable by legal employment in areas of strong consumer demand.

The lawyer first worked on a collective farm that produced canned and smoked fish. He obtained the desirable products of the collective farm in several ways. Fish products stolen from the collective farm warehouse were given to him by workers who sought legal advice on the evasion of criminal responsibility. As the individual responsible for certifying the loss of inventory of the farm's warehouse, the lawyer approved inventory reports documenting nonexistent losses. The lawyer, the manager of the warehouse and the manager of the *tsekh* (factory shop) were able to divide the goods that were reported to have spoiled. The shop manager, out of gratitude to the *iuriskonsult*, would permit him to buy smoked fish at a cost one-eighth that charged in stores, a privilege accorded by law only to the director. While the *iuriskonsult* interviewed could enrich himself through these three schemes, his profits were limited by the amount of the fish products he could obtain and the time required to resell the items. Therefore, as soon as he had amassed enough money to buy himself a more lucrative position, he left the collective farm.

The profits earned at the farm were used to acquire a legal position at the bureau for the purchase and sale of homes. (The *iuriskonsult* of a housing bureau approves all forms before they are notarized.) This position lends itself to two methods of enrichment. Individuals seeking to buy and sell homes have usually spent months or even years searching for desirable housing arrangements. Many are willing to pay the lawyer responsible for approving the deal. Such bribes were one important source of illegal income for the Baltic *iuriskonsult*, but even more money could be obtained if the lawyer himself entered the housing market.

This resourceful *iuriskonsult*, like many American real estate agents, would look for housing bargains. If he found a house that was being sold cheaply, he would offer the seller more than he would be paid by the proposed purchaser. Then he would register the home in the name of friends or family, as it is illegal in the USSR to have more than one home, and renovate the house for resale. After he had completed the physical repair of the house, he would sell it at a tremendous profit, as nothing in the USSR is more in demand than housing. Such activity would be deemed enterprising in the West, but in the USSR the *iuriskonsult* was violating many laws, including those on misuse of positions of responsibility and speculation.

Other less corrupt *iuriskonsulty* described the benefits available to them as a result of their job responsibilities. One lawyer in the Russian Soviet Republic reported that he sometime received bribes at the end of each quarter from the manager of his enterprise warehouse. Many financial claims (*pretenziia*) were made against the warehouse each quarter. The lawyer was required to prepare a finding (*zakliuchenie*) suggesting that the quarterly bonus of the warehouse manager be reduced to discourage such poor management practices. The warehouse manager would offer small payments to the *iuriskonsult* to avert not only a loss of rubles but more importantly to avoid drawing attention to his illegal economic activities that accounted for the large number of claims.

Iuriskonsulty sometimes received not cash but the preferable reward of desirable and scarce consumer goods. The chief *iuriskonsult* for a major trade organization in the Georgian Soviet Republic reported that because store managers were aware that the *iuriskonsult* might either do them harm or save them from prosecution, they tried to curry his favor. He was able regularly to buy scarce items at cost from the numerous stores under the jurisdiction of his trade organizations. But numerous other individuals—the chief inspector, the members of the inspection commission (five or six persons), heads of departments such as planning and personnel, the director and assistant director of the trade organization, the director of the city trade department, members of the OBKHSS (the police unit concerned with the protection of socialist property), members of the *militisiia* (the gendarmerie) and the procuracy received goods regularly from store managers and "most did not even pay for what they received." The differential treatment of the legal adviser was explained by a former Georgian *iuriskonsult*: "With all these people on take, not much depended on the *iuriskonsult*." The situation described by Georgian *iuriskonsult* was not confined to his republic, for interviews with former employees of the OBKHSS, the *militsia*, and the procuracy from many of the republics of the Soviet Union suggest that store managers throughout the USSR provide their best goods to legal professionals as well as Party personnel to save themselves and their families from criminal prosecutions.

Other nonmonetary opportunities are available to the *iuriskonsult* employed outside of the retail sector. One *iuriskonsult* formerly employed by a republic ministry of agriculture reported on the benefits associated with his visits to agricultural organizations:

> When I went to different agricultural organizations. . .they always entertained me, put cognac on the table. Sometimes they brought me food products. Apples, for example. All this was done so that if something unpleasant happened, I would fill out the documents to the advantage of the individual threatened with criminal charges. And these troubles could occur at any of the annual inspections.

Another *iuriskonsult* explained the costs of accepting such favors. A railways *iuriskonsult* normally did not accept bribes or favors. But awaiting a winter visit from an affluent relative in the United States, the lawyer was forced to use her position to acquire the foods necessary to properly entertain her foreign guest. As little food was available in the stores at the time, the lawyer asked the food manager of the railroad dining car office to purchase scarce items, bitterly aware that sometime in the future she would have to pay back this favor. Not long after this, the *iuriskonsult* was forced to "pay for the favor" by hiding the fact of the food manager's embezzlement.

Most *iuriskonsulty* do not enrich themselves through their illegal activities. Moreover, their legal violations are not so significant as to prevent the effective performance of their duties. Such illegal conduct is characteristic of that of much of the Soviet population who are forced to bend the law in order to survive.

While few *iuriskonsulty* involve themselves deeply in the second economy, their failure to prepare cases for criminal prosecution allows others to enrich themselves at the cost of the first economy. Other legal advisers are more deeply involved in the second economy—advising their supervisors on ways to avoid criminal activity. The different stances assumed by *iuriskonsulty* to the surrounding second economy were determined by the personality, values and work environment of the individual lawyer.

VI. *IURISKONSULTY,* MANAGERS AND THE SECOND ECONOMY

The *iuriskonsulty* uninvolved with the second economy either believed in the honesty of their supervisors or feigned ignorance of the manipulations. While directors sometimes change as frequently as every two or three years as a consequence of their inefficiency and corruption, *iuriskonsulty*, like the wily Talleyrand, manage to survive all upheavals. Even *iuriskonsulty* who serve as personal advisers to corrupt directors survive untouched because the Party apparatus views the lawyer as a petty bureaucrat of little consequence to the operations of his enterprise.

The legal adviser's immunity from suspicion permits him to advise his supervisor on ways to "legalize their actions." In conversations perhaps similar to those between Western corporation executives and their counsels, some *iuriskonsulty* would say to their directors, "If you prepare your documents in this way, you will be in violation of the law, but if you do it this way your behavior will be completely legal." Some lawyers would go even farther to assist their directors and would use the law to disguise acts of embezzlement. As one lawyer interviewed explained, he had advised his director to list missing merchandise as damaged and the 10% that could be written off in this way would be sufficient to cover the amount embezzled.

While some directors were sufficiently clever to cover up their illegal conduct and did not require counsel from their enterprise lawyer, many managers, especially those in Central Asia and the Caucasus, depend on their *iuriskonsulty* for assistance in escaping prosecution. One lawyer, an unofficial adviser to his director, boasted of his close relations with his manager, never realizing the revelations he made about his moral character. The lawyer reported that he and his director were in constant contact throughout the day. The consultations were so frequent that the director's secretary commented to the *iuriskonsult* interviewed, "He so hates to part from you that I am surprised that he does not take you to bed along with his wife." For his services, the factory manager paid him the ultimate compliment, "Dear Sasha, you constantly save me from the hands of the procuracy." The director also provided concrete benefits; he sent a work team to the lawyer's apartment to renovate and redecorate it, charging the lawyer only for the cost of the materials.

While few *iuriskonsulty* collude with management on means to evade the law, many more legal advisers choose to ignore minor violations of the law. A good example is provided by a *iuriskonsult* formerly employed at a clinic. He reported that as many as 50% of the doctors failed to register all their patients, as they maintained large private practices at the clinic. The two individuals responsible for enforcing the law at the clinic, the chief doctor and the *iuriskonsult*, both refrained from curtailing this illegal activity. The chief doctor had a large private practice of his own and did not want to jeopardize this income. The *iuriskonsult* refrained from reporting this misconduct because he did not want to antagonize the clinical staff and understood that they could not live on their monthly salaries of 100-120 rubles ($130-160). The illegal practices of Soviet doctors necessitated by their poor financial position are more understandable than those of their highly paid Western counterparts.[4] *Iuriskonsulty* in commercial enterprises would ignore cases of petty theft committed by poorly paid enterprise employees.

The lawyer almost never consciously decides to participate in the second economy; his activity is confined, through choice and circumstance, to tacit or overt collusion with its major beneficiaries—enterprise directors, managers and other supervisory personnel. The *iuriskonsult* lacks the opportunity to steal from the government and the authority to curtail the illegal conduct of others. Subservient to management, the *iuriskonsult* is rarely the initiator of illegal activity or a direct beneficiary of the second economy. Moreover, his lack of autonomy prevents him from divorcing himself from the illegal conduct of others.

VII. *IURISKONSULTY,* WORKERS AND THE SECOND ECONOMY

Although blatant misuses of a *iuriskonsult* position are rare, courageous acts by *iuriskonsulty* are also infrequent. Lawyers in many enterprises all too often decline to assist the victims of management's illicit schemes. The following cases drawn from two lawyers' experiences show how lawyer can aid the workers of their organization—but most decline to act, fearing management reprisal. The interest that these *iuriskonsulty* took in their enterprise workers provide examples of the personalization of law. In these cases the impact of the individual lawyer was more important than the laws.

The warehouse manager of a Ukrainian factory had stolen several thousand rubles worth of goods from his inventory, but when the losses were discovered he managed to shift the blame to a warehouse employee. The enterprise lawyer was instructed by his organization's management to sue the accused worker. If this suit were successful, hundreds or thousands of rubles would be deducted from the worker's salary to compensate the enterprise for its loss. The *iuriskonsult*, infuriated at the thought that an innocent worker would suffer irreparable financial harm while the culprit would not suffer for the crime, devised a strategy to help the worker. The *iuriskonsult* investigated the case and established that the documentation concerning the missing merchandise was so inadequate that the materials could have been damaged or stolen before they ever reached the warehouse. The courageous *iuriskonsult* recommended the worker to a skilled defense attorney and discreetly transmitted his collected evidence. The warehouse employee was rightfully absolved of responsibility by the court.

Similar assistance was provided a worker by one Central Asian lawyer who was required to prepare documents for the procuracy on large-scale embezzlement. A worker was accused of the disappearance of 56,000 rubles worth of food from a major canning plant in Central Asia. The *iuriskonsult* was convinced of the accused man's innocence and considered what might account for such a massive loss. It occurred to him that the fruits and vegetables that had reputedly disappeared might simply have dried out in the sun as a result of poor storage practice. He took two days away from a busy schedule to spend time at an adjoining plant learning about weight loss in fruits and vegetables due to the evaporation of waste. With this information he was able to account for some 30-35% of the missing goods. The *iuriskonsult* concluded in his disposition to the procuracy that some of the short weight might be attributable to loss of water rather than theft. He said, "I did not believe that the accused worker was guilty;

either the head of the storeroom was deceiving him, the poorly educated worker had signed for goods he had not received, or the loss was the result of management's failure to protect the items from the sun.'' When the investigator in charge came to the enterprise to discuss the case with the *iuriskonsult*, the lawyer elucidated how he accounted for 20,000 rubles of the loss and explained his conclusions regarding the rest of the missing food. The case was eventually dropped for insufficient evidence to implicate the worker under suspicion.

The Central Asian lawyer could afford to help the worker because he was the director's personal legal adviser. But most enterprise lawyers would not dare to protect an ordinary worker, fearing management's anger at their failure to recover rubles for the enterprise.

Neither the corrupt behavior of the employee of the Baltic housing project discussed earlier (Section V) nor the principal actions of the *iuriskonsult* at the Ukrainian factory are typical, as most legal advisers keep their avaricious or samaritan instincts in check. They intentionally remain purely bureaucratic functionaries removed from the second economy—neither participants in its schemes nor protectors of its victims. Detachment from the second economy has it own rewards. Lawyers guard their moral principles, avoid arrest and may gain rewards from managers appreciative of the lawyer's unseeing eye.

The relationship between Soviet *iuriskonsulty*, enterprise managers and administrative personnel is not unique. The extralegal activities described by these émigré lawyers do bear at least a superficial similarity to the activities described by Macaulay (1979, 1982) in his study of American corporate lawyers and contractual relationships. But the lawyer's advisory function described by Soviet émigré lawyers is more similar to that described by Heinz and Laumann (1981:Ch. 10) in their study of Chicago lawyers where the client controls the lawyer than it is to Macaulay's (1963) analysis of lawyer-client relationships where the lawyer exercises influence over his client. In the Soviet context, clients are more likely to control their relationship with their legal adviser than the reverse. Circumstances may affect the relationship, but the Soviet *iuriskonsult*, who lacks the independence and status of his American counterpart, is more often the subservient party in any lawyer-client relationship.

VIII. THE SECOND ECONOMY AND STATE GOALS

Not all individuals participate in the second economy to improve their personal financial position. Managers engage in unauthorized negotiations, conclude unofficial contracts for the delivery of scarce commodities and resolve disputes without recourse to arbitration. All this illegal economic activity is done to further the economic interests of the enterprise. These actions may result in intangible benefits to the manager, but they may also result in his prosecution.

The lawyers interviewed were not as good informants on the illicit economic activity engaged in to promote state financial objectives because they were rarely privy to the secret maneuvers of their superiors. While illegal economic activity engaged in for personal gain often resulted in shortages of essential materials that could not be overlooked by the lawyer, managers' participation in the second economy to achieve plan objectives often resulted in fewer financial and legal problems for the organization. Lawyers only became aware of unofficial negotiations and contracts when they resulted in inadequate deliveries to the enterprise or when a suit was initiated against their organization for failure to deliver promised goods. Only in these cases might the lawyer discover the reason for this organization's failure to deliver goods that had been produced. Often the *iuriskonsult* would not even be aware that interorganizational disputes were settled without resorting to arbitration because no evidence of the economic disagreement would reach his desk. In these cases managers would resolve delivery schedules or problems of quality through telephone calls or over vodka. As maintenance of good relations with trading partners is more important than the ruble penalites that can be extracted through arbitration, it is most frequently in the organization's favor to conclude unofficial deals with trading partners rather than to resolve disputes through formal legal channels.

The Soviet system provides no alternatives for the manager but to participate in the second economy. Unless a manager can promise the director of a trading partner either personal benefits or needed supplies, he will never obtain a desirable commodity even if it is promised to his organization by a legally binding contract. As goods rather than money are at a premium in the USSR, illegal negotiations prevail because legal channels fail to resolve fundamental supply problems. Recourse to the second economy becomes a necessity for any Soviet manager who chooses to fulfill his plan.

Managerial participation in the second economy for the good of the enterprise is generally untouched by the legal order unless the behavior is particularly egregious or the official annoys Party apparatchiks who seek means to punish the offender. In either case, the enterprise lawyer is uninvolved and disciplinary action is initiated by higher Party functionaries, often extralegally. But the enterprise *iuriskonsult* is still responsible for dealing with the financial damages inflicted by those employees of the enterprise and its trading partners, as well as of the transport industry, who participate in the second economy.

IX. *IURISKONSULTY* ADDRESS THE COSTS
OF THE SECOND ECONOMY

Iuriskonsulty address the costs of the second economy by suing both organizations and individuals responsible for *nedostachi* (shortages). The *iuriskonsult* can recover significant sums from individuals and can receive goods and fines that aid the production, trade and profits of his enterprise (Bulgakbaev, 1975:8-9). By assisting the enterprise comrades' court and the procuracy (Shor, 1960:117-24) in their prosecution of employees who steal from the organization, the lawyer is helping to stem the flow of goods from the legal first economy to the illegal second economy.

Management is rarely interested in revealing criminal conduct, as the presence of illegal economic activity is often interpreted by the Party as a sign of poor administration. Managers, therefore, with or without the assistance of the lawyer, try to hide financial misconduct. The first step taken by management to recover any loss is to ascertain the identity of the perpetrator. If the individual responsible is identified, he may be summoned by the *iuriskonsult* and warned that legal penalties might well follow if he fails voluntarily to return the goods or money. Sometimes this approach is taken even with the loss of several thousand rubles. Occasionally, the individual responsible for the loss will attempt to make a gift (*prinoshenie*) to the director (Grossman, 1977:32) in order to free himself from criminal liability. Directors interested in preserving their image may accept such gifts. If the director chooses to impose a penalty, he may select the appropriate disciplinary action or may do so only after consulting with his legal adviser. One of the punitive measures most frequently recommended by legal advisers is the removal of individuals from their positions for a prescribed period of time with a commensurate reduction in salary. This measure is neither very harsh nor visible to external parties.

Despite management's interest in hiding cases of embezzlement, cases of theft by workers and supervisory personnel are often uncovered. Thefts committed by employees are detected in several ways. Inspections conducted by inspection commissions or the OBKHSS, the police arm concerned with the protection of socialist property, often uncover missing inventory. In consumer goods factories, workers are sometimes frisked by guards when departing the premises to detect theft of state property. Arbitrators sometimes alert police and procuratorial authorities when they believe that the losses in a case under review are ascribable to the embezzlement of socialist property (Braginskii and Eremeev, 1969:79-80).

These methods of detecting the theft of state property only sometimes lead to a concrete perpetrator. Criminal law can be used to combat the pervasive second economy only when it is possible to fix the blame to a particular individual. In other cases the civil law can be used to remedy the damages inflicted by illicit economic activity. The lawyers interviewed reported that they spend much of their time preparing civil suits and documenting cases of criminal activity for the procuracy. The effect of these legal measures is limited, and few lawyers interviewed had any illusions that their actions resulted in long-term reduction in illegal economic activity. Despite the limited effectiveness of the civil and criminal law in combatting the second economy, these legal tools are among the few means available to Soviet authorities to curb this most widespread criminality.

A. Suits Against Enterprises

Civil suits are used to combat the costs of the second economy when embezzlement by employees of a trading partner results in deliveries of inadequate supplies of goods (*nedostachi*) when criminal responsibility cannot be established or when financial preparations are desired from a convicted embezzler. The suits initiated against trading partners for missing merchandise comprise the largest share of the lawyer's litigation work. Examples drawn from the experiences of several legal advisers suggest the problems that a *iuriskonsult* must face in assisting his enterprise to combat the second economy through civil law.

A manager of a tile factory participated in the second economy because if provided benefits to himself and his enterprise. Because tiles are in short supply, the manager of a construction firm was willing to pay a significant sum to the director and a premium to the enterprise to conclude an unofficial contract. The construction firm that was designated by contract to receive the rechanneled tiles filed suit against the floor tile factory for its failure to ship sufficient tiles. The clever director of the tile factory, not wanting to be detected by the arbitrator, bribed his employees and the inspection commission to certify that their tiles were not deliverable because "they had been damaged." The tile factory *iuriskonsult* presented the falsified documentation in arbitration, explaining that "it was not my job to investigate what lies behind pieces of paper." The arbitrator may have suspected the cause of the tile shortfall, but he did not investigate. All the arbitrator did was to fine the tile factory; he could not force the enterprise to deliver goods that it did not have. But the construction firm suffered an irreparable loss: the fine it received was much less useful than the tiles it needed to fulfill its contracts. If the construction trust that lost the tiles had employed a shrewder lawyer, he would merely have threatened suit and then let his manager negotiate an unofficial payment and an alternative shipment plan. In dealing with the second economy, the lawyer is often more useful as a *tolkach* (a facilitator) than as the upholder of the law.

A Ukrainian meat factory sent a refrigerator car of ducks and chickens to a trade distribution center. By the time the freight car arrived all the poultry had spoiled. The workers unloading the shipment failed to detect the condition of the birds before they signed the documentation accepting the shipment. Knowing that they would be held financially responsible for a signficant loss that was not their fault, they devised a strategy to transfer the costs of the loss to the shipper. The next time the distribution center received a shipment of good meat from the Ukrainian factory, the workers prepared documentation certifying that the goods were in poor condition. To obtain the signature of the government inspector necessary to document the loss, they bribed the inspector with money and meat expropriated from this shipment. The commission which received the goods presented the falsified documentation to the *iuriskonsult* of the trade distribution center. He then proceeded to file suit against the meat factory.

But luckily for the *iuriskonsult* of the meat factory, the arbitrator assigned to this case was shrewder that the arbitrator assigned to the tile case. He was aware of the possibility of fraud in the documents submitted by the *iuriskonsult*. The arbitrator carefully studied the work hours indicated in the inspector's report. He found that "In one document it was shown that the inspector worked from nine to twelve. In another document describing the receipt of a completely different shipment it was indicated that the same inspector worked from ten to one. Together the documents showed that in the course of a single day, this one inspector had worked 28 hours." This was a clear case of fraud. The arbitrator dismissed the case against the meat factory and alerted the appropriate authorities of indications of criminal conduct.

Unless there is a shrewd *iuriskonsult* or arbitrator, civil cases arising from the damages inflicted by the second economy often just compound the harm caused by the initial illegal conduct. Many participants in illegal economic activity are not only clever enough to perpetrate these crimes but are sufficiently shrewd to find the means to camouflage their criminal behavior. Furthermore, unless the lawyers can outwit the participants in the second economy, enterprises may suffer greatly—first, from the initial costs of the illegal economic activity; and, secondly, from the failure of the enterprise to recover damages to compensate for the loss. But if the law is used and applied with sophistication, illegal economic activity can be sharply curtailed and significant sums can be recovered. A Soviet legal scholar in Kazakhstan reported on the tens of thousands of rubles recovered by different enterprises through civil suits against responsible parties (Bulgakbaev, 1975:8-9).

B. Court Suits Against Employees

Most *iuriskonsulty* interviewed had initiated court suits against workers of their organizations. While they might be reluctant to initiate such actions when the carelessness of the workers had resulted in a loss to the enterprise (as in the case of the workers who accepted the spoiled ducks and chickens), most lawyers would neither resist management pressures to recover damages nor find means to aid unfortunate workers. The lawyers' stance in these cases is a clear indication of their lack of autonomy; they are forced to side with management against workers.[5] The lawyers found it easier to execute their responsibilities when workers' illicit activity accounted for losses to the enterprise. As one lawyer explained, he would not hesitate to sue the workers of his enterprise who had lost 5% of a particular shipment if he were sure that they had retained 5% for themselves. Suits such as this not only brought needed funds to the enterprise but warned other workers of the costs of engaging in the second economy.

C. Criminal Penalties

If it were determined that the workers had appropriated part of the shipment, they would not escape merely with civil penalties but would be subjected to criminal sanctions. In this case, the lawyer might be instructed by management to prepare documentation concerning the theft for the procuracy.[6]

Prosecution of offenders is not always a certainty in cases of petty theft. If there is only small-scale embezzlement of state property, the *iuriskonsult*, with the permission of the administrator of his enterprise, may succeed in diverting the case from the procuracy to the comrades' court of his enterprise. As the need to prosecute workers is seen as a sign of poor management practices, directors are often willing to have cases heard by the comrades' courts.

D. Comrades' Courts

Comrades' courts consist of workers at an enterprise or housing complex who judge the misconduct of their colleagues (Butler, 1977). Every factory or major enterprise has such a court, which meets periodically. Often the legal adviser of the organizations serves as the presiding officer and guides the procedure as well as the selection of a penalty. The comrades' courts handle cases related to labor code violations, drinking, hooliganism and theft. Most *iuriskonsulty* interviewed reported that theft of state property is these courts' primary concern. In some enterprises, petty thievery is so pervasive that comrades' courts meet twice a month to review the large number of cases. Only minor sentencing options are available. Most thieves of state property who come before the comrades' court escape imprisonment and usually receive only a fine of under 50 rubles and some kind of official *poritsanie* (group condemnation) of their activity. In addition, the individual might be entrusted to the collective to ensure that there is no repetition of his illegal conduct.

E. Criminal Prosecution

In more serious cases of theft, the *iuriskonsult* had no option but to prepare cases for criminal prosecution. *Iuriskonsulty* in some organizations had few cases to transmit to the procuracy, but in many consumer goods plants preparation of cases for the procuracy was almost a daily concern of the legal adviser. A *iuriskonsult* employed by the railroads had so many cases of embezzlement to transmit to the procuracy that she became well acquainted with the investigator of her regional procuratorial office. A lawyer for a complex of supermarkets found that one of the first things she had to learn on her job was to prepare cases for criminal prosecution. These documents required little investigative work by the *iuriskonsult* as they usually could be completed based on previously collected evidence. The documents would simply state that a theft of a certain amount of goods had occurred under certain circumstances with the named individual found responsible. Only in the rarest of circumstances when the lawyer was convinced of the innocence of the named individual might he probe more deeply into the facts of a case before transmitting the papers to the procuracy. Otherwise, most lawyers would perform this function, adhering to all established formalities.

F. Circuit Court Sessions

The transmission of papers to the procuracy does not always terminate an enterprise's involvement with an illegal act. If officials of the procuracy feel that the case is representative of large-scale illegal activity at the enterprise, they might suggest that a circuit court session (*vyezdnaia sessiia*) be held at the organization. In this case, a public trial conducted by an ordinary judge in accordance with the standard rules of criminal law and procedure would be held in the largest available space at the enterprise and workers would be excused from their jobs to hear the trial. It is the responsibility of the *iuriskonsult*, in conjunction with management, to ensure good attendance at the circuit court session. Often the accused party may be given a particularly harsh sentence to serve as an example to the other workers. Even if the workers disapprove of the sentence, as they often do, most are afraid to reveal their feelings in public. Following the trial, the *iuriskonsult* is required to give lectures to the workers of his organization to emphasize the possible penal consequences of illegal activity.

Almost all the *iuriskonsulty* employed in factories, trusts or trade organizations reported that circuit trials had been conducted at their enterprises. Most *iuriskonsulty* concluded that these trials had little long-term effect on the workers, as they did not inhibit their participation in the second economy. Soviet authorities may have sensed the ineffectiveness of this preventative measure because few *iuriskonsulty* reported observing more than a couple of such trials during their careers.

The failure of the lawyer to instill respect for the law is not confined to these circuit court sessions. Even though most *iuriskonsulty* spend much of their time dealing directly or indirectly with the second economy, both the civil and criminal weapons available to them are unsuccessful in curbing the widespread illegal economic activity. The reason for this failure is that managers, who have the ultimate authority in institutions, are more concerned with their financial well-being than with upholding the law. Moreover, personal benefits achieved by violating the law are greater than the punitive disincentives. Consequently, almost all participants in the Soviet workplace, even the lawyers whose function it is to uphold the law, are involved in the pervasive second economy.

X. ARBITRATORS AND THE SECOND ECONOMY

The foregoing generalization also extends to arbitrators, the lawyers who must resolve economic disputes between enterprises. Arbitrators, like iuriskonsulty, have a complex relationship to the second economy. They address the costs of the second economy at the same time that they benefit from its existence. For arbitration is the legal mechanism by which enterprise lawyers recover damages from other organizations for losses due to the operation of the second economy. But arbitrators, because of the nature of their work assignments, are generally supposed to be less subject to corruption than most other members of the legal profession. Yet, even while they are deciding cases caused by the existence of the second economy and are informing the procuracy of evidence of corruption, many are themselves benefiting from the existence of the second economy.

A. Combatting the Second Economy

Arbitrators play an important role in combatting the second economy (Tadevosian, 1980: 154-57). They provide notice (*signalizatsiia*) to the supervisory organization, Party organs and the procuracy when there are indications of financial misconduct or production and delivery problems. These signals are sent when an organization has sent a shipment of particularly poor quality goods or a shipment of very insufficient quantity. Arbitrators may also notify the authorities when an enterprise is failing to provide documentation of receipt of goods or is failing to fill out forms in the appropriate manner, both frequently signs of illicit economic activity. However, according to former arbitrators, these signals rarely result in tangible changes in the operation of an organization. All that ever results from these signals is a formal criticism of an individual (*poritsanie*) or a damage suit against a responsible party to recover part of the losses. An explanation for the failure of these signals to curb the second economy was provided by one former Soviet arbitrator: "To bring any order to the system is impossible. The fault lies in the system and the actions of no one person or group of individuals can remedy these fundamental problems."

B. Are Arbitrators Beneficiaries of the Second Economy?

At the same time that the arbitrator is combatting corruption in the workplace he might also be a participant in the second economy. Lawyers and managers will often provide arbitrators with small gifts to receive favorable treatment for their organization. These gifts can be readily made because bribes given to arbitrators are not easily detected. Circumstances facilitate this bribery because no established procedure exists for hearing cases and reviewing evidence. Moreover, no decision can be viewed as against governmental interests because both parties in the dispute are state-owned enterprises, a cover for corruption not available in capitalist societies. The informality of the arbitration process and the limited possibilities of detection provide wide latitude for bribery that is not present in the judiciary.

Despite the ease with which arbitrators can be bribed, large-scale corruption is not known. Whereas many judges collect tens of thousands of rubles as a result of their positions, an arbitrator is fortunate if he or she receives a sweater, a case of apples or some bottles of wine. Some defense attorneys and prosecutors interviewed had difficulty naming judges in their districts who were not willing to accept bribes in exchange for favorable treatment of offenders. Every lawyer working in the criminal justice system acknowledged the pervasive corruption of judicial and prosecutorial personnel. Many judges are prosecuted for bribe taking, and even special labor camps exist to isolate convicted members of the judiciary and the procuracy. But such extreme measures are not taken against arbitrators, for no one interviewed mentioned trials of arbitrators, even in response to specific questions on corruption in arbitration. Arbitrators are not spared prosecution because of the benevolence of the judicial system but because their corruption is not sufficient to merit procuratorial attention.

Structural as well as personal reasons explain the absence of corruption in arbitration. Arbitrators are less frequently offered bribes because there is less advantage in bribing an arbitrator than in bribing a judge. Judges preside over cases that determine the fate of individuals, whereas all that arbitrators resolve are economic disputes between state-owned enterprises. If an individual faces a lengthy period of incarceration, he may be willing to pay large sums of money to shorten his prison term or be charged with a less serious crime. If he seeks a way out of an unhappy marriage, smaller bribes may be given to secure a divorce at a time when government policy is encouraging the strengthening of families. But such strong incentives do not exist to bribe arbitrators; managers have more to fear from Party disagreements than from economic mismanagement. Financial losses incurred through arbitration do not jeopardize the positions of Soviet managers as similar losses would threaten the job security of Western corporate executives.

The absence of incentives is not the only reason that bribery is minimal in arbitration. Arbitrators lack the Party protection that shields many members of the judiciary from prosecution; but even the Party is powerless to help in many overt and blatant cases of corruption. Arbitrators are not always members of the Party, whereas Party membership is a prerequisite to selection for the judiciary in over 95 percent of cases (Sharlet, 1979:326-28). Arbitrators who are Party members are not as closely associated with the local Party apparatus as are judges because they are spared the calls from the Party concerning particular cases. The remoteness of arbitrators from Party influence gives them more independence, but not the degree of Party protection needed to take significant bribes.

Bribery is particularly circumscribed in cities like Moscow, Leningrad and

Kiev and in the Baltic republics where the quality of legal decisions is high and any decision that appeared to be influenced by corruption would easily be detected. As one former arbitrator from a Slavic republic explained, "The most that I could do for an organization that offered me a bribe was to find a loophole to aid their case." In the Caucasus and Central Asia there is wider latitude for corruption in arbitration because the level of legal competence is generally lower. Arbitrators in these Asian republics could take gifts with impunity because even a poorly constructed decision does not arouse suspicion. Nationalism, however, eliminates the need for many such gifts. When cases involve organizations from outside the republic, arbitrators generally decide the case in favor of his republic's enterprise regardless of whether a gift or payment has been made. Then the organization that has benefited from the arbitrator's decision often provides him with a gift as a reward for favorable treatment. But these gifts are small compared to those offered members of the *militsiia*, procuracy and judiciary in these republics.

Only small-scale corruption exists in arbitration because of the nature of arbitration and the quality of personnel it attracts. But the limited corruption in arbitration is not a testimony to this legal institution but a reflection of the powerlessness of arbitration to have a significant impact on the operation of Soviet organizations. If arbitration could affect the life of enterprises as courts affect individuals, corrupt individuals would seek arbitration work and managers would press Party officials to select "influenceable" arbitrators. Moreover, if managers thought that the arbitrators' decisions affected their standing, they would not limit gift giving to arbitrators but would use the extensive financial resources at their disposal to obtain desirable results.

But little incentive now exists among managers to influence the decision making of arbitrators because so many decisions are purely formalistic and have little impact on the economic welfare of an organization. The institution of arbitration does not affect the ability of an organization to accomplish its most important objective—plan fulfillment; it merely affects costs and profits, which lack the significance in the Soviet context that they have in Western capitalist societies. Ironically, the absence of large-scale corruption in arbitration is the ultimate testimony that the decisions made by arbitrators are not of vital concern to the parties affected.

XI. CONCLUSION

Management's reluctance to interfere in the arbitration process is further evidence that the law is often allowed to govern the planned economy but not to curb the operation of the second economy. This "hidden" economy has survived and proliferated, in direct violation of both civil and criminal law, because it provides tangible benefits to millions of individuals. This massive disobedience and evasion of the law might be viewed as a sign of large-scale rebellion against the Soviet system. But its major beneficiaries are those in management and the Party *apparat* ruling the Soviet state. Although these individuals do indeed enjoy the monetary rewards of the second economy, it is unlikely that they would permit large-scale violation of the law to persist if they felt that it threatened the stability of the Soviet regime. The second economy has survived and proliferated because it performs vital functions for the Soviet state—it introduces flexibility and incentives into the Soviet system. Because the second economy plays these significant roles, Soviet authorities have failed to use the legal weapons necessary to combat this major economic drain on the first economy. As the second economy functions to the society's and the Party's benefit, management has resisted a more forceful legal presence in their organizations. The individuals assigned responsibility for enforcing the economic law, *iuriskonsulty* and arbitrators, are denied the authority and the power necessary to combat effectively widespread illicit economic activity. Moreover, these enforcers are sometimes themselves drawn willingly or unwillingly into the pervasive second economy.

Law is still not an important tool in fighting the Soviet second economy. As in capitalist societies, disciplinary action against high-level managerial personnel who participate in the second economy is still infrequent. The reason is that high-level personnel in both societies have the personal connections and status that protect them from prosecution. *Iuriskonsulty* and arbitrators, because they lack the institutional clout necessary to make them effective fighters against the second economy, only help remedy the damage inflicted by the widespread illicit economic activity. Soviet bureaucrats and the Party elite generally fail to identify their personal welfare with that of enterprises within the planned economy and are therefore unwilling to grant greater power to law enforcement personnel. As in the West, conflict betwen institutional responsibility and personal financial interests allow the second economy to flourish in the USSR.

NOTES

1. A conference on the second economy was organized by the economists Gregory Grossman and Vladimir Treml on January 24-26, 1980 and was held at the Kennan Institute of the Smithsonian. A book based on this conference is forthcoming.

2. Evidence of the problems inherent in the railroad system is that one of the first actions of the new General Secretary, Yuri V. Andropov, after his accession to power was the removal of the minister of railroads.

3. It is not possible to switch price tags in the USSR because customers in most stores do not have direct access to the merchandise. Moreover, prices for items are printed on them, as goods sell for the same price all over the country.

4. While working at LEAA (Law Enforcement Assistance Administration) I was informed of an investigation of stolen IBM typewriters that had been traced to doctors who had traded care for this stolen property. Similar enforcement activity or type of corruption would be unlikely in the Soviet Union.

5. This contradicts Soviet sources that speak of the independence of the *iuriskonsulty* (e.g., see Aristakov et al., 1970:26).

6. This is part of a major effort to combat theft at the workplace. See Tadevosian (1980:154-57) and Selivanov (1975:61-72).

REFERENCES

Aristakov, Iu. M., A.B. Godes, A.V. Lavrin and A. N. Raevski
   1970   Pravovaia rabota na predpriiatii, Moscow: Iuridicheskaia Literatura.
Braginski, M. and D. Eremeev
   1969   Arbitrazhi i predpriiatie. Minsk: Belarus.
Bulgakbaev, A. (ed.)
   1975   Iuridicheskaia sluzhba na predpriiatiiakh Alma Alta: K pomoshehu iuriskinsultov.
Butler, W.E.
   1977   "Comradely justice revisited." 3 Review of Socialist Law 325.
Clinard, Marshall B.
   1968   "White collar crime." International Encyclopedia of the Social Sciences New York. Macmillan 483.
Geis, Gilbert (ed.)
   1968   White Collar Crime. New York: Atherton
Grossman, Gregory
   1977   "The second economy of the USSR." 26 Problems of Communism 25.
Heinz, John and Edward Laumann
   1981   Chicago Lawyers: The Professions of the Bar. New York: Russell Sage Foundation.
Henry, Stuart
   1978   The Hidden Economy. London: Martin Robertson.
Macaulay, Stewart
   1963   "Non-contractual relations in business: a preliminary study." 28 American Sociological Review 55.
   1979   "Lawyers and consumer protection laws." Law and Society Review 115.
   1982   "Law schools and the world outside their doors II: (some notes on the margins of Heinz and Laumann and Zemans and Rosenblum." Disputes Processing Research Program Working Paper, University of Wisconsin Law School.
Moore, Sally Falk
   1978   Law as Process. London: Routledge and Kegan Paul.
Selivanov, A.D.
   1975   "Iuridicheskaia sluzhba bor'be za okhrannost' sotsialisticheskoi sobstvennosti." In A. Buigakbaev (ed.), Iuridicheskaia shuzhba na predpriiatiiakh. Alma Alta: K. Pomoshu iuriskonsultov.
Sharlet, Robert
   1979   "The Communist Party and the administration of justice in the USSR." In Donald B. Barry et al. (eds.) Soviet Law After Stalin, Part 3, Alphen aan den Rijn: Sijthoff and Noordhoff.
Shor, I.M.
   1960   Organizatsiia iuridicheskoi sluzhbu na predipriiatii i v sovnarkhoze. Moscow: Gosiurizdat.
Tadevosian, V.S.
   1980   Ukreplenie sotsialisticheskoi zakonnosti v narodnom khozaistve. Moscow: Nauka.

JUVENILE DELINQUENCY IN ISRAEL 1948-1977:

PATTERNS AND TRENDS

Yael Hassin

I. INTRODUCTION

This study was designed to investigate the main trends and patterns of the phenomenon of juvenile deliquency in Israel, as reflected in the official criminal statistics of the past 30 years, from the establishment of the State in 1948 until 1977.

Three main topics are discussed: the extent of the problem of juvenile delinquency during these years; the types of offenses involved in juvenile delinquency; and the connection between country of origin and juvenile delinquency. This last issue will receive the most attention.

II. METHOD

The research population includes those Jewish youngsters (male and female) who are defined by law as minors for whom a criminal file has been opened

Research in Law, Deviance and Social Control, Volume 5, pages 25-50
Copyright © 1983 by JAI Press, Inc.
All rights of reproduction in any form reserved
ISBN: 0-89232-334-5

with the police and who have been referred to the Juvenile Probation Service. In fact, only 50% of these youngsters actually stand trial in the juvenile courts: in the other cases, the file is closed by the police. For the purposes of this study, however, the more complete population will be discussed, i.e., all those minors who have been apprehended by the police as suspected of criminal activity (hereinafter referred to as juvenile deliquents).

Data were collected from a number of sources: annual reports from the Israel Police;[1] annual reports from the Juvenile Probation Service;[2] and data from the Central Bureau of Statistics.[3] These sources were partially parallel and partially complementary. It was not possible to locate official reports of juvenile delinquents for the year 1963, but only the number of files opened. Thus, the year 1963 is not represented in this study.

Most of the data will be presented in the form of the rate of the group of offenders to the total number of the same age group in the general population.[4] Such a method provides a more relevant description of the situation than that published in the criminal statistics. For this study, such a method has the following advantages: it allows for standardization of the data on offenders and a comparison over time; it demonstrates the criminal group's tendency toward illegal behavior; and its compares the characteristics of the group to the same age group of the general population.

This study does not go beyond 1977 because in 1978 boys aged 17-18 were included in the definition of minors.[5] For security reasons (this age group has to serve in the Israeli army), it was not possible to discuss the data about this group separately in calculating the rates for a particular age group. Another statutory amendment concerning the definition of minors came into force in between 1948 and 1974, the study covered boys aged 9-16 and girls aged 9-18; in the last three years of the study (1975-1977) boys aged 16-17 were also included.

There is a consensus among researchers that official criminal statistics cannot serve as an adequate measure of criminality (Empey, 1978). Although at present most empirical study in criminology is based on the official statistics, the literature points out three main faults: (a) Representation of the offenders is only partial, and in order to receive a more reliable, alternative source two others types of data must be considered, namely, victim surveys and self-reporting (Sparks, 1981; Reiss, 1981; Winslow, 1969; Wheeler, 1967; and Wolfgang, 1964; Kitsuse and Circourel, 1963; Short and Nye, 1958). (b) The official statistics reported by the police tend to favor or bias against certain population groups (Box, 1971); Black and Reiss, 1970; Hirschi, 1969; Neiderhoffer, 1969; Matza, 1969; Wilson, 1968a,b; Wheeler, 1967; Piliavin and Briar, 1964[6] (c) There is a significant discrepancy between the number of offenders for whom criminal files are opened and the numbers who are indicted (Box, 1971. Chap. 6, Hood and Sparks, 1970: 70-79). There is another drawback: the criminal statistics do not take into consideration the interaction between two factors which vary over the years—the distribution of the offender population, and opportunity for committing offenses (Reiss, 1981: 11-12, 15-16).

The official criminal statistics in fact describe two dimensions of delinquent behavior: (1) the criminal behavior of those apprehended by the police, and (2) the socioeconomic background of those apprehended. Nevertheless, these data are the only existing source for describing the known criminality in a given population and the only means for discerning changes in the patterns and trends of criminality over a period of years. Moreover, the societal reaction, which includes allocation of resources both in manpower and in institutions, is based exclusively on these statistics.

III. FINDINGS: THE DISTRIBUTION OF JUVENILE OFFENDERS

In Figure 1, we show the rate of offenders relative to the age group in the general population (absolute numbers in Appendix 1). A number of principal findings emerge from this graph: the middle curve, which represents the rate of male and female offenders is relatively stable for the years 1949-1960, about 7.5:1000 (except for the rise in the years 1953-1956, when it reached 10:1000). There is a steep rise from 1961 to 1962 (from 7.7:1000 to 15.9:1000); relative stability in the years 1962 to 1969 (from 15.9:1000 to 17.4:1000, except for 1967, the year of the Six Day War); and a downward trend from 1969 onward (from 17.4:1000 in 1969 to 11.0:1000 in 1977).

The uppermost of the three curves is the most prominent, representing the rate of male juvenile offenders. Since the curve of female offenders is almost constant, it is the rate of male offenders which in fact influences the trend evident in the middle curve. The rate of female offenders remains almost constant over the years, never exceeding 4:1000. The ratio of girls to boys fluctuates between 1:7 to 1:10, i.e., only about 10% of all the known juvenile offenders in Israel are girls.

The offenders were divided into three age groups: With respect to the first (ages 9-12) there was a decline, commencing in 1962, from 39% of all reported juvenile offenders in that year to 10% in 1977. The second (13-16 years) and largest group comprised 50-70% of all known offenders. The third group, which contained only girls comprised between 2% and 10% of all offenders.

With the departure of the British from Israel in 1948, all the previous records were removed preventing any comparative study between the periods before and after the establishment of the State (Israel Police, [1948] 1960: 1-3). We have defined as recidivists all those youngsters who have been referred twice or more to the Juvenile Probation Service; new offenders are those who are referred for the first time only. Figure 2 shows the distribution of Jewish offenders according to the division between first offenders and recidivists.[8] It indicates that the

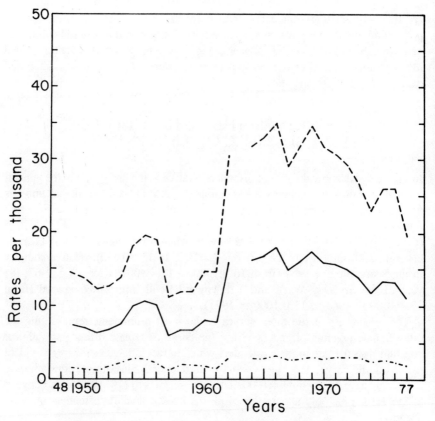

Figure 1. Rates of Juvenile Offenders (per thousand)
of the Age Group in the General Population.
Key: – · – , girls; - - - - , boys; ———— , girls and boys.

28

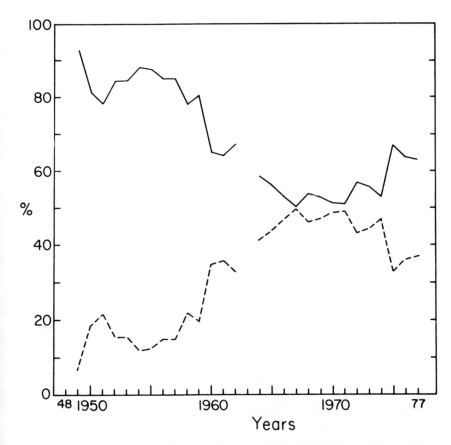

Figure 2. Juvenile Offenders: First Offenders and Recidivists (in percent).
Key: ———, first offenders; - - - - , recidivists.

proportion of recidivists rose up to 1967. From then on, the ratio of first offenders and recidivists was stable, except for 1976, when a new age group (16-17 years) was included in the definition of minors and entailed an increase in the proportion of first offenders. A similar picture emerged when the separate rates (per 1000) of first offenders and recidivists were calculated (see Appendix 2).

Recidivists were divided into two subgroups, according to the number of offenses committed: youngsters who have committed from two to five offenses, and those who have committed six or more offenses. This distribution is represented in Figure 3.[9] We see that over the years a type of continuous internal ratio of first offenders to recidivists was mentioned. The upper curve depicts the first offenders, and it includes between 50% and 60% of all the known juvenile offenders. The middle curve represents those offenders who have committed from two to five offenses. It includes about 30% of youngsters apprehended. The third curve, which represents youngsters who have committed six or more offenses, includes about 15% of all the youngsters.

It is therefore apparent that in spite of the drop in the absolute number of offenders, as well as the downward trend of the rate of offenders, a type of internal balance has been maintained among the three groups of offenders.

We must consider, in particular, the group of hard-core delinquents who have committed six or more offenses. In recent years, the types of crimes committed by these youngsters have become more serious. They, for example, are largely responsible for the rise in crime against the person, as indicated in Figure 4 (see below).

The likelihood that these youngsters will commit further offenses is high. Wolfgang (1980), in his cohort study in Philadelphia, found that the probability of youngsters who have committed four offenses to continue committing offenses is .80, and the likelihood that the further offenses will be more serious is between .300 and .722. On the Israeli scene, too, there is evidence of this phenomenon: in 1977, in the Tel Aviv region, 7% of the youngsters apprehended by the police were charged with 52.3% of all offenses (Report of the Commission for Investigating Crime in Israel, 1978 Jerusalem p. 20, Shimron Rept). This group, then, will continue to keep the law enforcement agencies busy, and a large number of these offenders will almost certainly follow a career of crime (Clinard and Quinney, 1967: 131-4).

The contribution of the treatment and justice system to the prevention of crime is debatable. One can always argue that, were it not for this system, the number of juvenile recidivists would be growing rather than remaining constant. But even if we accept this argument, we are still left with the grave problem that the law enforcement system has failed both in preventing these youngsters from committing their first crime and in deterring them from the commission of additional offenses. Attempts at rehabilitating this group have also failed.

We may assume that all the possibilities for dealing with these youngsters have been exhausted. Thus, should there be no changes in the rehabilitation and

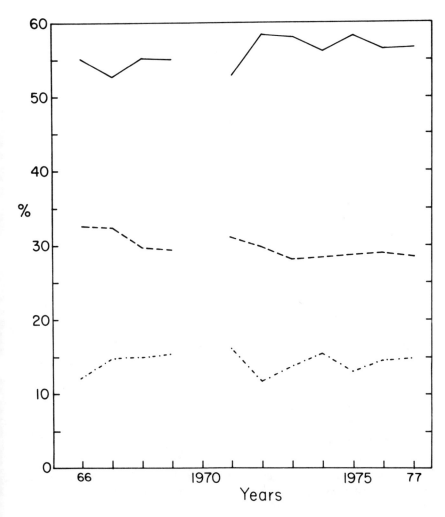

Figure 3. Juvenile Offenders According to Number of Offenses (in percent). Key: ———, first offenders; - - - -, two to five offenses; · — · —, six and more offenses.

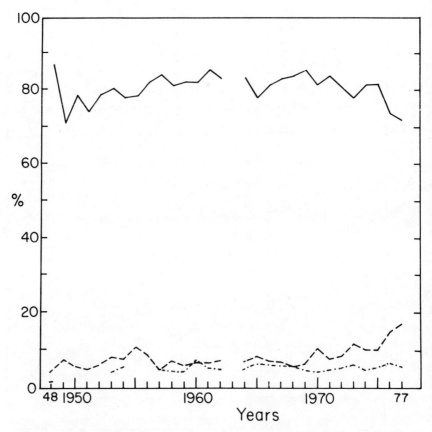

Figure 4. Juvenile Offenders According to Type of Offenses (in percent).
Key: ———, offenses against property; - - - -, offenses against the person;
· — · —, offenses against the public order.

law enforcement systems—and the chances of any change are low—there will be no option but to concentrate on protecting society from these criminals and on findings ways of dealing with or punishing them so that they will be unable to harm society.

It appears, in effect, that Israel should follow the latest trend in the United States, that is, to allocate maximal resources to the identification of recidivists and violent offenders so as to incapacitate them from committing further crimes (Sykes, 1978: 488-93). Such an approach would emphasize the need to deal with hard-core recidivists, instead of with the entire delinquent population. [see Editors Note]

The second problem investigated in the study related to the types of crime that youngsters commit. Figure 4 depicts the division of male and female Jewish youths according to the three most prevalent types of offense: offenses against property; offenses against the person; and offenses against the public order.[10] The figure shows the internal relationship, in percentages, of all the offenses with which juveniles were charged.

As is true in other countries it seems that offenses against property are the most prevalent in juvenile crime, and they hover around 80% of total juvenile offenses over all the years of the study. In the last two years (1976-1977), there was a slight drop in offenses against property, as opposed to a rise in offenses against the person. Offenses against the person have also maintained a constant level. About 10% of the youngsters committed such crimes, and the same is true for offenses against the public order, which do not exceed 10% of all juvenile crime. Notwithstanding the slight increases and decreases, we can discern a fixed pattern of juvenile delinquency throughout the years in this respect.

The extent of the drug-related offenses is far behind these other offenses. However, it has increased significantly, inter alia due to the fact that following the 1967 war and the expansion of Israel's borders Israel has become a stopover in the drug-smuggling routes. Although the phenomenon of drug use was known before 1967, it has increased and intensified since that year and the population using drugs has become more varied, including both marginal/criminal youths and those defined as middle class.

Table 1 presents the percentages of juvenile suspects with respect to all people charged with drug-related offences.[11] Whereas the percentage of adults charged with drug-related offenses out of all adult suspects has approximately doubled over these years (from 2.47% in 1972 to 5.27% in 1977), the percentage of youngsters so charged has increased sixfold (from 0.4% of all juvenile suspects in 1972 to 2.86% in 1977).

It may be assumed that as of 1978 the picture reflected in the criminal statistics relating to juvenile crime in Israel has changed, both because of the broadening of the definition of minors with its application to the 17-18 age group and because the age of criminal liability was raised from 9 to 13 years (*Sefer Hahukkim*, 900, 1978: 148). Since there is a different pattern of criminality among the 17-

Table 1.   Drug-Related Offenses—Juveniles
(in absolute numbers and percentages)

	1972	1973	1974	1975	1976	1977
Usage	43	47	65	144	50	289
Dealing	—	—	9	10	6	24
Export/import	—	—	—	—	2	—
Total	43	47	74	154	58	313
Percentage of total juvenile suspects	0.48	0.54	0.88	1.66	0.84	2.86
Adult drug suspects as percentage of all adult suspects	2.47	3.03	3.84	4.72	3.19	5.27

18 age group (more sophisticated and violent crime), the changes should be studied both with respect to the extent of the phenomenon of juvenile crime and with respect to the fixed pattern of criminality determined in the present study, in which about four-fifths of the offenders committed offenses against property.

The official statistics distinguish between three ethnic groups: (1) natives of Africa and Asia and their offspring (hereinafter referred to as ''the Afro-Asian group''); (2) natives of Europe and America and their offspring (hereinafter referred to as the ''Euro-American group''); (3) native Israelis and their offspring born in Israel (hereinafter referred to as the ''Israeli group'').[12]

This classification is very crude, since it does not take into account the differences among the various countries included in the group: the socioeconomic, demographic and cultural characteristics of Moroccan immigrants are unlike those of the Iraqis, and the Yemenite community differs from the Persian community, but they are all included in the Afro-Asian group. The data, however, do not allow for finer distinctions.

It must also be kept in mind that country of origin is not an independent variable such as age, but rather a complex variable which, in the Israeli reality, is closely connected with social indicators such as level of education, income, housing conditions or family size. Even though the gap between the Afro-Asian and the two other groups narrowed during the years of the study, the Afro-Asian group still lags behind the Euro-American and Israeli groups. In 1977, the percentage of the Afro-Asian groups that acquired a tertiary education was one-third that of the other two groups (Appendix 3).[13] The Afro-Asian group's total annual monetary income is low ((Appendix 4). Their average family size is higher than that of the other two groups (Appendix 5), and they live in more crowded conditions. Furthermore, they frequent the welfare agencies more than six times as often as the others Appendixes 7 and 8).

The limitations of the data made it impossible to analyze juvenile crime by country of origin over all the years of the study. We can make only a sample presentation for the 1950s, and a continuous presentation from 1964 onward.

Large-scale migration of Asians and Africans to Israel began at the beginning of the 1950s. The arrival changed the size of the Israeli population and its ethnic composition in a very short span of time. For these immigrants, the first years were a period of adjustment to the conditions of life in the receiving country. Although there was a general rise in the real income and standard of living of immigrants from all countries between 1951 and 1960, the gap between the Euro-American immigrants and the Afro-Asian immigrants widened (Hanoch, 1961). There was also an increase in the crime rate of the Afro-Asian group: from 8.3 juvenile offenders per 1000 in 1951 (10.0:1000 in 1953; 13.0:1000 in 1957; 15.0:1000 in 1958) up to 23.7:1000 in 1960, i.e., nearly three times as high. During the same period, juvenile delinquency among the Euro-American immigrants, which from the outset was much lower, rose by only about 50% from 3.4:1000 persons in 1951 (5.0:1000 in 1953 and 1957: 6.0:1000 in 1958) up to 5.6:1000 in 1960.

As of 1964, the data are continuous, and Figure 5 depicts the rates per thousand of juvenile offenders according to the three groups of ethnic origin (the rates are also shown in Appendix 9).[14] If we disregard the two wars in 1967 and 1973 (on the relationship between war and crime, see Hassin and Amir, 1976) and the periods immediately following them (when the police were less concerned with youth and disclosure of crime) we learn from Figure 5 that the upper curve, representing the Afro-Asian crime rate, showed a significant and constant decline beginning in 1969 (from 28.0:1000 to 18.5:1000). This decrease is in keeping with that indicated in Figure 1. Hence, it is the drop in the crime rate of the Afro-Asian group which caused the significant drop in the total crime rate.

The rate of offenders of the Afro-Asian group is three to four times as high as that of the Euro-American group and the second-generation Israeli group. Offenders of Afro-Asian origin are overrepresented relative to the proportion of Afro-Asians in the general population of the same age group, and the second two groups are underrepresented (see Appendix 10). The crime rate for the Israeli groups showed a decrease for the years 1965-1967 (from 12.0:1000 to 6.76:1000), and a leveling off thereafter, except for small fluctuations, until the last year of the study, in which there was a further drop (4.7:1000). The curves for the Euro-American and the Israeli groups are more or less similar, which means they were comparatively low and had only small fluctuations.

Another phenomenon worth noting is the internal relationship among offenders apprehended by the police according to their country of origin. Appendix 11 shows that despite the decrease in the crime rate of the Afro-Asian group over the years of the study, they constituted around 80% of all known offenders. On the other hand, the Euro-American and the Israeli groups constituted about 10% and 5% of all known offenders, respectively.

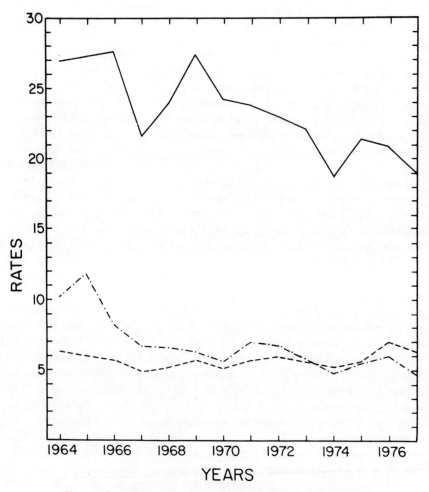

Figure 5. Rates (per thousand) of Juvenile Offenders
According to Place of Origin
Key: ———, Afro-Asian migrants and their children;
- - - -, Euro-American migrants and their children;
· – · –, Israel-born children of Israeli natives.

This phenomenon of a constant high proportion of Afro-Asians in official statistics is somewhat misleading. It is true that the proportion is high, but the 80% over the years is a result of a drop in the crime rate of the Afro-Asian group multipled by an increase in this group's proportion of the general population of the relevant age groups multiplied by the decrease in the crime rate of the survey population:

$$\frac{\text{Afro-Asian crime}}{\text{Afro-Asian population}} \times \frac{\text{Afro-Asian population}}{\text{general population}} \times \frac{\text{general population}}{\text{general crime}}$$

In fact, even more than a pattern of crime of the three groups, we see here the impact of police work, as mentioned earlier (Section II).

IV. SUMMARY OF FINDINGS

We can summarize our findings as follows:

a. From 1948 till 1969, the rate of juvenile crime increased. From 1969 until 1977, there was a general, gradual downward trend in the rates of juvenile offenders (per thousand). This trend was influenced primarily by the decrease in the crime rates of the Afro-Asian group (from 27 in 1966 to 18.5 in 1977).

b. During the period of the study, the ratio of first offenders to recidivists remained relatively stable, i.e., the percentage of juveniles who have committed only one offense, juveniles who have committed two to five offenses, and juveniles who have committed six or more offenses.

c. The patterns of juvenile delinquency by offense also remained relatively stable: offenses against property constituted about 80% of all offenses; offenses against the person constituted between 8% and 10% of all offenses, and offenses against the public order account for about 6-7% of all offenses.

d. We were able to discern a significant decrease in the crime rate (per thousand) of the Afro-Asian group relative to the total number of offenders (from 27.0 in 1966 to 18.5 in 1977).

Israel is regarded as one of the developed Western states. Research studies carried out in both capitalist and socialist countries have shown that juvenile delinquency is an inevitable result of industrial and economical development. In all developed states, including Japan and Switzerland, where the general crime rate is low, there has been an increase in the juvenile delinquency rate (Shelley, 1981: 80-82). For many years explanations for this increase have focused on the influenced of urbanization, mass media, family disintegration, parental occupations, peer group influence, and the like.

In Israel, however, there is an opposite tendency. Since 1969 there has been a decrease in the juvenile delinquency rate. We must, therefore, find explanations for the difference between Israel and other Western countries in this respect.

A decrease in juvenile delinquency was found among youths of Afro-Asian origin, but not among the two other groups—youths of Euro-American origin and second-generation Israelis. Since 80% of the reported crimes are committed by youths of Afro-Asian origin, the decrease in that group affects the general rate of juvenile delinquency. In this context, two main questions arise:

1. Why is the crime rate higher for the Afro-Asian immigrants than for the other two ethnic groups?
2. What is the social significance of the drop, commencing in 1969, in the crime rate of the Afro-Asian group?

The answer to these questions comprises several components:

First, Jewish immigration to Israel differs from the migration of other nationals from country to country. It was not only the ideology of the "ingathering of the exiles" which formed the backdrop to the immigration to Israel but also, as a natural outcome of this, the ideal of equality between veteran and newcomer, and between Westerners and Easterners. In the Law of Return, the new immigrant is granted full rights, from the moment of his arrival in Israel. Against this background, the immigrants to Israel developed high expectations of being one among equals in the economic and social framework. But even though Israel was undergoing a process of accelerated industrialization and economic growth, it could not satisfy these elevated expectations for a number of reasons: (a) the population of the receiving country was also a migrant one, still in the process of consolidation; (b) the receiving country was populated mainly by people from a Western background, whereas most of the immigrants came from the Islamic countries; (c) in the process of accelerated technological and industrial development, the absorption of immigrants with a lower level of education was neglected, and their former cultural background prevented their assimilation into the technological society (Eisenstadt, 1954).

Second, the transition from one country to another, each so different in its economic development and cultural background, upset the traditional patterns of life to which the immigrants were accustomed and caused strain on the family framework, challenged patriarchal authority, disturbed communal patterns and to a great extent brought about a loss of all social orientation.

Third, the children of the immigrants were youngsters in the midst of the crisis of adolescence: they were confronted with an unfamiliar language and failure at school; they lived, for the most part, in conditions of economic hardship and poverty; they had to face the obstacle of integration into an alien culture, and they bore a sense of interethnic disparity, of inequality and helplessness. All of these factors contributed to manifestations of alienation, isolation, deviation and eventually crime.

Most of the studies that investigated the connection between the waves of migration and deviant behavior were based primarily on criminal statistics, and they attempted to relate the statistics to Sellin's theory of culture conflict—a theory which stressed the contribution of such conflict to deviant behavior (see, e.g., Amir and Shichor, 1975; The Prime Minister's Committee for Distressed Children and Youth, 1973; Shoham et al., 1966; Shoham, 1962; Milo, 1960). But all those studies ignored the other changes in the social indicators of the population. Against this wider background, we can explain the rise in the crime rate of the Afro-Asian group in the 1950s, as well as the downward trend in the same crime rate from 1969 onward.

We have already noted that, during the 1950s, the gap between the Afro-Asian population and the Euro-American population widened and created interethnic tension and a sense of discrimination. At the same time, there was a rise in the Afro-Asian crime rate, which doubled the rise for the Euro-American group. In the 1960s, however, the Afro-Asian group slowly narrowed the gap in certain areas: education, the acquisition of power in municipal, bureaucratic and political arenas, and the purchase of commodities (Samuha and Peres, 1974). From 1967 (the year of the Six Day War) onward there was a rise in the level of income and in the employment ladder, which mainly affected the Afro-Asian immigrants. In the same period, the Afro-Asian housing density was somewhat alleviated and there was a surge in the development of primary and secondary prevention programs with most of the resources allocated to the Afro-Asian immigrants. This trend continued into the 1970s. Although the effects of all these factors are gradual, it may be assumed that they contributed to the persistent downward trend in the crime rate of the Afro-Asian group.

Hence, it is possible to contend that the gap in the standard of living between the different ethnic groups (not only from the economic but also from the social and cultural aspects) is a central factor in the crime rates of these groups; consequently, a narrowing of the gap will contribute to diminishing disparities in the crime rates, i.e., to a drop in the crime rate of the Afro-Asian group. We can assume that distress creates crime, and since the distress of the Afro-Asian immigrants and their children in Israel is greater, their crime rate, too, is higher.

This, however, is only a partial explanation, since the narrowing of the gap between the ethnic groups is measured by means of the average. This measure does not reflect the distance between the lowest and the middle 10 percentile, both within the same ethnic group and for the population at large. In other words, there are some families, irrespective of country of origin, who belong to the lower 10 percentile of the socioeconomic strata and for whom the gap has not narrowed, although their standard of living may have improved. The important question for which the criminal statistics provide no answer remains open: What are the effects of socioeconomic factors, without regard for ethnic origin on juvenile crime?[15] We do know that most juvenile offenders come from families which are at the bottom of the socioeconomic ladder, particularly families which have a tradition of crime, and with respect to which the country of origin is not a distinguishing factor.

It is possible, then, that most of the offenders represented in the last years of the study come from families facing a double disadvantage: the first, an extraethnic one, i.e., a gap between themselves and other ethnic groups in Israel; the second, an intraethnic one, i.e., a gap between themselves and natives of their own country and their children. If this supposition is correct, then the variable of country of origin loses its customary significance as being related to juvenile crime and may be replaced by the variable of families in distress, who belong to the lower strata of society and who are faced with the double disadvantage described above.

If this is indeed the case, then one should conclude that since there will always be a socioeconomic gap, and consequently a feeling of distress, discrimination and tension, there will also always be juvenile offenders who come, for the most part, from the bottom rungs of society. At the same time, due to the link between the size of the gap and the crime rate, a narrowing of the gap would result in a decrease in crime. These two processes are, of course, slow and drawn out.

Israel, like other industrial states, has discovered that crime is a phenomenon of developing societies. Although displaced ethnic groups in all industrial countries significantly contribute to the crime rate, in Israel there has been a relative *decrease* in crime in these groups. We estimate that the cause of this decrease is to be found, mainly, in the narrowing of economic, cultural and social gaps between groups.

While the relative deprivation of the lower percentiles of the population cannot explain the etiology of all types of crime, it can provide a line of thought for understanding the inner motivation of criminal behavior. Additional studies should be conducted that analyze the link between families in the lower socioeconomic strata, without regard to their country of origin, and the crime rate of their minor children.

EDITOR'S NOTE

While it may be argued that existing crime-control measures have failed to stamp out juvenile crime in societies like Israel and the United States, there is no reason to assume that incapacitation of "hard-core" recidivists remains the only viable alternative to achieve the "protection of society."

Appendix 1. Juvenile Offenders, Male and Female, Jewish
(absolute numbers)

Year	Number		Year	Number
1948	1450		1963	—
1949	1082		1964	7301
1950	1182		1965	7643
1951	1234		1966	8208
1952	1347		1967	6773
1953	1541		1968	7292
1954	2133		1969	7940
1955	2471		1970	7216
1956	2623		1971	7126
1957	1709		1972	6941
1958	2069		1973	6463
1959	2224		1974	5516
1960	2872		1975	6301
1961	3012		1976	6214
1962	6598		1977	5878

Appendix 2. First Offenders and Recidivists
(rate per 1000 of the age group)

Year	First Offenders	Recidivists
1949	6.80	0.54
1950	5.65	1.30
1951	4.90	1.36
1952	5.67	1.04
1953	6.37	1.17
1954	8.75	1.19
1955	9.27	1.32
1956	8.57	1.51
1957	5.07	0.89
1958	5.26	1.48
1959	5.38	1.31
1960	5.20	2.79
1961	4.97	2.78
1962	10.66	5.20
1963	—	—
1964	9.52	6.74
1965	9.42	7.35
1966	9.53	8.41
1967	7.45	7.38
1968	8.60	7.37
1969	9.21	8.18
1970	8.14	7.75
1971	8.00	7.70
1972	8.52	6.46
1973	7.70	6.12
1974	6.24	5.53
1975	8.98	4.43
1976	7.98	4.54
1977	6.98	4.10

Appendix 3. Age 14+ According to Years of Schooling and Place of Birth (in %)

	1961					1966					1971					1977			
	0	*1-4*	*5-8*	*9-12*	*13+*	*0*	*1-4*	*5-8*	*9-12*	*13+*	*0*	*1-4*	*5-8*	*9-12*	*13+*	*0*	*1-4*	*5-8*	*9-12*
Asia/ Africa	31.3	10.0	36.0	19.0	3.0	27.9	10.0	36.7	22.2	3.2	23.5	8.6	36.4	26.5	5.0	20.1	6.2	32.8	33.2
Europe/ America	3.2	7.5	37.6	38.2	12.7	3.1	9.5	34.4	38.7	14.3	2.4	8.3	32.4	38.5	18.4	2.5	6.4	27.8	39.5
Israel	2.2	1.9	26.1	53.9	15.2	1.7	1.3	25.5	54.8	16.7	1.0	1.3	20.5	59.4	17.8	0.7	0.5	14.6	61.7

This material was processed according to the *Israel Statistic Annual*

1961: Table 38   1963, p. 653
1967: Table 20/34   1967, p. 547
1971: Table 22/1   1972, p. 575
1977: Table 22/2   1978, p. 653

Appendix 4. Average Gross Annual Income
per Urban Household by Place of Birth
(in thousands of lirot)[a]

Year	Africa/Asia	Europe/America	Israel
1965	6.2	8.5	9.4
1970	9.7	13.2	13.6
1975	27.5	33.4	33.4
1977	54.2	66.8	66.0

[a]This material was processed according to the *Israel Statistics Annual*, 1978, Table 11/8, p. 303.

Appendix 5. Average Jewish Family Size by Place of Birth

Year	Africa/Asia	Europe/America	Israel
1961	4.8	3.2	3.4
1966	4.8	3.0	3.3
1971	4.6	2.8	3.4
1977	4.4	2.7	3.5

[a]This material was processed according to the *Israel Statistics Annual*:

1961—Table 2/22, p. 59, 1962;	1971—Table 2/28, p. 55, 1972;
1966—Table 2/19, p. 45, 1967;	1977—Table 2/30, p. 66, 1978.

Appendix 6. Jewish Families According to Number of Persons
per Rooom and Place of Birth[a]

Year	No. of Persons	Africa/Asia	Europe/America	Israel
1961	Less than 1	3.1	10.2	10.0
	1.0-1.9	26.8	56.4	58.1
	2.0-2.9	30.4	27.0	22.8
	3.0+	39.7	6.4	9.1
1966	Less than 1	5.9	18.2	10.1
	1.0-1.9	35.8	63.4	62.8
	2.0-2.9	31.1	15.7	17.9
	3.00+	27.2	2.7	9.2
1971	Less than 1	9.2	28.0	15.8
	1.0-1.9	45.6	60.5	61.1
	2.0-2.9	29.8	10.1	15.7
	3.0+	15.4	1.4	7.4
1977	Less than 1	14.5	40.2	21.1
	1.0-1.9	55.2	54.4	67.1
	2.0-2.9	24.1	5.0	9.2
	3.0+	6.2	0.4	2.5

[a]This material was processed according to the *Israel Statistics Annual*:

1961—Table 14, p. 1978, 1962;
1966, 1971—Table 11/15, p. 281, 1972;
1977—Table 11/21, p. 315, 1978.

Appendix 7. Families Handled by the Welfare Bureaus, According to Place of
Origin[a]

Year	Africa/Asia	Europe/America	Israel
1960	61.2	28.9	9.8
1966	66.2	29.4	4.4
1971	65.0	27.4	7.6
1977	61.7	27.9	10.4

[a]This material was processed according to the *Israel Statistics Annual*:

1961—Table 21/1, p. 503, 1962;   1971—Table 24/15, p. 628, 1972;
1966—Table 21/3, p. 553, 1967;   1977—Table 25/21, p. 746, 1978.

[b]Includes non-Jewish families in mixed neighborhoods for the years 1969, 1971, 1977.

Appendix 8. Families in the Care of Social Welfare Bureaus,
According to Place of Origin
(per hundred households in the general population)[a]

Year	Africa/Asia	Europe/America	Israel
1960	31.7	8.9	15.7
1966	33.0	10.2	6.1
1971	31.7	9.8	7.7
1977	35.4	11.7	8.7

[a]This material was processed according to the *Israel Statistics Annual*:
1961—Table 2/22, p. 59, and Table 21/1, p. 503, 1962;
1966—Table 2/19, p. 45, and Table 21/3, p. 553, 1967.
1971—Table 2/28, p. 55, and Table 24/15, p. 628, 1972;
1977—Table 2/31, p. 67, and Table 25/21, p. 746, 1978.

Appendix 9. Rates (per Thousand) of Representation of an
Age Group in Criminality, According to Place of Origin

Year	Afro-Asian Group	Euro-American Group	Israeli Group
1964	27.0	6.3	10.2
1965	27.3	6.0	11.9
1966	27.6	5.7	8.2
1967	21.6	4.9	6.7
1968	23.9	5.2	6.6
1969	27.4	5.7	6.3
1970	24.2	5.1	5.6
1971	23.8	5.7	7.0
1972	23.0	6.0	6.8
1973	22.1	5.6	5.8
1974	18.8	5.2	4.8
1975	21.4	6.6	5.5
1976	20.8	7.0	6.0
1977	18.5	6.3	4.7

Appendix 10.   Ratio Between Representation in Crime and
Representation in the Age Group[a]

Year	Afro-Asian Group	Euro-American Group	Israeli Group
1964	1.47	0.34	0.56
1965	1.42	0.31	0.62
1966	1.37	0.28	0.41
1967	1.30	0.29	0.40
1968	1.32	0.29	0.36
1969	1.39	0.29	0.32
1970	1.34	0.28	0.31
1971	1.34	0.32	0.40
1972	1.35	0.35	0.40
1973	1.40	0.36	0.36
1974	1.40	0.39	0.36
1975	1.41	0.43	0.36
1976	1.40	0.47	0.41
1977	1.42	0.48	0.36

[a] Greater than 1 = greater representation than their proportion of their age group; less than 1 = lower representation than their proportion of their age group.

Appendix 11.   Juvenile Offenders According to Place of Origin
(as a percentage of all reported offenders)

Year	Afro-Asian Group	Euro-American Group	Israeli Group	Unknown
1957	76.56	15.13	4.06	4.25
1958	77.46	14.90	4.87	2.77
1959	73.33	17.48	5.74	3.43
1960	80.64	17.96	—	1.39
1961	78.19	19.99	—	1.83
1962	67.19	21.28	3.38	8.16
1963	—	—	—	—
1964	73.86	14.41	4.52	7.22
1965	74.57	12.38	4.70	8.35
1966	74.89	10.54	3.24	11.33
1967	72.77	10.26	3.38	13.58
1968	75.72	9.66	3.30	11.31
1969	80.99	9.30	3.09	6.62
1970	79.27	8.63	3.24	8.85
1971	79.09	9.57	4.43	6.91
1972	80.61	10.04	4.58	4.77
1973	82.78	10.15	4.53	2.54
1974	82.40	10.77	4.88	1.96
1975	82.16	11.38	5.37	0.89
1976	80.30	12.54	6.42	0.74
1977	80.53	12.61	6.11	0.75

NOTES

1. Up to 1971 (inclusive) material on crimes and offenders in the police reports was collected manually, and there may therefore be slight discrepancies in the number; as of 1972, the material was transferred to the police computer. Until 1971 (inclusive) the number of persons accused by the police was listed as the number of files opened on them during that year; as of 1972, the accused are listed only once a year, according to the most serious offense. The reports of the Juvenile Probation Service refer only once to every minor according to the most serious offense, and we shall therefore present in this study the number of juvenile offenders according to the reports of the Juvenile Probation Service.

2. Organized reports of the Juvenile Probation Service exist only as of 1962. In these reports, as in others, information on the year 1963 is missing.

3. Up to 1956 (inclusive) material was collected from the sources at the Central Bureau of Statistics. For 1948-9, *Israel Statistics Monthly*, No. 4, and *Israel Statistics Monthly*, No. 7; for 1950-1956; *Israel Statistics Annual*, Nos. 2-8; for 1957-1959; Ministry of Welfare, *Statistical Survey of Juvenile Offenders* 1957-1959; 1961; for 1960-1 Central Bureau of Statistics, *Juvenile Delinquency*, 1960, 1961 (Jerusalem, 1964).

4. In calculating the rates, the definition of "minority" and the changes in this definition over the years were taken into account: until Oct. 1, 1975, "minors" applied to girls aged 9-18 and boys aged 9-16. As of Oct. 1, 1975, the definition applied to boys aged 16-17 as well; see Youth (Adjudication, Punishment and Treatment) Order, 1975, K.T. 3315, of Mar. 3, 1975, p. 1274.

5. As of April 1977, the definition of minors applied also to boys aged 17-18; see note 4, *supra*.

6. This is only a partial list of the studies dealing with the subject of bias. For a comprehensive list of studies on the subject, see Box, 1971, Chaps. 3 and 6.

7. In the criminal statistics, there is no record of those youngsters for whom the police decided not to open criminal files and to register only "no charge" files (diversion). As such, this population is not represented in the study.

8. In order to have an idea of the level of recidivism, it would have been necessary to examine the number of Jewish offenders to the number of charges (for the number of files opened for these offenders). This was impossible since the criminal statistics upon which this study was based did not distinguish between Jews and non-Jews with respect to the variable of the number of files opened.

9. Owing to the limitations of the data, it was possible to make this division only as of 1966.

10. These three offenses are among the most common for youth and therefore Figure 4 deals with them alone. For this reason, the percentages in the graph do not total 100.0%. Drug-related offenses are discussed later in Section III.

11. Owing to problems in the police reports (*supra*, note 1), in Table 1 we have used reports only from 1972-1977. The small number of youngsters apprehended for drug-related offenses is a result of two factors:

    a. In the offence of drug-usage, there is no complainant, and therefore, the apprehension of these youngsters depends exclusively on the goals of the police.

    b. The Israel Police follows a clear policy, based on the directives of the Attorney General, of not enforcing the law in all its severity with respect to minors who are first apprehended for drug use, i.e., the Police does not open criminal files, does not indict, but uses diversion. As such, this offense finds limited expression in the police statistics.

12. In 1948, the Jewish population in Israel totaled 716,700. By the end of 1977, the population had grown to 3,077,300, that is, the Jewish population had grown 4.29 since the establishment of the State; see Central Bureau of Statistics, *Israel Statistics Annual*, 1980, No. 31. Table B/1, p. 31. It is interesting to note that from May 15, 1948, until the end of August 1949, 272,000 immigrants (Jewish) arrived in Israel. See *Government Annual*, 1959, p. 147.

48   YAEL HASSIN

13. Owing to the limitations of the data, it was possible to examine the averages of this social indicator only as of 1961.

14. We are presenting the data from 1964 onward, for prior to this the Central Bureau of Statistics did not have data according to the division into countries of origin (natives and their children).

15. None of the sources of criminal statistics in Israel contain classification of offenders according to the ten percentiles of the socio-economic strata.

REFERENCES

Amir M. and D. Shichor
    1975 "The ethnic aspect of juvenile crime in Israel." Crime and Social Deviance, Vol. 3, no. 1,2, Pp. 1-15; 1-18.
Black D.J. and A.J. Reiss
    1970 "Police control of juveniles." American Sociological Review, No. 35, Pp. 63-78.
Box, S. Deviance, Reality and Society.
    1971 Holt, Rinehart and Winston, Ltd., Chaps. 3 and 6.
Central Bureau of Statistics
    1949 Israel Statistics Monthly, no. 4.
Central Bureau of Statistics
    1956 Israel Statistics Monthly, no. 7.
Central Bureau of Statistics
    1959 Israel Statistics Annual. no. 2-8.
Central Bureau of Statistics
    1964 Juvenile Delinquency, 1960-1 Special Publication no. 186, Pp. 28-9.
Central Bureau of Statistics
    1980 Israel Statistics Annual 1980, no. 31, Table b/1, p. 31.
Clinard, M.B.
    1978 Cities with Little Crime. Cambridge University Press: London, p. 122.
Clinard, M.B. and R. Quinney
    1967 Criminal Behavior Systems, second edition. Holt, Rinehart and Winston, Inc.: New York.
Eisenstadt, S.N.
    1954 The Absorption of Immigrants. London: Routledge and Kegan Paul, p. 46.
Empey, L.T.
    1978 American Delinquency, Its Meaning and Construction. Dorsey Press, part two.
Government Annual
    1950 p. 147.
Hanoch, G.
    1961 "Income disparities in Israel," Fifth Report 1959 and 1960. Falk Centre for Economic Research in Israel," p. 94.
Hassin, Y. and M. Amir
    1976 "Business (Crime) as usual in wartime conditions among offenders in Israel." The Journal of Criminal Law and Criminology, Vol. 66, no. 4, Pp. 491-495.
Hirschi, T.
    1969 Causes of Delinquency. University of California Press, Pp. 41-47, 81, 205-212.
Hood, R. and R. Sparks
    1970 Key Issues in Criminology. London: Weidenfeld and Nicolson, Pp. 70-79.
Israel Police
    1960 Annual Report, 1959, Tel Aviv.
Kitsuse J.I. and A.V. Circourei

1963 "A note on the uses of official statistics." Social Problems, Vol. 11, Pp. 131-139.
Kobrin, S.
1970 "The Conflict of Values in Delinquent Areas." In M.E. Wolfgang, I. Savitz and N. Johnston, The Sociology of Crime and Delinquency. Second Edition, John Wiley, New York: pp. 190-198.
Law of Return
1950 S.H. 51, (6.7.50), p. 159.
Matza, D.
1969 Becoming Deviant. New Jersey: Prentice-Hall, p. 183.
Milo, E.
1960 Prevention of Types of Criminality Resulting from Social Changes and Accompanying Economic Development in Less Developed Countries. Jerusalem, Ministry of Social Welfare
Ministry of Welfare
1959 Statistical Survey of Juvenile Offenders.
Niederhoffer, A.
1969 Behind the Shield: The Police in Urban Society. New York: Anchor, pp. 101-2.
Piliavin, I. and S. Briar
1964 "Police encounters with juveniles." American Journal of Sociology. Vol. 70, Pp. 206-214.
Prime Minister's committee for Distressed Children and Youth
1973 Jerusalem, (October).
Reed, J.P and F. Baali, (eds.)
1972 Faces of Delinquency. Prentice-Hall: Englewood Cliffs, N.J., pp. 25-39.
Reiss, A. Jr.
1981 "Understanding changes in crime rates." In S.E. Fineberg and A.J. Reiss, Jr., (eds.), Indicators of Crime and Criminal Justice: Quantitative Studies, U.S. Government Printing Office, Washington, D.C., Pp. 11-17.
Report of the Commission for Investigating Crime in Israel
1978 Jerusalem: p. 20 (Shimron Report).
Samuha, S. and Y. Peres
1974 "Ethnic gap in Israel." Megamot. 20, no. 1.
Schmelz, U. and D. Saltzmann
1965 Criminal Statistics in Israel. Publications of the Institute for Criminology. Vol. 1, Pp. 182-4.
Sefer Hahukkim
1978 900 (5738 in Hebraic calendar), p. 148.
Sellin, T.
1938 Culture Conflict and Crime. New York: Social Science Council.
Sellin, T. and M.E. Wolfgang
1964 The Measurement of Delinquency. John Wiley
Shaw C.R. and H.D. McKay
1942 Juvenile Delinquency and Urban Areas. Chicago: University of Chicago Press.
Shelley, L.I.
1981 Crime and Modernization. Carbondale and Edwardsville:Southern Illinois University press.
Shoham, S.
1962 "The application of the culture-conflict hypothesis for the criminality of immigrants in Israel." Journal of Criminal Law, Criminology and Police Science. Vol. 53, no. 2, Pp. 207-214.
Shoham, S. M.N. Shoham and A. Abed-El Rasak
1966 "Immigration, ethnicity and ecology as related to juvenile delinquency in Israel" British Journal of Criminology, Vol. 6, no. 4, Pp. 391-409.

Short, J.F.Jr., and F.I.Nye
    1958   "Extent of unrecorded juvenile delinquency: Tentative conclusions." Journal of Criminal
            Law Criminology and Police Science. Vol. 49, no. 4, Pp. 296-302.
Sykes, G.M.
    1978   Criminology. Harcourt Brace Jovanovich: New York.
Sparks, R.F.
    1981   "Criminal opportunities and crime rates." In S.E. Fineberg and A.J. Reiss, Jr. (eds.),
            Indicators of Crime and Criminal Justice: Quantitative Studies, U.S. Department of Justice,
            Bureau of Justice Statistics, U.S. Government Printing Office, Washington, D.C., pp. 18-
            27.
Wheeler, S.
    1967   "Criminial statistics: a reformulation of the problem". Journal of Criminal Law, Crimi-
            nology and Police Science. Vol. 58, no. 3, Pp. 317-324.
Wilson, J.Q. (a)
    1968   "The police and the delinquent in two cities." in S. Wheeler (ed.), Controlling Delinquents.
            New York: John Wiley, pp. 9-30.
Wilson, J.Q. (b)
    1977   "Police discretion." (1968) in Sir Leon Radzinowicz and M.F. Wolfgang (eds.), Crime
            and Justice. Vol. II, The Criminal in the Arms of the Law, Basic Books, pp. 129-145.
Winslow, R.W.
    1969   Crime in a Free Society. Belmont, California: Dickenson, Pp. 43-4.
Wolfgang, M.E.
    1980   "The longitudinal study of delinquency and crime." Papers presented at the 2nd Israel
            Society of Criminology Meeting (April), p. 10.
Youth (Adjudication, Punishment and Treatment) Order.
    1975   In K.T., 3315, of 30.3 1975, p. 1274.

THE ANTI-ALIEN CONTRACT LABOR LAW OF 1885 AND "EMPLOYER SANCTIONS" IN THE 1980s

Kitty Calavita

I. INTRODUCTION

"Illegal" migration to the United States has recently been pushed to the top of the already crowded agency of controversial political issues for the 1980s. In fact, immigration policy in general and the issue of "illegals" in particular is consistently declared "one of the most significant domestic and international issues confronting this nation" (Ochi, 1981:381).

Recognizing that the phenomenon of immigration represents primarily the movement of a work force, recent proposals to reduce "illegal" migration center around the reduction of employment opportunities for the undocumented. "Employer sanctions," which would make it illegal for employers knowingly to hire "illegal" aliens, have provided a central component of the Carter administration's 1977 proposal, the more recent Select Commission on Immigration and

Research in Law, Deviance and Social Control, Volume 5, pages 51-82
Copyright © 1983 by JAI Press, Inc.
All rights of reproduction in any form reserved
ISBN: 0-89232-334-5

Refugee Policy's recommendations, President Reagan's immigration policy package, and the current Simpson-Mazzoli proposal.

As is so frequently the case, this central element of recent proposals is also one of the most complex and controversial, particularly with regard to its enforcement possibilities and potential impact. The proposal is not only politically controversial given the myriad civil rights and justice dilemmas it raises, but it adds to the enigmas that scholars face when they attempt to make theoretical sense out of the apparent maze that is American immigration policy. This paper represents an effort to sort out those enigmas surrounding the issue of employer sanctions, utilizing historical data and a comparative, theoretical approach.

The context within which the contemporary employer sanctions proposal is formulated, as well as the shape it is taking and its potential for significant impact, bears striking resemblance to a previous labor/immigration law, enacted nearly a century ago—the Anti-Alien Contract Labor Law of 1885. This paper provides an in-depth investigation of that earlier piece of immigration legislation. It then goes on to flesh out the apparent similarities between that law and the contemporary employer sanctions proposal. It is hoped that this historical comparison will not only contribute to a more adequate understanding of the prospects and pitfalls of the employer sanctions proposal but will also suggest the utility of an historically informed approach to immigration issues.

II. THE ANTI-ALIEN CONTRACT LABOR LAW OF 1885[1]

A. Immigration and Industrial Expansion

The last four decades of the nineteenth century were unique in U.S. history in terms of industrial and capital expansion. Between the end of the Civil War and the turn of the century the number of manufacturing establishments in the United States more than doubled and production increased fourfold (Clark, 1929). The value of manufactured products rose from $1.9 billion in 1860 to $11.4 billion in 1900 (Bimba, 1927).

As early as 1791, Alexander Hamilton (1791:123) had warned Congress that if America were to industrialize, immigration must be encouraged so as to "mitigate" the "dearness of labor." The second half of the nineteenth century witnessed the success of Hamilton's idea and the crucial role immigration played in U.S. industrialization.

Twenty-five million immigrants entered the country in this period, most of them remaining in the cities and entering the industrial work force. By 1880, more than 70% of the population in each of our largest cities was made up of immigrants or their children, and the proportion of immigrants to native-born was not much lower in the smaller industrial towns of the east (Gutman, 1976:40). The foreign-born increasingly made up the bulk of the industrial work force. Samuel Lane Loomis noted in 1887 that "not every foreigner is a workingman, but in the cities at least, it may almost be said that every workingman is a foreigner" (quoted in Gutman, 1976:40).

As Boyer and Morais (1977:21-22) characterize this era, in the midst of this unparalleled expansion of industry, "everything would have been perfect in a perfect world had it not been for certain unfortunate aspects of the rising industrial system." Paramount was the fact that this "industrial system" was producing class struggle and a militant labor movement as systematically as it produced commodities. Labor journalist John Swinton (1894:Preface) put it succinctly: "The times are revolutionary. There is a new spirit abroad."

In fact, the Balitmore & Ohio Railway strikes of 1877, the successful Gould strike of 1885 and the Homestead and Pullman strikes of the 1890s were merely the landmarks of a 30-year period of class struggle more intense and prolonged than any in our history. By 1885, the Knights of Labor spearheaded a national labor movement of unprecedented proportions. Promoting labor solidarity by providing the arena in which the various craft unions could unify their strength nationally, the Knights of Labor brought together for the first time the skilled and the unskilled, the native- and the foreign-born, into one national organization. With nearly a million members, a stable financial base, and a network that potentially united all the nation's workers, the Knights of Labor backed skirmish after skirmish on the industrial battlefield and came through with a significant record of success.

B. The Distribution of Immigrant Labor

During and immediately following the Civil War, employers regularly imported immigrant workers for the express purpose of breaking strikes and, more generally, undermining unions. The *Workingman's Advocate* (1869:2), a prominent Chicago labor paper, noted the trend:

> Ever since the completion of the Atlanta telegraph, it has been the threat of unprincipled employers, in every state where unpleasantness has occurred, to threaten the importation of foreign workmen, and in many instances they have been able to put their threats into execution.

Despite occasional successes by employers, the practice of breaking strikes by importing immigrants had one major drawback. The very union strength that made such importations necessary also made it likely that the union, through concerted efforts, might succeed in persuading these imported workers to break their contracts and join the union—or leave the area. Among imported miners and ironworkers, such prounion activity appears to have been frequent (*Workingman's Advocate*, 1873:1; Grossman, 1945; Erickson, 1957:53).

When employers directly imported immigrant strikebreakers, they risked not only losing the strike and strengthening the union as imported workers joined the strikers but also forfeiting the advanced passage money. To make it worse, because of these uncertainties in the system, it was frequently necessary to engage many more men than were actually necessary. Clearly, the payment of passage money for many more immigrants than were used was financially impractical. The fluctuations in the economy made formal contracts with European workers even more burdensome. The plague of economic collapse every six or seven years made it quite likely that contracted workers would have to be carried over periods of depression by the employer.

The private labor exchange fit very well into this set of circumstances, and it remained the mechanism by which immigrant labor was distributed for several decades. Most of these private labor bureaus were concentrated in New York City. By 1906, there were 61 such labor exchanges located on Greenwich and Mulberry Streets directly opposite Castle Garden. Nor were these agencies small concerns. One agency's circular boasted that 20,000 workers could be supplied if necessary (*John Swinton's Paper*, 1885). One order was filled for 500 workers in 1885; in 1883, 11,000 had been sent to the New York and West Shore Railroad; one batch of 3,000 was supplied to the Baltimore & Ohio Railroad in 1884 (Erickson, 1957:100-101). All were apparently supplied "at a moment's notice" (*Congressional Record*, 1885:1633), and none was at superfluous expense or risk to the employer. For each worker they supplied, the labor exchanges typically received $1.00—a small cost to the employers, considering that the workers often received less than the usual pay scale. Hungarians, Poles and Italians supplied by the exchanges were working in the Pennsylvania mines for as little as 80 cents a day when the usual rate was $1.50-$1.75 (*John Swinton's Paper*, 1884a:1; 1884b:1). The New York City Italian Labor Bureau supplied workers at 50 to 60 cents a day and even stipulated "that the laborers will serve from one to five years without demanding an increase" (U.S. Congress, Senate Committee on Education and Labor, 1885:810-11). The higher fee of $2.00 per worker for strikebreakers if they succeeded in breaking the strike was a small price to pay for the freedom to ignore workers' demands.

The use of immigrants from these labor exchanges became a regular weapon in capital's arsenal against striking miners. In the three-year period between 1872 and 1875 when the Miners National Association under the leadership of John Siney backed strike after strike, 14 strikes were broken in Ohio, Pennsylvania and Indiana, by the introduction of Swedish, German, Italian and black strikebreakers (Gutman, 1976). Coming directly from the New York exchanges, the immigrants arrived under heavy guard, both to protect themselves and, more importantly, to isolate them from the strikers.

Swedish strikebreakers who arrived in the Blossburg district of Pennsylvania in 1873 were taken under guard to the special barracks that had been constructed to house them (Roy, 1970:104). Italians came from New York to the western

Pennsylvania mines in the midst of a general strike in 1874 "armed as a regiment of soldiers"(*Iron Molders Journal*, 1874:104-105), and other immigrant strikebreakers arrived in Westmoreland County in the same year armed with breech-loading rifles (McNeill, 1888:260). Throughout the rest of the century, miners, railway workers, construction workers—in fact, the workers of almost every American industry—watched their strikes defeated by newly arrived immigrants and gun barrels (Berthoff, 1953; Erickson, 1957:112; Gutman, 1976).

We should note here that no contracts were signed between employers and these immigrants who were "bought" from the urban labor exchanges.

The fact that this unskilled immigrant labor provided the cutting edge with which to frustrate union efforts did not go unappreciated by the capitalists of the period. Andrew Carnegie (1886) referred to the influx of immigrants as a "golden stream" and valued each at "at least $1500 apiece." The editor of the *Engineering and Mining Journal* (1880) noted approvingly that "Castle Garden, with its hosts of immigrants, appears to be solving the labor question."

C. Labor Makes Legal Demands That Cannot be Ignored

In the immediate sense, the foregoing comment was partially true. However, the inherent conflict between capital and labor was *not* solved; its symptoms were merely transformed and conflict recreated, as organized labor began to make legal demands for protection from capital's use of immigrants to undermine their efforts.[2]

Much of organized labor's agitation in the early 1880s for protection from immigrant "pauper labor" and strikebreakers was formulated in broad, general terms. At a labor rally in Pittsburgh in 1882, for example, workers protested being forced to compete with "the pauper labor of Europe" (*Philadelphia Times*, 1882:1). During the elections of 1880, labor newspapers across the country made an issue of the harmful effects on unions of unrestricted immigration.

In March 1883, a relatively small group of craft unionists, the Window-Glass Workers of America, formulated and submitted to Congress an anti-alien contract labor bill that came to be viewed by politicians and capitalists of the period, as well as labor historians, as the culmination of organized labor's demands for protection from immigrant labor.

It has already been pointed out that for most sectors of American industry it was no longer feasible to import workers on contracts, nor was it necessary. Rather, the immigrant strikebreakers that were the Achilles' heel of labor unions were obtained at the urban labor exchanges. Only highly skilled craftsmen continued to be imported from Europe under contract. It is not surprising then that the real impetus for the Anti-Alien Contract Labor Law came from a small group of skilled craftsmen. It was only after the glassworkers had sent their bill to Washington that Terence V. Powderly and other leaders of the Knights of Labor were informed of the bill and agreed to back it.

For the next three years, organized labor's discussion of the restriction of immigration was limited to the issue of contract labor. The protection of American labor via some kind of immigration regulation became synonymous with the prohibition of contract labor. It is not difficult to understand why the Knights of Labor, although they had not themselves formulated the issue in these terms, came to see the Anti-Alien Contract Labor Law as their salvation. The Slavic, Hungarian, Italian and other unskilled immigrants who were repeatedly brought from the New York exchanges and used by employers to break crucial strikes were almost invariably brought en masse to the strike location under armed guard, surrounded by employers' men and police contingents hired for the occasion. It understandably appeared—and in one sense, but not the crucial one, the appearance was real—that these immigrants were of *captive status*, owned, transported and guarded by employers.

The dilemma for congressional lawmakers was this: Just at the time when the new-found strength of organized labor made it even more crucial for employers to have continued access to the "golden stream," that same strength made it no longer possible for Congress to ignore labor's insistent pleas for protection. The need to sustain a surplus and, therefore, tractable labor force versus the simultaneous need not to jeopardize the political status quo with that strategy was by now, and would continue to be, a central dilemma for immigration policymakers.

D. Symbolic Action as a Response

Congress was confronted with two equally unacceptable policy options: it could continue to promote the short-term interests of employers and jeopardize its own legitimacy and political stability, or it could address labor's grievances by numerically limiting the "golden stream," thereby interfering with the interests of employers.

Stearns (1979), in her examination of occupational safety and health laws in Sweden, notes that there is frequently a less painful "resolution" of such dilemmas—that of "symbolic action." That is, political disturbances and protests can often be curbed through symbolic legislation which appears to address the concerns of the protesting groups but does not significantly alter conditions nor threaten even the short-term interests of capital. For example, Stearns suggests that the ideal "solution" to the conflict in Sweden between the need for uninterrupted capital accumulation and the need for the social democratic state to show its concern for working-class interests was the creation of a large occupational safety and health bureaucracy whose ostensible purpose is to ensure safe and healthful working conditions but which in effect does little of the kind. Edelman (1964, 1977) similarly demonstrates the utility of this concept of "symbolic action" in reference to both legislation and linguistics.

It would seem that legislation can be rendered purely symbolic in any of four ways: (1) loopholes can be incorporated into the legislation so that it can be easily circumvented; (2) it can address only a narrow and relatively insignificant aspect of the issue involved; (3) Congress can fail to designate enforcement procedures or fail to appropriate funds for its enforcement; or (4) the courts' interpretation of the legislation can be such as to eliminate any potential effect. The Anti-Alien Contract Labor Law of 1885—also known as the Foran Act— was victim to all four.

The Foran Act, first introduced by Martin Foran in the House of Representatives in January 1884 and referred to the newly created Committee on Labor, was passed a year later on February 18, 1885. It stipulated that:

> **Section 1**. . .[I]t shall be unlawful for any person, company, partnership, or corporation. . .to prepay the transportation or in any way assist, any foreigner or foreigners, into the United States. . .under contract or agreement, parol or special, express or implied, made previous to the importation or migration of such alien. . .to perform labor or service of any kind in the United States.
>
> **Section 5**. . .That nothing in this act shall be construed to prevent any person, or persons, partnership, or corporation from engaging, under contract or agreement, skilled workingmen in foreign countries to perform labor in the United States: *Provided*, that skilled labor for that purpose can not be otherwise obtained (*Congressional Record*, 1885:1622).

The debates surrounding the Foran Act are worth examining in some detail. These discussions make it clear that the bill was above all an attempt to placate organized labor without exacting sacrifices from capital.

The first requirement of symbolic legislation is that it seem to respond to the demands being made by the protesting group. There is no doubt that the participants in the debates surrounding the Foran Act in the House in June 1884 and in the Senate in February 1885 were above all concerned with demonstrating to American labor that the bill was to serve them. Without exception those who spoke in favor of the bill rhetorically pronounced that the bill was to be the salvation of the American laborer, protecting him against both immigrant labor and the "greedy capitalists" who imported it. Foran, an Ohio Republican and the bill's spokesman in the House, introduced the bill:

> Mr. Speaker. . .its object is to prevent and prohibit men whose love of self is above their love of country and humanity from importing into this country large bodies of foreign labor to take the places of and crowd out American labor. . . .No greater evil could be inflicted upon American workingmen than to bring them into competition with this species of slave labor (*Congressional Record*, 1884:5349).

Others in the House reiterated: "I am in favor of protecting American labor. . ." (*Congressional Record*, 1884: 5349). And: "I am a protectionist. I want to protect American labor against degrading competition both abroad and at home" (*Congressional Record*, 1885:5364).

In the Senate, John Sherman of Ohio—the father of the 1864 Contract Labor Law which had made foreign contract labor legally binding—applauded the Foran

58   KITTY CALAVITA

Bill: "This bill (protects)...our laboring men...from the men who are not free, who are slaves...who...are brought here under contracts to drive out of the field the honest laboring men of the country" (*Congressional Record*, 1885:1785-86).

Thomas M. Ferrell, in the House, outshone all others with page after page of "American labor" rhetoric:

> I rejoice that I am enabled, from this exalted position to raise my voice and to aid by my vote the toiling millions of my countrymen who are made to suffer unjustly the bitter discrimination of this system, in assisting them to procure relief by the enactment of wholesome and just laws....I sincerely hope the time has come when the great labor associations and the poor toilers who know how this system affects their social condition in this beautiful land of perpetual harvest, are to soon proclaim from the mines in the bowels of the earth to the workshop in every valley and on every hilltop, that Congress here assembled has passed a bill to prevent pauper-wage prices for their labor, and that the dismal period has passed from the land forever...(*Congressional Record*, 1884:5364).

So repetitive were such pronouncements that the bill's few opponents complained, rather perceptively as we will see:

> Representatives have unloaded their choicest rhetoric, heavily freighted with glittering generalities, upon the laborer until he must be akin to Atlas, or blessed with sinews of iron and legs of brass to bear the burden (*Congressional Record*, 1884:5364).

That it was pressure from an organized and potentially disruptive labor movement that made some legislative response necessary was well recognized. Again, it is the bill's few opponents whose words are most revealing:

> In our eager desire to gratify public demands...I should regret very much—it makes no difference what might be the clamor in this country, it makes no difference if the labor union societies were ten to where there is one—I would regret very much as Senator to feel compelled to yield to a demand made on me from that direction (*Congressional Record*, 1885:1631).

If the congressional discussions make it clear that the bill was a response to organized labor's demands for protection, close attention to the debates makes it equally clear that no such protection was to be forthcoming. In the first place, an amendment was added immediately specifying that new industries which required skilled labor that could not be otherwise obtained, were exempt from the provisions of the act.

That this amendment was particularly important to the bill's supporters is clear from the response to a suggestion that the clause be struck out. It was immediately declared an affront to labor to even consider striking out a clause of a bill which labor had helped labor frame:

> The bill was not framed by children and babes, but by men whose interests it undertakes to guard and conserve....The provisions which the Senator moves to strike out is one which

they were particularly careful to have included in this bill and to strike it out, in the general estimate of all those who take any affirmative interest in the enactment of the bill in to law, entirely emasculates it. *They very likely then would prefer its defeat*, or at all events would become indifferent to its enactment (*Congressional Record*, 1885:1622; my emphasis).

This, in spite of the fact that the provision with regard to "new industries" had been added not by organized labor but by the Committee on Labor in the House. Labor's only comment on the provision had been Powderly's noncommital remark, "I would not object to men being brought to start new industry."[3]

More important than these amendments in ensuring the bill's lack of impact, the bill itself referred only to the narrow issue of foreign labor actually on contract. Since most of the immigrant labor used to break strikes and reduce wages had no preemigration contract with the employer but was obtained at the labor exchanges, the law had no potential effect on the real scourge of American workers. An amendment introduced in the House on the first day of debate stipulated that only those contracts made *before* emigration were covered in the act (*Congressional Record*, 1884:5370-71), thus exempting contracts made between the immigrant upon arrival and the labor exchanges, leaving untouched that very segment of immigrant labor that was most detrimental to organized labor.

If the bill was to placate organized labor beyond the small minority of highly skilled craft workers to whom it potentially applied, it must *seem* to address their concerns. This it did admirably. Speaker after speaker denounced the "pauper labor of Europe," the unskilled Hungarians, Poles, Slavs and Italians who broke strikes, who were *not* broke, however, on contract:

Large numbers of degraded, ignorant, brutal Italian and Hungarian laborers...This is the class of persons, this is the species of immigration with which this bill seeks to deal...(*Congressional Record*, 1884:5349).

And:

That large numbers of inferior, unskilled, degraded laborers are annually imported under contract to perform labor in the United States is known to everybody (*Congressional Rrd*, 1884:5351).

The emphasis throughout the debates was on the so-called new immigrants—the Italians, Poles, Hungarians and Slavs—and the issue was diverted to the allegedly inferior living standards of these groups. These "new immigrants" were denounced as "slaves," "serfs," and "lowest beings," and as receiving "30 to 50% less wages than American laborers" (*Congressional Record*, 1884:5350). It was even declared that "this servile contract is worse than the African slaves of the South" (*Congressional Record*, 1885:1625). This concentration on the living standards of "new immigrants" had two consequences. Not only did it make the bill seem to apply to the kind of labor that most threatened American workers, but it also stressed the repugnancies of such "slave labor."

By using vague and ambiguous terminology, the bill's spokesmen were able to accomplish the appearance of protecting American labor against this monstrous evil of slave labor while fashioning the bill so as not to exact any substantial changes. "Contract labor" was never explicitly defined, nor was there consensus on what the bill actually prohibited. Its many supporters apparently found it irksome that there were a few uncooperative naysayers who preferred to understand the bill's terms and how it would actually affect labor. Thus, while Foran and others often referred to the "slave labor" obtained at Castle Garden and the labor exchanges, they had to admit under questioning that their only data on contracts made abroad had to do with 200 glassworkers (*Congressional Record*, 1884:5350). Similarly, after Senator Henry Blair of New Hampshire had read out petitions citing contracts made with glassworkers and skilled goldbeaters, he too was forced to concede that the bill was directed at *contract* labor, "not necessarily pauper labor" (*Congressional Record*, 1885:1834).

Neither its spokesmen nor its few opponents were unaware that the bill was "crude and imperfect" (*Congressional Record*, 1885:1796). With regard to its ambiguities, one of the bill's opponents commented: "Whoever it was that proposed this bill...he was a very poor lawyer..." (*Congressional Record*, 1885:1631). And later:

> Almost everyone who has risen to advocate the bill, has got up and explained that the bill was crude and imperfect....The whole door of mischief that is intended to be closed out by this bill is left wide open...and yet this is the bill about which so much is said and about which every Senator's judgment is challenged when he presumes to make a criticism of it (*Congressional Record*, 1885:1796).

Another stated briefly in the House:

> After what I have heard spoken on the floor of this House today, my faith in the infallibility of language to convey its true meaning, or at least its intended meaning...has been sadly shaken (*Congressional Record*, 1884:5364)

Speaker after speaker who rose in *favor* of the bill similarly "complained" of its loose terminology:

> I expect to vote for this bill. I think the bill is immature and crude, but I shall vote for it on account of the salient principle which it announces (*Congressional Record*, 1885:1780).

Without exception those who spoke in favor of the bill, yet admitted to its ambiguities and imprecisions, *rejected amendments whose purpose was to clarify its terms*. Senator John Morgan of Alabama urged, for example, "If we have got to amend it so that it has to go back to the House...why not make the bill so that it shall be clearly intelligible?'' Senator James George of Mississippi responded impatiently, ''That is a very immaterial difficulty'' (*Congressional Record*, 1885:1794).

Amendments to clarify the intent of the bill were repeatedly rejected by overwhelming margins, and criticisms that the bill was ''an absurdity'' were conspicuously ignored. Increasingly, the attention was focused on more comfortable subjects:

> I should like to have a verbal transposition made of the words 'service or labor' in the 6th line of the second section, so as to read 'labor or service.' That would be altogether more poetic, while the other savors rather of blank verse (*Congressional Record*, 1885:1839).

This amendment was agreed to.

More important for our purposes here, the bill was recognized as unenforceable, by proponents and opponents alike:

> From a careful examination of it, there is no part of it which seems to me to be at all effective. The penalties in this bill I do not think can ever be enforced. . . . I expect to vote for the bill, but I want to put on record my understanding of it (*Congressional Record*, 1885:1628).

Similarly, Senator Wilkinson Call of Florida declared:

> I shall vote for this bill. . . . I think the bill will fail to have any effect upon the laboring people of this country, that it is impossible that it should be of any service to them. . . . I shall support the bill. And I do so with the conviction that the bill will be no benefit to them [the laborers] (*Congressional Record*, 1885:1785; my emphasis).

Senator William Frye of Main concurred:

> Under the provisions here. . . I agree with the Senator from Connecticut that *it is not drawn for an indictment by any manner of means*. . . . I do not believe that any man on earth would ever be punished (*Congressional Record*, 1885:1628; my emphasis).

Not infrequently, it was even implied that this very unenforceability was an asset:

> I do not myself believe that there is any efficacy whatever in this idea or that it will affect anything of the protection of the American laborer that is anticipated. . . . Still I cannot see that there is any harm in gratifying this desire (*Congressional Record*, 1885:1628).

In response to a comment that the bill would be difficult to enforce, Blair (*Congressional Record*, 1885:1629; my emphasis) patiently explained, ''*If it cannot be enforced, will it do any hurt?*'' And later, ''I do not understand the harm [it] can do it if has no effect.'' Finally, and perhaps most revealingly,

62   KITTY CALAVITA

I do not believe that any of the provisions of the bill will work hardship or do any substantial harm, but I do believe that we shall do infinite harm if we fail now, this subject having come to the consideration of the Senate, to put on record our adherence to the principles which I believe are contained in this bill (*Congressional Record*, 1885:1782).

The bill's few opponents were even more explicit in their analysis of the purely symbolic nature of the bill. After three days of debate, Senator Matthew Butler of South Carolina concluded:

Taking the assertion of the advocates of this bill that they are really anxious to prevent what is said to be an evil, it has occurred to me that this bill offers a premium upon its very face for its own violation.... This bill as it stands reaches nobody. It is and will be found to be whenever the attempt is made to enforce it, absolutely inoperable, and in its operation a *sham and a pretense*; it has no penalty whatever which can reach anybody and which may not be evaded at any moment. It will be evaded, because a premium is offered in the bill itself for doing so.... When American labor clamors for recognition by Congress we provide a bureau of labor, as we did last year.... *The laborers literally asked for bread and we have given them a stone, and we propose to give them another in this bill if it passes*.... My objection to this bill... is that *it pretends to do something and really and practically does nothing except to throw a sop to Cerberus, and to pat the American laborer on the head by giving him a bill which amounts to nothing*.... We throw him his taffy to satisfy the clamor of the American laborer, *giving him a sham* when he wants something real.... I do not intend to vote for a measure that will be as inoperable as a blank piece of paper (*Congressional Record*, 1885:1835; my emphasis).

Another senator remarked simply, "There is a scorpion in it" (*Congressional Record*, 1885:1835).

The political maneuverings within the debates make it clear that both the bill's proponents and its opponents were vividly aware that the bill's success was actually dependent on its anticipated inoperability. Butler, one of the most vehement opponents of the bill, introduced a simple amendment that would make it illegal for contract laborers to land. It was introduced under the pretense that it would improve the bill, because it might thereby be made effective. "There is no ambiguity about it. It is distinct. It has its penalties. Its penalties can be enforced" (*Congressional Record*, 1885:1835). It soon became clear that the attempt was to add to the bill an amendment which might supply an enforcement mechanism, and thereby cause the bill to be defeated. Blair, the major spokesman for the bill in the Senate, was duly suspicious:

I feel reminded of the proverb that it is well to beware of the Greeks when they come bearing gifts. I have examined his amendment with a suspicion that he might not be from the very bottom of his soul the most anxious to conserve this bill.

The amendment was soundly defeated.

In spite of the fact that the bill had been declared "inoperable," "crude," "ambiguous," "a sham," the Senate motion that it be referred to the Committee on the Judiciary to be reworded "so as to more effectively reach the ends aimed at" was rejected, 41 to 15 (*Congressional Record*, 1885:1839).

Charles O'Neill (*Congressional Record*, 1884:5357) summarized the proceedings in the House: "There are often circumstances arising in connection with debate which cause us to pause to understand motives. . . .Friends of labor? *Heaven save workmen from such friends!*" (The italics are mine.)

The bill passed in the House by a voice vote almost unanimously. In the Senate it passed 50 to 9, being favored by both Republicans and Democrats, Northerners and Southerners (see Table 1).

Industry, when not conspicuously silent on the issue of the Foran Act, displayed a telling indifference, grounded in the knowledge that the bill's terms would leave it unaffected. Articles in the *Anglo-American Times* (October 28, 1887; November 4, 1887; August 9-30, 1889; November 15, 1889; May 23, 1890) revealed industry's indifference to the Act. Neither the *Railroad Gazette* nor the *Engineering and Mining Journal* even mentioned the Act, even though the congressional discussions of the Foran Act had emphasized the alleged role of mining and railroad companies as importers of contract labor, and trade journals frequently reported on factors which would affect the supply of labor.

E. Symbolic Law in Action

Industry had calculated correctly. The history of the operation of the Foran Act indicates that it exacted no sacrifices from capital. In the 14 years between 1887 and 1901, out of an immigration flow of about 6 million, no more than 8,000 immigrants were barred as "contract laborers" (see Table 2).

It was estimated that only one employer of contract labor in 1,000 was convicted (Testimony of Ullo, U.S. Congress, House, *Reports of the Industrial Commission*, 1901). After several hundred pages devoted to the Anti-Alien Contract Labor Law, the Industrial Commission concluded in 1901, "This law is practically a nullity. . ." (p. LVII). As the lawyer who had for six years been in charge of preparing for court the contract labor cases at the port of New York stated, "If it is advisable to restrict contract labor, the law as it stands does not restrict it" (Testimony of Ullo, *ibid.*, p. 14).

It had not been written with enforcement in mind. Congress had in fact appropriated no funds, nor established any machinery, for the enforcement of the Foran Act, for three years after the bill's enactment into law. During this time, no landing immigrants were even questioned with regard to their contract labor status.

Furthermore, the law as originally written applied only to the *importer* of contract labor and nowhere barred the contracted laborer from landing. An amendment in 1888 provided that contract laborers must be returned to their country of emigration. The same year Congress for the first time appropriated

Table 1.   Senate Vote on Foran Act, February 18, 1885

Yeas

Nelson W. Aldrich—Rhode Island (R)	Howell E. Jackson—Tennessee (D)
William B. Allison—Iowa (R)	John P. Jones—Nevada (R)
Henry W. Blair—New Hampshire (R)	John E. Kenna—West Virginia (D)
Thomas M. Bowen—Colorado (R)	Lucius Lamar—Mississippi (D)
Joseph E. Brown—Georgia (D)	Elbridge G. Lapham—New York (R)
Wilkinson Call—Florida (D)	Samuel J. R. McMillan—Minnesota (R)
Johnson N. Camden—West Virginia (D)	John R. McPherson—New Jersey (D)
Angus Cameron—Wisconsin (R)	William Mahone—Virginia (D)
Jonathon Chace—Rhode Island (R)	John F. Miller—California (R)
Omar D. Conger—Michigan (R)	Warner Miller—New York (R)
Shelby M. Cullom—Illinois (R)	John I. Mitchell—Pennsylvania (R)
Henry L. Dawes—Massachusetts (R)	Justin S. Morrill—Vermont (R)
Joseph N. Dolph—Oregon (R)	Thomas W. Palmer—Michigan (R)
James D. Fair—Nevada (D)	Austin F. Pike—New Hampshire (R)
William P. Frye—Maine (R)	Orville H. Platt—Connecticut (R)
James Z. George—Mississippi (D)	Preston B. Plumb—Kansas (R)
Randall L. Gibson—Louisiana (D)	James L. Pugh—Alabama (D)
Arthur P. Gorman—Maryland (D)	Matt W. Ransom—North Carolina (D)
Eugene Hale—Maine (R)	Dwight M. Sabin—Minnesota (R)
Isham G. Harris—Tennessee (D)	Philetus Sawyer—Wisconsin (R)
Benjamin Harrison—Indiana (R)	William J. Sewell—New Jersey (D)
John J. Ingalls—Kansas (R)	John Sherman—Ohio (R)
Charles H. Van Wyck—Nebraska (R)	James D. Walker—Arkansas (D)
George G. Vest—Missouri (D)	James F. Wilson—Iowa (R)
Daniel W. Voorhees—Indiana (D)	

Nays

Matthew C. Butler—South Carolina (D)	John T. Morgan—Alabama (D)
James B. Groome—Maryland (D)	Eli Saulsbury—Delaware (D)
Wade Hampton—South Carolina (D)	Zebulan Vance—North Carolina (D)
Joseph R. Hawley—Connecticut (R)	John S. Williams—Kentucky (D)
Samuel B. Maxey—Texas (D)	

*a*R = Republican; D = Democrat.

Source: *Congressional Record*, Senate, 48th Congress, 2nd Session, 1885, p. 1839.

a small budget for the enforcement of the law that had been enacted almost unanimously three years earlier.

Pari passu with amendments which might have had a tightening effect on the already small traffic of contract labor, court interpretations and the administration of the law by immigration inspectors became increasingly liberal, nullifying any potential impact.

After 1891, the contract labor inspection procedure was the following: The aliens, upon arrival, filed past a registry clerk who questioned them as to their

Table 2. Number of Contract Laborers Debarred for
Every 10,000 Immigrants Admitted

Year	Number Debarred	Year	Number Debarred
1892	16	1902	4
1893	12	1903	13
1894	19	1904	18
1895	27	1905	11
1896	23	1906	21
1897	14	1907	11
1898	18	1908	25
1899	24	1909	16
1900	19	1910	17
1901	7		

Source: Jeremiah Jenks, *The Immigration Problem*. New York: Funk & Wagnalls, 1913, p. 624.

health and other aspects of their eligibility for landing. *No questions were put to the immigrants with regard to their contract labor status.* Rather, a "contract labor inspector" stood beside the registry clerk, listening to the questions and answers, and if the inspector became suspicious he took the alien aside and questioned him individually (*ibid.*, p. 125).

Ultimately, the enforcement of the law depended on the discretion of those port inspectors and special boards of inquiry. Their attitudes with regard to the law were therefore crucial. Although there is little direct documentation on the subject, the U.S. Commissioner-General of Immigration (in his *Annual Report*, 1904:38) remarked that enforcement of the law was lax because there was the general opinion that labor had forced the law on Congress! Samuel Gompers, president of the American Federation of Labor (AFL), referring to the negative attitudes of port inspectors with regard to the law, testified before the Ford Committee in 1888 (U.S. Congress, House, *Ford Committee Report*, 1888:401) "officers of the government seem to make it their purpose to bring odium and ridicule upon the law by its non-enforcement...."

While these port inspectors determined whether an alien should be debarred, federal courts were responsible for prosecuting the importers, and court convictions of importers were far more rare even than the debarring of contract laborers. In fact, the Industrial Commission (p. 125) reported in 1899 that in six years *only one case had resulted in the conviction of an importer.* The crux of this low conviction rate lay in the courts' narrow interpretation of what constituted a contract, side by side with their very liberal interpretation of which kinds of laborers were legally exempt from the provisions of the law. Nor was this a coincidental or purely legally inspired formula. Rather, a New York district attorney expressed what he called the "contempt the U.S. judges have for the contract labor law" (*cited in* U.S. Congress, House, *Report of the Industrial Commission*, 1901:125).

In 1888, the Supreme Court dealt the law a decisive blow, when it maintained the right of the court to examine Congressional Debates in order to ascertain the "true intent" of the lawmakers. In 1899, the courts inferred from an inspection of the congressional debates surrounding the Foran Act that "Congress intended to exclude only those whose labor or service is manual in character, and that all other classes could be admitted even under contract" (U.S. Congress, House, *Industrial Commission*, 1901:LX). In a circuit court of appeals in 1899, it was determined that not only were professional classes exempt from the provisions of the law, but *all skilled labor*. In fact, "Congress *never intended to include in the act skilled labor of any kind*"! This, in spite of the fact that even a cursory examination of the debates reveals repeated references to both unskilled and skilled labor. Furthermore, the only documentation of contract labor that Congress had been able to provide was among the highly skilled window glass-workers. The Industrial Commission (*ibid.* pp. LX-LXI) summarized the effect of this court decision:

> The cheap labor from East and South Europe does not come under contract, and so evades the law, while skilled laborers, who naturally would be more likely to enter into contracts, are by this decision exempt.

The courts had capitalized on the diversion of the issue in the congressional debates, from the issue of "contract labor" to the "living standards" of the new unskilled immigrants—a diversion which was part of an attempt to present the bill as the salvation of American labor. Thus, ironically, the concentration on the unskilled in the debates served not only to promote the law as labor's salvation but was used subsequently to guarantee that labor was in fact unaffected.

F. Summary

To summarize the argument made here, the conflict in the last decades of the nineteenth century between organized labor's new-found strength and industry's need to produce a maximum profit was "resolved" by the continuing use of an ever-expanding immigrant labor supply. Another conflict was thus produced, however, as labor increasingly protested the use of "imported" immigrant strikebreakers. At just the moment that organized labor's strength made continued access to immigrant labor even more crucial to American employers, that same strength required that Congress make some response to American laborers' insistent demands for protection from that use of immigration. Labor's unfortunate, but understandable, emphasis on contract labor made the symbolic resolution— in the form of the Anti-Alien Contract Labor Law of 1885—practically a foregone conclusion, unopposed in Congress and unresisted by industry.

III. EMPLOYER SANCTIONS IN THE 1980s

The recommendations of the Select Commission on Immigration and Refugee Policy (SCIRP) in 1981, Reagan's immigration policy package, and, most recently, the Simpson-Mazzoli proposal, all include "employer sanctions" as a major component.[4] Under these proposals, it would be illegal for employers knowingly to hire undocumented workers. The logic behind employer sanctions begins with the recognition that it is the undocumented workers' ability to procure employment in the United States that encourages them to immigrate and concludes that, if the American employer were precluded from hiring the undocumented, illegal immigration would be reduced.

The model proposed here, in which the construction and application of legislation is seen as a dialectical process and in which symbolic law constitutes an attempted "resolution" to prevailing contradictions, may be helpful in understanding the recent popularity of this employer sanctions approach and its potential for future impact. It will be argued (1) that the recent employer sanctions proposals share with the 1885 case a labor law approach to immigration regulation; (2) that, as with the 1885 legislation, employer sanctions can be seen as one stage in an ongoing series of contradictions and legislative "resolutions"; and (3) that this employer sanctions "resolution" constitutes a similar symbolic response.

A. The Labor Law Approach

Both the employer sanctions approach and the 1885 Anti-Alien Contract Labor Law are *labor* policies whose ostensible purpose is the regulation of immigration. Just as the 1885 law was introduced as the "salvation of American labor" by protecting it from the "slave labor of Europe," the rationale for employer sanctions is that they will eliminate the unfair competition of an "illegal" class of laborer and preserve the America labor market for American—or at least documented—workers. This rationale is frequently accompanied by discussions of the large number of "illegals" in the United States and the exploitability of the undocumented worker, much as Congress complained of "coolie labor" (as they referred to alien contract labor) in 1885.

Furthermore, the employer sanctions proposal is comparable to the 1885 legislation in that it too must be seen as an attempt to juggle contradictory economic, political, and ideological demands. The following subsections outline the nature of those contradictions and the potential of employer sanctions as a symbolic response.

B. The "Illegalization" of Immigration

With the 1920s quota restrictions on European immigration to the United States, American employers increasingly turned to the "back door" as an alternative source of cheap labor. Mexicans were early seen as an ideal substitute for the European immigrant worker. Above all, they returned home—or could be made to return—during periods of depression or in the off-season, thereby constituting a work force par excellence: that is, without the political and fiscal hazards of more permanent immigration.[5] As early as 1911, the Dillingham Commission reported on the advantages of Mexican immigration:

> Because of their strong attachment to their native land . . . and the possibility of their residence here being discontinued, few become citizens of the U.S. The Mexican immigrants are providing a fairly adequate supply of labor. . . . While the Mexicans are not easily assimilated, this is not of very great importance as long as most of them return to their native land. . . . [I]n the case of the Mexican he is less desirable as a citizen than as a laborer (U.S. Congress, Immigration Commission, *Reports of the Immigration Commission*, 1911, Vol. 1:690-91; see also 'Prohibition of Immigration.' House Hearings, 65th Congress, 3rd Session, 1919:24-25).

With the increase in Mexican immigration to the United States, there has been a corresponding increase in "illegal" entrants. The difficulties of estimating the number of such illegal immigrants to the United States have been reported extensively in the literature (see, for example, Garcia y Griego and Estrada, 1981; Select Commission on Immigration and Refugee Policy, *Final Report*, 1981; Cornelius et al., 1982). Nonetheless, the fact that the number of legal Mexican immigrants to the United States has since 1930 been consistently surpassed by the number of apprehended Mexican illegal aliens is undoubtedly representative of the overall pattern (Stoddard, 1976; Marshall, 1978:166-7; Teitelbaum, 1980).

Several policy changes over the last decades have precipitated this increase in illegal immigration in rather predictable ways. In the first place, although numerical restrictions on Mexican immigration were not established until 1965, severe qualitative limitations were placed on aspiring Mexican migrants beginning with the depression of the 1930s, as U.S. consuls in Mexico were urged to interpret strictly the existing "public charge" clause. Not surprisingly, as documented immigration from Mexico was limited, the number of Mexicans who entered without papers increased.

The Bracero Programs of 1942-1964, in which Mexican contract laborers were imported through a number of bilateral agreements between the United States and Mexico, further increased illegal migration, as the number of aspiring braceros always far exceeded the legal allotment (Hadley, 1956; Scruggs, 1961; Galarza, 1964; Grebler, 1966). Formal and informal U.S. policies during the bracero period explicitly *encouraged* the illegal traffic. The bracero agreement of 1949, for example, provided that "such illegal workers, when they are located in the United States, *shall be given preference for employment* under outstanding U.S. Employment Service certification" (quoted in Galarza, 1964:63; emphasis mine). Illegals ("wetbacks," as they were called) were "dried out" by the U.S. Border Patrol, who escorted them to the border, made them step symbolically to the other side, and brought them back as lawful braceros. In the notorious "El Paso Incident," the Mexican government had excluded Texas from the bracero agreement as a result of the failure of Texas growers to abide by established wages and working standards. In response, U.S. border officials opened the border at El Paso for a five-day period in October 1948, letting in thousands of aspiring—but undocumented—braceros, "apprehending" them, and transporting them to the local cotton growers, to whom they were "paroled."

In 1952, the McCarran-Walter Act made it illegal to "harbor, transport, or conceal illegal entrants, or directly or indirectly induce their entry into the U.S." (66 Stat. 163). However, the so-called Texas Proviso—an amendment to the 1952 Act in response to pressure from Texan growers—explicitly excluded employment per se from the category of "harboring, transporting, or concealing" (66 Stat. 163, Chap. 477, June 27, 1952). While its author made it clear in congressional debate that "*knowing*" employment would indeed constitute "harboring. . ." (*Congressional Record*, 82nd Congress, 2nd Session, Senate, 1952:794), the amendment has been interpreted by the U.S. Immigration and Naturalization Service (INS) to exclude "employment" entirely from the provisions of the statute (for discussion of the INS interpretation and its departure from congressional intent, see Greene, 1972:453-5).

In other words, it makes little sense to account for the increase in "illegal" immigration that has resulted from these policies simply in terms of bureaucratic blunders, congressional shortsightedness, or INS corruption. It is a highly predictable consequence of our policies since the Quota Restrictions—policies which represent the responses of policymakers faced with myriad contradictions and dilemmas which constrain them to a juggling act on which the curtain never falls.[6] And if earlier, temporary Mexican workers helped resolve the problem of the need for cheap labor versus the political and fiscal burdens associated with massive *permanent* immigration, so the "illegalization" of this flow just takes the marginalization of the immigrant worker one step further. One scholar of Mexican immigration, summarizing the debate over possible restrictions on Mexican immigration in the 1920s, paraphrased Congress's antirestrictionist sentiment:

> The Mexican, they pointed out, was a *vulnerable* alien living just a short distance from his homeland. In the event that he did create serious racial or social problems, he, unlike Puerto Ricans or Filipinos. . .could easily be deported. No safer or more economical unskilled labor force was imaginable" (Reisler, 1976:181, paraphrasing Hearings of the House Committee on Immigration, 1929).

Right in his logic, Reisler was empirically wrong: the "illegal" worker who by definition is "criminal" is "safer" and more "economical" even than the legal Mexican immigrant.

Politically, the "illegal" must remain invisible, thus virtually immunizing the United States against the kind of guest-worker political movements that Western Europe has recently experienced (Bustamante, 1977; North American Congress on Latin America (NACLA), 1979). Economically, the "illegal" is preferable to legals because they dare not apply for any kind of cash assistance programs, so the old problem of "public charges" is resolved (North and Houstoun, 1976; NACLA, 1979:30-31; Select Commission on Immigration and Refugee Policy, *Background Papers*, 1980).

Finally, it is hard to conjure up a more beneficial arrangement from the employer's point of view. While the undocumented worker today undoubtedly plays a smaller role, proportionately, than the immigrant worker of whom American labor complained in 1885, nonetheless the "illegal alien" is pivotal in certain labor-intensive, highly competitive sectors of American industry. The centrality of undocumented workers to southwestern agriculture has been amply documented (U.S. Congress, House, Subcommittee No. 1. . . . Hearings, June 19 and 21, 1971; Bustamante, 1978; Corwin and Fogel, 1978; Marshall, 1978; Cornelius et al., 1982), but their utility is not confined to the agricultural sector. According to a Manpower Administration Survey in 1976, 19% of undocumented workers were employed in agriculture, while the majority were engaged in light manufacturing, garment shops, the hotel and restaurant industries, and microchip assembly plants (survey cited in Omi, 1981:86).

The success of these "new sweatshops" (Koeppel, 1978:22-26) frequently depends on the violation of protective labor laws. For example, the garment shops of New York, San Francisco, Los Angeles and other major urban areas of the United States—in competition with similar shops in Taiwan, South Korea and other cheap-labor countries—thrive on an almost exclusively female immigrant work force, many of whom are undocumented (Dygert and Shibata, 1975; Koeppel, 1978; Maram, 1980; Garcia, 1981). Receiving less than the minimum wage, frequently working on a piece-rate system, under working conditions similar to those of turn-of-the-century sweatshops, these workers-economically desperate and of an "outlaw" status—rarely file formal complaints against their employers (Human Rights Commission of San Francisco, 1969; Dygert and Shibata, 1975; Koeppel, 1978; NACLA, 1979).

Nor are such sweatshop conditions confined to the garment industry. In a recent study of the Los Angeles hotel and restaurant industries, Maram (1980) found that 86% of the busboys and dishwashers were undocumented and that 21% reported receiving less than the minimum wage. Studies on the wage levels of undocumented farm laborers are inconclusive (Smith and Newman, 1977; Marshall, 1978; Ross, 1978; Lewis, 1979; Mines, 1981; Mines and Anzaldua, 1981; Select Commission on Refugee and Immigration Policy, 1981; Cornelius et al., 1982). Even assuming, however, that most undocumented farm laborers receive the legal minimum wage, it is easy to understand the grower's enthusiasm for this work force. Arduous, seasonal and hazardous, farm labor is "acceptable" only to those who have little choice, and in this respect recent illegal aliens are eminently qualified. As summarized by ex-Secretary of Labor F. Ray Marshall (1978:169), "Illegal aliens are preferred. . .because they tend to work 'scared and hard'."

In other words, these "new immigrant" workers, saddled with both economic desperation and an illegal status, are of special utility to their employers, particularly in certain seasonal and/or labor-intensive, highly competitive sectors— constituting a new "golden stream," as it were.[7]

C. Economic Structure vs. Ideology

It has often been observed that historically, during periods of economic downturn in the United States, anti-immigrant rhetoric tends to increase (Stoddard, 1976; Portes, 1977; Bach, 1978; Bustamente, 1978; Koeppel, 1978; Omi, 1981). Fernandez (1981), for example, documents a positive correlation between media coverage of the illegal alien and recessive trends in the American economy.

Beginning in the early 1970s, illegal immigration became a major source of concern both in the media and in statements by public officials. The front headline of the *Wall Street Journal* (September 29,1971) warned of a "LEAKY BORDER." Subheadlines urged that "Illegal Immigrants. . .Pose Economic Threat. . .At Home, Idleness and Poverty" and "the 'Wetback's Impact on the U.S. Economy is Sizable." The front page of the *Los Angeles Times* (October 22, 1971) carried a similar warning: "Illegal Alien: Growing Peril to U.S. Worker." The *San Francisco Examiner* (August 23, 1971) echoed, "Illegals Pour into the U.S." and "Tide of Illegals Rising. . .Hurts California Farm Workers" (August 25, 1971). The *Sacramento Union* (May 28, 1976) warned, "The cost to the taxpayer is heavy," and "Illegal aliens prey on the economy" (May 4, 1976). *The Los Angeles Herald-Examiner* (February 25, 1977) called illegal Mexican immigration "an unstoppable flood of humanity" urging that "jobs and crime are by-products of the illegals." *U.S. News and World Report* (May 30, 1977:30) editorialized that illegal aliens are "outlaws, figuring only as a frightening burden." A *New York Times* News Service story produced the following headline in newspapers across the United States in March 1981: "ILLEGAL ALIENS RECEIVING U.S. HOUSING AID" and, later, "hundreds of thousands of citizens wait months or years for similar assistance."[8] The *Los Angeles Times* (August 10, 1980) announced that "Residents, Illegal Aliens Vie for Scarce Farm Jobs."

In 1970, Senator Walter F. Mondale, in undisguised repugnance, called illegal Mexican immigration "a hemorrhage along the Mexican border," adding "It's the ugliest phenomenon in the United States today" (quoted in the *Long Beach*

Press, April 15, 1970). California Assemblyman Ray Seeley (*Press Release*, October 21, 1971) expressed concern that illegal Mexican immigrants might damage the American economy "beyond repair." Commenting on high unemployment figures among Mexican-Americans, the Regional Manpower Administrator of the U.S. Department of Labor declared that the "illegal alien is the worst enemy of the Mexican-American" (quoted in the *People's World*, December 11, 1971).[9] William Colby, Director of the Central Intelligence Agency (CIA), in an interview published in the *Los Angeles Times* and *Playboy Magazine* in June 1978, warned that the illegal alien "invasion" from Mexico would in the future constitute a greater threat to national security than any other phenomenon.[10]

Many have noted that this focus on the immigrant during periods of high unemployment constitutes "scapegoating" and has the consequence of deflecting attention away from broader, structural causes of economic downturns: "In depression, large numbers of immigrants provide a scapegoat and deflect many workers' attention away from the roots of unemployment, which are in the economic system itself" (David Gordon, quoted in Koeppel, 1978:26). Portes (1977:36) similarly underlines this function of the "denunciations of illegal immigration by the press and public officials." Bach (1978:77) has noted that "if the state must confront Mexican immigrant labor as a constitutive part of more generalized working-class conditions, *rather than a cause of those conditions*, then. . .a strategic weapon of the state in defusing working-class struggles would be lost and the political problem would fall heavily into the laps of current state managers" (my emphasis).

Whether deliberate or not, this political/ideological use of the immigrant parallels and occurs simultaneously with their economic function as described above. The paradox inherent in this situation is evident. For, while the ideology of immigrant scapegoating may serve to rationalize the symptoms of recession, it simultaneously generates demands that something *be done* about illegal immigration. In other words, while undocumented workers are of special utility to their employers, the ideology which links them to the deepening recession generates political demands to eliminate that cheap and flexible labor supply. Employer sanctions proposals must be seen within the context of this contradiction between the economic and the ideological—in this case an ideology which, on the one hand, resolves certain legitimation problems but which, on the other, comprises an element of this new dilemma.

As with the 1885 legislation, the employer sanctions proposal constitutes a response to—or an attempt to resolve—the contradiction between the immigrant's economic utility versus political demands to limit that supply of cheap labor. The contemporary proposal furthermore shares with the 1885 case a narrow focus on a particular *kind of immigrant worker* as the way to resolve this contradiction. Just as the issues of immigrant strikebreaking and wage reductions were redefined as problems of "contract labor" in 1885, so now the employer sanctions approach does not directly address the low wages and hazardous working conditions that are the raison d'être of illegal alien employment, but rather focuses on a particular *category of worker*. While many scholars and several commissioners of the Select Commission of 1981, have pointed out that strict enforcement of *existing* protective labor laws would minimize the incentive to employ undocumented workers, this approach to reducing illegal immigration is not seriously considered. In fact, it is ironic that at the same time that the employer sanctions proposal is enjoying increasing popularity there has been a de facto *relaxing* of the enforcement of protective labor laws in the United States.[11]

Two consequences follow from the kind-of-worker approach of employer sanctions proposals:

In the first place, such proposals carry a symbolic message with regard to responsibility and blame. Edelman (1977) has commented on the symbolic impact of certain types of government programs:

> A reference in an authoritative public statement or in a social security law to 'training programs' for the unemployed is a metonymic evocation of a larger structure of beliefs that job training is efficacious in solving the unemployment problem, that workers are unemployed because they lack necessary skills, that jobs are available for those trained to take them (p. 16).

Similarly,

> Campaigns urging car owners to drive safely. . .*focus attention on the driver* as the cause of accidents: on his negligent or risky habits and his failure to keep his car in good working order.... Whether or not a 'drive safely' campaign makes drivers more careful, it creates an assumption about what the problem is and who is responsible (p. 36; my emphasis).

In exactly the same way, a law which addresses unemployment and budget deficits by focusing on the employment of the illegal alien metonymically generates a whole set of political beliefs with regard to responsibility.

Secondly, this kind-of-worker approach leads to almost insurmountable enforcement problems. Convictions under an employer sanctions law will require that the employer *knowingly* hired illegals and will rely, therefore, on some counterfeit-proof system of identification. Despite this fact, the Select Commission in 1981 conspicuously avoided recommending any specific means of identification, without which it will be impossible to demonstrate employer intent. In fact, Commissioner Elizabeth Holtzman noted, ''For some inexplicable reason the issue of a national identification card was never directly voted on'' (1981:342). President Reagan's Task Force explicitly recommended *against any* such identification system. Instead, the Task Force has built in a loophole that would result in the employer's complete invulnerability to the proposed law. It has recommended the use of a ''certification form'' to be signed by employer and employee. This signed statement would provide the worker's reassurance to the

employer that he is a lawful resident and, thus, supply future evidence of the
employer's good intentions in hiring him. Under such a system, not only would
it be impossible to demonstrate legally that an employer "knowingly" hired an
"illegal," but the onus would be shifted entirely to the worker.

The Simpson-Mazzoli Bill requires that job applicants show some "proof"
of legal immigration status, such as a birth certificate, a driver's license or a
social security card. It is common knowledge that "Along the Mexican border
there is. . .a brisk trade in bogus documents of every kind" (*New York Times*,
December 8, 1980:Al) and that a Social Security card is no indication of one's
immigration status since the Social Security Administration asks no questions
relevant to immigration status in issuing the card. A new national identification
system would be required if employer sanctions legislation is to have any impact,
yet the civil liberties implications of such an identification system make it politically unfeasible.

Such potential enforcement problems are underlined by the dismal track record
that employer sanctions legislation has achieved in the 12 states that already
have such sanctions on the books. Indeed, as the *Briefing Papers* of the Select
Commission on Immigration and Refugee Policy (April 21, 1980) report, there
has only been *one* successful prosecution under these laws. Although California
has one of the heaviest illegal migration traffics in the country and has had an
employer sanctions law since 1971, the California law—ensnared in political
and legal difficulties—has *never* been implemented.

The state experience not only highlights the inherent enforcement problems
of the employer sanctions approach[12] but may also help clarify the nature of the
dilemma with which these legislators now find themselves grappling and the
impact of this dilemma on the shape the legislation ultimately takes. In California,
for example, the employer sanctions bill of 1971 (A.B. 528; also known as the
Arnett Bill, after its Assembly sponsor) was continually weakened in the legislative process and made more "ambiguous" in order to obtain the votes of
those legislators who were hesitant to "harass" employers (personal interview
with Dixon Arnett, January 28, 1982). Through the amendment process, those
provisions which might have made it an effective threat to employers, were
eliminated.[13] In the clash between economic reality, ideology and political demands, the temporary solution in California was a statute which, while retaining
its ideological and political (symbolic) components, interfered not at all with the
economic reality.

Furthermore, a comprehensive report by the U.S. General Accounting Office
(GAO) in 1982 revealed that employer sanctions have consistently failed to
reduce undocumented migration in the 20 other countries in which they have
been legislated. Even those countries with relatively secure identification systems
and fines of up to $40,000 per violation report dismal track records under the
law. According to the study, this is in large part because "judges have not

considered the hiring of illegal aliens a serious violation'' and are reluctant to impose harsh penalties (General Accounting Office, 1982:13-14).

Like its 1885 predecessor, federal employer sanctions legislation constitutes an attempt to resolve contradictory economic and political/ideological demands; hence the result, as in 1885, is likely to be legislation which is merely symbolic— a monument to the ideology which produced it, but devoid of objective impact. This contemporary symbolic resolution is conceptually different from the 1885 case in at least two ways. In the first place, unlike the 1885 legislation, the employer sanctions approach is not primarily a response to pressure from organized labor. Rather, the political impetus to ''do something'' about illegal immigration is derived from the ideology which places at least partial responsibility for many of the symptoms of the current recession on the influx of illegal aliens—an ideology which provides a scapegoat for the economic downturn but also generates in dialectical fashion demands that something *be done* about the ''problem.'' Secondly, although the legislative outcome is likely to be symbolic, serving only the function of subjective reassurance while not altering objective conditions, there is little evidence that policymakers are in the *conscious* pursuit of an empty law. Perhaps because employer sanctions are less a response to direct pressure from outside interest groups than they are derived from an ideology prevalent among the legislators themselves, the causal process which produces the symbolic outcome will probably be somewhat different from the apparent ''voluntarism'' behind the 1885 law. Whereas the congressional legislators of 1885 appear to have intentionally produced a preconceived ''token gesture'' with which to placate labor, it is more likely in the present case that the legislation will be *rendered* symbolic in stages not by hypocritical legislators but by the clash of contradictory forces in the political arena. The focus on a *category of worker*, rather than on working conditions themselves, comprises the first stage in this evolution toward symbolic law; the second stage is likely to be—as in the California case—an amendment process which significantly softens any potential impact; the third and final stage may well include the predictable enforcement complications inherent in such an approach.

Thurman Arnold (1937:207-13), describing the origins of the Sherman Anti-Trust Laws, has observed that the *ideal* of competition and an antibigness ideology ran head-on into the *economic* pressures toward monopolization:

In order to reconcile the ideal with the practical necessity, it became necessary to develop a procedure which constantly attacked bigness on rational/legal and economic grounds, and at the same time never really interfered with combinations. . . . Granted an insistent demand, which opposes a deeply felt ideal, and a conflict of this kind between two institutions (the economic and the ideological), the result is as inevitable as the reaction of a man sitting on a hot stove. . . . In various ways the actual enforcement of the anti-trust laws was completely emasculated. . . because such a process is inevitable when an ideal meets in head-on collision with a practical need.

The future of employer sanctions legislation is likely to resemble "the reaction of a man sitting on a hot stove." Caught between the economic utility of the undocumented worker and the immigrant-as-scapegoat ideology, legislators have constructed a response which *in its very approach* is fated to remain purely symbolic—an unenforceable monument to and means of reproducing that ideology.

IV. CONCLUSION

This analysis has traced emergence of the Anti-Alien Contract Labor Law of 1885 as an example of symbolic legislation in response to the specific political and economic dilemmas of the period. In particular, the strength of organized labor by 1885 made a continued influx of immigrant labor ever more crucial to employers, while requiring some response from Congress to workers' pleas for protection from that immigrant influx. The law of 1885 was in many ways an ideal "resolution" to such a dilemma. While addressing labor's grievances in page after page of prolabor rhetoric, the resulting legislation included ample loopholes, was followed by no enforcement provisions and had no substantial impact.

The underlying purpose of this historical and theoretical analysis is to help decipher the otherwise perplexing scenario surrounding recent "employer sanctions" proposals. This necessarily brief discussion of such proposals suggests that the labor law approach to immigration regulation, as with the 1885 legislation, must be seen within the context of an ongoing set of economic, ideological and political contradictions. As in 1885, the employer sanctions "resolution" of these contradictions is a symbolic response. Pressed through the filter that is economic reality, the legislation will consist of little more than the political/ ideological residue.

NOTES

1. Portions of Section II of this paper are adapted from a larger manuscript by the author, *U.S. Immigration Law and the Control of American Labor, 1820-1924*, forthcoming by Academic Press.

2. The double irony of this dialectical sequence of contradictions, conflicts and resolutions is not only that previous "resolutions" precipitate later conflicts in the abstract but, in this case, the same immigrant groups—the Irish and Germans—which had provided capital with a cheap and compliant work force earlier in the century, now are the very ones who, like a Trojan horse welcomed into this midst, comprise the backbone of the class struggle via strikes and union activity. This necessitates the further immigration of cheap labor—a condition which contributes to the class conflict nature of the situation as this tactic is protested. This irony—that the same national groups which now advance the class struggle had once been elements of its "resolution"—is intuitively appealing because it paints human faces into the abstract dialectic. It also underlines the fact that the dialectical process is not propelled by personal attributes of individuals or individual ethnic groups but is *structurally* driven.

3. It is interesting that once the move to strike this clause had been soundly defeated, a motion was introduced to strike that *part* of the clause which stipulated, "Provided that skilled labor for that purpose cannot be otherwise obtained." While Senator Blair had earlier refused to touch the section on the grounds that labor had "framed" it, he was now less protective: "I have no objection to the Senator's moving to strike that out," even though the deletion would have affected labor adversely, while the provision as a whole had been essentially a proindustry loophole.

4. Employer sanctions proposals have enjoyed a recent flurry of popularity. There have been eight major employer sanctions proposals put to Congress in the last 10 years: the Rodino bills of 1972 and 1975; the Kennedy bill of 1975; the Eastland bill of 1976; the Carter proposal of 1977; the Select Commission on Immigration and Refugee Policy recommendation of 1981; President Reagan's proposal of 1981; and the Simpson-Mazzoli proposal of 1982.

5. For a discussion of those hazards and contradictions associated with unregulated legal immigration of a permanent sort, see Calavita (1981).

6. For a more extensive discussion of the stimulation of illegal migration as a consequence of the formal and informal immigration policies of the U.S. government, see Stoddard (1976).

7. It must be recognized that the qualitative difference today with regard to this "golden stream" is that transnational capital is no longer dependent on the movement of the work force but "may" simply relocate production to the *source* of the cheap labor supply, as has been the case with microchip assembly plants. Nonetheless, for certain sectors of the economy—agriculture and services, for example—it is concretely impossible to relocate the "production" process.

8. The "information" for this article was supplied by the U.S. General Accounting Office, which apparently had stated that it "believed" that some illegal aliens may receive housing assistance (cited in Cornelius, 1982).

9. Abundant evidence now indicates that (1) the displacement of resident workers out of jobs by undocumented workers is probably minimal, given a two-tiered occupational system in which most undocumented workers fill jobs for which resident workers generally do not apply, and (2) the undocumented worker in fact pays more in taxes than he or she receives in benefits, constituting not a "tax burden," as these California legislators suggested in 1971, but a source of net revenue (North and Houstoun, 1976; Koeppel, 1978; Cockcroft, 1982; Cornelius et al., 1982).

10. Indicative of the prevalence of this new nativist ideology, an Associated Press-NBC News Poll in August 1981 found, on the basis of national samples, that 65% of respondents favored a decrease in legal immigration (cited in the *San Diego Union*, August 17, 1981:A9). A Gallup Poll (cited in the *San Diego Union*, November 30, 1980:A22) in 1980 reported that 76% of its respondents favor a law against the employment of illegal aliens.

11. In fact, President Reagan's "enterprise zone" proposal for revitalizing blighted urban areas includes suggestions that many protective labor laws be officially eliminated in those areas.

12. Several of the Select Commissioners' statements with regard to this issue of the enforceability of a federal employer sanctions law are eerily reminiscent of congressional comments in 1884 and 1885 on the enforceability of contract labor prohibitions: on the one hand, "I voted in favor of employer sanctions...."; on the other, "I have little confidence...[they] will be effective....They have been effective at best in States where they have been imposed" (Commissioner Elizabeth Holtzman, 1981:341-2). And "The Commission ignored the evidence that nowhere have such laws been shown to be effective" (Commissioner Rose Matsui Ochi, 1981:384).

13. The final form of the California bill eliminated any explicit requirement that employers question aspiring employees with regard to their immigration status and required only that they not *know* their workers are undocumented. In addition, an "adverse effect" clause was added to the final form of the bill, making the knowing employment of undocumented workers illegal only if that employment has an "adverse effect" on lawfully resident workers, an ambiguity which the bill's Assembly author—Dixon Arnett—says "got the legislation passed" (personal interview, January 28, 1982).

REFERENCES

Anglo-American Times,October 28, 1887; November 4, 1887; August 9-30, 1889; November 15, 1889; May 23, 1890.

Arnett, Dixon
  1982   Personal interview. (January 28).
Arnold, Thurman W.
  1937   The Folklore of Capitalism. New Haven: Yale University Press
Bach, Robert
  1978   "Mexican immigration and U.S. immigration reforms in the 1960s." Kapitalistate. 7:63-80.
Berthoff, Rowland T.
  1953   British Immigrants in Industrial America. Cambridge: Harvard University Press.
Bimba, Anthony
  1927   The History of the American Working Class. New York: International Publishers.
Boyer, Richard and Herbert Morais
  1977   Labor's Untold Story. New York: United Electrical, Radio, and Machine Workers of America.
Bustamante, Jorge A.
  1978   "Commodity-migrants: structural analysis of Mexican immigration to the United States." In Stanley R. Ross (ed.), Views Across the Border, the United States and Mexico. Albuquerque: University of New Mexico Press.
  1977   "The 'wetback' as deviant: an application of labelling theory." American Journal of Sociology. 77(4):706-718.
Bustamante, Jorge and James Cockcroft
  1982   "Unequal exchange in the binational relationship: the case of immigrant labor." In Carlos Vasquez and Manual Garcia y Greigo (eds.), Mexican-U.S. Relations: Conflict or Convergence. Los Angeles: UCLA Chicano Studies Research Center.
Calavita, Kitty
  1981   "United States Immigration Law and the control of American Labor." Contemporary Crises. 5:341-368.
Carnegie, Andrew
  1886   Triumphant Democracy, or Fifty Years' March of the Republic. New York: Charles Scribner's Sons.
Clark, Victor
  1919   History of Manufacturing in the United States. Vol. 1, 1607-1860. New York: McGraw-Hill.
Cockcroft, James
  1982   "Mexican migration, crisis and the internationalization of labor struggle." Contemporary Marxism, 5(July).
Congressional Record
  1884   48th Congress, 1st Session. House: 5349-5371.
  1885   48th Congress, 2nd Session. Senate: 1622-1839.
  1888   50th Congress, 2nd Session. House: (Ford Committee Report).
  1952   82nd Congress, 2nd Session. Senate: Volume 98:794.
Cornelius, Wayne
  1976   Mexican Migration to the United States. Cambridge: Center for International Studies. Massachusetts Institute of Technology.
Cornelius, Wayne
  1982   "America in the era of limits: nativist reactions to the 'new' immigration." Working

Papers in the U.S.-Mexican Studies, No. 3. La Jolla, California; Program in U.S.-Mexican Studies, University of California, San Deigo.

Cornelius, Wayne, Leo R. Chavez, and Jorge G. Castro
1982 "Mexican immigrants and Southern California: a summary of current knowledge." Working Papers: U.S.-Mexican Studies, No. 36. La Jolla, California: Program in U.S.-Mexican Studies, University of California, San Diego.

Corwin, Arthur and Walter Fogel
1978 "Shadow labor force: Mexican workers in the American economy." In Arthur Corwin (ed.), Immigrants—and Immigrants. Westport, Connecticut: Greenwood Press.

Dygert, Harold Paul, III and David Shibata
1975 "Chinatown sweatshops: wage law violations in the garment industry." University of California, Davis Law Review. 8:63-83.

Edelman, Murray
1964 The Symbolic Uses of Politics. Chicago: University of Illinois Press.
1977 Political Language: Words that Succeed and Policies that Fail. New York: Academic Press.

Engineering and Mining Journal
1880 (May 15):335.

Erickson, Charlotte
1957 American Industry and the European Immigrant, 1860-1885. Cambridge: Harvard University Press.

Fernandez, Celestino
1981 "Undocumented Mexican migration: three perspectives." Presentation to San Deigo State University Latin American Lecture Series, (October 9).

Fogel, Walter
1979 "Mexican illegal alien workers in the United States." Institute of Industrial Relations Monograph Series, 20. University of California, Los Angeles.

Galarza, Ernesto
1964 Merchants of Labor: The Mexican Bracero History. Santa Barbara: McNally and Loftin.

Garcia, Victor Quiroz
Undocumented Mexicans in Two Los Angeles Communities: A Social and Economic Profile. Monographs in U.S.-Mexican Studies, N.Y. Las Jolla, California: Program in U.S.-Studies, University of California, San Deigo.

Garcia y Griego, Manuel and Leobardo F. Estrada
1981 "Research on the magnitude of Mexican undocumented immigration to the U.S.: a summary." In Antonio Rios-Bustamante (ed.), Immigrant Workers in the United States. Los Angeles: Chicano Studies Research Center, UCLA (Anthology Series, No. 2).

General Accounting Office of the U.S.
1982 "Information on the enforcement of laws regarding employment of aliens in selected countries." Washington, D.C.: U.S. Government Printing Office, (August 31).

Grebler, Leo
1966 Mexican Immigration to the United States: Its Record and its Implications. Los Angeles: UCLA Mexican-American Study Project, Advance Report 2.

Green, Sheldon
1972 "Public agency distortion of congressional will: federal policy toward non-resistant alien labor." George Washington Law Review, 40, No. 3:440-463.

Grossman, Jonathan Philip
1945 William Sylvis, Pioneer of American Labor: A Study of the Labor Movement During the Era of the Civil War. New York: Columbia University Press.

Gutman, Herbert
1976 Work, Culture, and Society in Industrializing America. New York: Alfred A. Knopf.

Hadley, Eleanor M.
1956 "A critical analysis of the wetback problem." Law and Contemporary Problems. 21:334-357.
Hamilton, Alexander
1791 "Report on manufacturing." American State Papers. Finance, I:123.
Holtzman, Elizabeth
1981 "Supplemental statements by commissioners." Appendix B, U.S. Immigration Policy and the National Interest, The Final Report and Recommendations of the Select Commission on Immigration and Refugee Policy to the Congress and the President of the United States, (March 1):341-352.
Human Rights Commission of San Francisco
1969 "Analysis of Chinatown garment workers survey questionnaire." 1.
Iron Molders Journal
1874 (November 10):104-105
Jenks, Jeremiah
1913 The Immigration Problem. New York: Funk and Wagnalls.
John Swinton's Paper
1884 (January 6):1; (August 3):1.
1885 (February 1).
Koeppel, Barbara
1978 "The new sweatshops." Progressive. 42 (November):22-26.
Lewis, Sasha G.
1979 Slave Trade Today. Boston: Beacon Press.
Long Beach Press
1970 (April 15).
The Los Angeles Herald-Examiner
1977 (February 25).
The Los Angeles Times
1971 (October 22).
1980 (August 10).
Maram, Sheldon L.
1980 "Hispanic workers in the garment and restaurant industries in Los Angeles County." Working Papers in U.S.-Mexican Studies. No. 12. La Jolla, California: Program in U.S.-Mexican Studies, University of California, San Deigo.
Marshall, F. Ray
1978 "Economic factors influencing the international migration of workers." In Stanley R. Ross (ed.), Views Across the Border, the United States and Mexico. Albuquerque: University of New Mexico Press.
McNeil, George E.
1888 The Labor Movement: The Problem of Today, Comprising a History of Capital and Labor, and its Present Status. New York: M. W. Hozen.
Mines, Richard
1981 Developing a Community Tradition of Migration: A Field Study in Rural Zacatecos, Mexico, and California Settlement Areas. Monographs in U.S.-Mexican Studies, No. 3. La Jolla, California: Program in U.S.-Mexican Studies, University of California, San Deigo.
Mines, Richard and Ricardo Anzaldua Montoya
1981 New Migrants vs. Old Migrants: Alternative Labor Market Structures in the California Citrus Industry. Monographs in U.S.-Mexican Studies, No. 9. La Jolla, California: Program in U.S.-Mexican Studies, University of California, San Deigo.
New York Times
1980 (December 8):A 1.

North American Congress on Latin America (NACLA)
   1979   A Special Report on the Undocumented. Volume XII (November-December).
North, David and Marion Houstoun
   1976   The Characteristics and Role of Illegal Aliens in the U.S. Labor Market: An Exploratory
          Survey. Linton and Company, Inc.
Ochi, Rose Matsui
   1981   "Supplemental statements by commissioners." Appendix B, U.S. Immigration Policy and
          the National Interest, The Final Report and Recommendations of the Select Commission
          on Immigration and Refugee Policy to the Congress and the President of the United States,
          (March 1): 381-389.
Omi, Michael
   1981   "New wave dread: immigration and intra-third world conflict." Socialist Review. 60:77-
          87.
The People's World
   1971   (December 11).
Philadelphia Times
   1882   (June 18):1
Portes, Alejandro
   1977   "Labor functions of illegal aliens." Society. Vol. 14 (September-October):31-37.
Reisler, Mark
   1976   By the Sweat of their Brow: Mexican Immigrant Labor in the United States, 1900-1940.
          Westport, Connecticut: Greenwood Press.
Rosenblum, Gerald
   1977   Immigrant Workers: Their Impact on American Labor Radicalism. New York: Basic Books.
Ross, Stanley, R.
   1978   Views Across the Border, the United States and Mexico. Albuquerque: University of New
          Mexico Press.
Roy, Andrew
   1970   A History of the Coal Miners of the United States. Westport, Connecticut: Greenwood
          Press.
The Sacramento Union
   1976   (May 4); (May 28).
The San Diego Union
   1980   "Gallup Poll." (November 30):A22.
The San Diego Union
   1980   "Gallup Poll." (November 30)A22.
   1981   "AP-NBC Poll." (August 17):A9.
The San Francisco Examiner
   1971   (August 23); (August 25).
Scruggs, Otey M.
   1961   "The United States, Mexico, and the Wetbacks 1942-1947." Pacific Historical Review
          30 (May):149-164.
Seeley, Assemblyman Ray
   1971   Press Release. (October 21).
Select Commisison on Immigration and Refugee Policy (SCIRP)
   1979   Briefing Papers. (October 29); (December 17).
   1980   Briefing Papers. (February 4); (April 21).
   1980   Background Papers. "The economic impact of illegal aliens."
   1981   Final Report. U.S. Immigration Policy and the National Interest. The Final Report and
          Recommendations of the Select Commission on Immigration and Refugee Policy to the
          Congress and the President of the United States. (March 1).

Smith, Barton and Robert Newman
    1977   "Depressed wages along the U.S.-Mexican border: an empirical analysis." Economy
            Inquiry (January).
Stearns, Lisa R.
    1979   "Fact and fiction of a model enforcement bureaucracy: The labor inspectorate of Sweden."
            British Journal of Law and Society. 6:1-23.
Stoddard, Ellwyn R.
    1976   "A conceptual analysis of the 'alien invasion': institutionalized support of illegal Mexican
            aliens in the U.S." International Migration Review. Volume X No. 2 (Summer).
Swinton, John
    1894   Striking for Life. New York.
Teitelbaum, Michhael S.
    1980   "Right versus right: immigration and refugee policy in the U.S." Foreign Affairs. 59
            (Fall):21-59.
U.S. Commissioner-General of Immigration
    1904   Annual Report of the Commissioner-General of Immigration. Pp. 38.
U.S. Congress
    1919   House Committee on Immigration and Naturalization. "Prohibition of immigration." House
            Hearings, 65th Congress, 3rd Session: pp. 24-25.
U.S. Congress
    1888   House. Ford Committee. Ford Committee Report. House Miscellaneous Documents. p.
            401.
U.S. Congress
    1901   House Industrial Commission. 57th Congress, 1st Session. House Document No. 184,
            Volumes XIV, XV.
U.S. Congress
    1971   House. Subcommittee No. 1 of the Committee on the Judiciary, "Illegal aliens." Hearings.
            June 19, June 21. 92nd Congress, 1st Session. Washington, D.C.: U.S. Government
            Printing Office.
U.S. Congress
    1911   Immigration Commission. The Dillingham Commission. Reports of the Immigration Com-
            mission, 42 Volumes. Washington, D.C.: U.S. Government Printing Office.
U.S. Congress
    1885   Senate Committee on Education and Labor Report on the Relations Between Capital and
            Labor. Volumes I-III.
U.S. News and World Report
    1977   (May 30).
U.S. Statutes at Large
            66 Stat. 163.
Van Arsdol, Maurice, et al.
    1979   Non-Apprehended and Apprehended Undocumented Residents in the Los Angeles Labor
            Market. U.S. Department of Labor
The Wall Street Journal
    1971   (September 29).
Workingman's Advocate
    1867   (September 28).
    1869   (February 27).
    1869   (December 25).
    1873   (November 29).

WOMEN'S BODIES AS DISEASED AND DEVIANT: HISTORICAL AND CONTEMPORARY ISSUES

Alexandra Dundas Todd

I. INTRODUCTION

The current women's health movement is an outgrowth of the general feminist reawakening of the late 1960s. This movement has been concerned with the treatment of women by the medical profession both in their role as patients and as medical workers. The tendency in the medical model to approach reproductive issues through the prism of disease has been heavily criticized and attacked as oppressive to women in a growing literature which springs from this reawakening.

One of the major methodologies employed in this critique has been historical. These insights have been gathered to shed light on alternative visions of the social organization of reproduction and contraception as they have related to women's lives. This has not been an easy task, since most written reproductive history has been dominated by a male, medical perspective—a view which reinforces present status quo definitions of women's bodies.

Research in Law, Deviance and Social Control, Volume 5, pages 83-95
Copyright © 1983 by JAI Press, Inc.
All rights of reproduction in any form reserved
ISBN: 0-89232-334-5

Feminist scholarship, however, has offered insights into the historical trends in the conceptualization of reproduction and the control of female anatomy. Both the diseasing of reproduction and the sinfulness of female sexuality in Western society have been scrutinized by researchers and journalists in recent years. This process has uncovered a legacy of women's bodies being defined, by virtue of their very existence, as deviant. The relationship between the rise of a male-dominated medical profession in the nineteenth century and historical shifts in women's health care has been explored. Further, these historical trends provide insights important to an understanding of women's reproductive concerns today.

II. SOME HISTORICAL NOTES

Midwives were the predominant deliverers of babies, birth control and women's health needs in America as well as the rest of the Western world until the twentieth century. Birth control in nineteenth century America was considered extremely immoral. Sexual values required a close relationship between sexual intercourse and procreation. Historically, definitions of female sexuality have been class bound and culturally specific. For example in Victorian England, lower-class women were defined as lasciviously and evilly oversexed, whereas upper-class women were supposed to be passive, asexual creatures incapable of arousal. What little birth control was available was transmitted through midwives and women's networks. During the nineteenth century the foundations of women's reproductive networks were shaken, and a process which undermined women's control of women's health was set in motion (Barker-Benfield, 1976; Gordon, 1976).

The nineteenth century was a period of increasing professionalization in the United States. While there were anti-elitist sentiments such as the popular health movement, the medical profession made systematic headway in regularizing and centralizing an exclusive allopathic practice (Ehrenreich and English, 1979). Medical education promoted this new exclusivity with more systematized and regulated licensing which excluded women from training. The American Medical Association (AMA) was formed in 1847, restricting membership to those trained and licensed in the new model. Journals began to flourish, standardizing information between doctors whether rural or urban. Following the Civil War hospitals became more firmly entrenched, providing the seeds for centralization and specialization in medicine. Hospitals provided further control by dictating who was eligible to practice in them and who was not. These changes in the organization of medicine, combined with national tendencies toward urbanization, standardization and increased communication between the states, provided a setting for the development of a professional, elite, highly educated, predominantly male medical core. (Stevens, 1971).

This professionalization of medical practice seriously affected the definition and treatment of women's health needs. Historically, childbirth had been understood as a natural process under the control of women. Midwives and neighborwomen were the attendants at births. In other words, this area was considered "women's work." However, with the rise of male obstetricians, childbirth became defined as a process fraught with danger and in need of expensive, scientific, expert care, i.e., male doctors (Ehrenreich and English, 1979). The notion of childbirth as a healthy function was progressively changed into a definition of childbirth as a disease and illness (Wertz and Wertz, 1977). It was during this period that a new consciousness was formulated around what I will call the "diseasing of reproduction." With the professionalization of medicine, midwives were portrayed by the medical men as dirty, dangerous and unreliable. Obstetricians claimed intellectual superiority in terms of education (although this education rarely included clinical birth experience) and technical superiority through equipment such as forceps which nondoctors were not allowed to use by law (Ehrenreich and English, 1979).

Further, hospitals were slowly becoming recognized and used by the general population. Obstetricians were welcome in these settings; midwives were not. In fact, the onset of the delivery of babies by male doctors introduced a plague of puerperal fever which lasted until the end of the nineteenth century. Doctors would treat ill or dead patients and then proceed to deliver babies, whether in the home or the hospital, without washing their hands. This practice spread disease and increased maternal mortality until the connection was made in the late nineteenth century. Midwives with their limited practices did not come in contact with or spread disease, resulting in safer childbirth. In the light of this information, the idea that "filthy midwives" were replaced by "antiseptic" obstetricians and gynecologists becomes a myth perpetuated by gynecological historians (Rich, 1976).

The rise of obstetrics and gynecology as male domains has been related to a more general trend in America for men to take over and control women and their sexuality (Barker-Benfield, 1976). While the oppression of women was certainly not new to the nineteenth century, a new rationale for control did develop. Whereas female sexuality had in the past been predominantly a sin in need of religious control, it now also became a sickness—a sickness in need of medical control. In mid-nineteenth century America, one reaction to this male control was the flowering of feminism and interest in women's rights. Feminism was characterized by an interest of women in (1) expanding their right to freedom and choice under the label "voluntary motherhood," (2) changes in diet and clothing to allow for more activity and better health controlled in the home, and (3) maintaining midwives who were known to be knowledgeable in methods of birth control. All of this was perceived by the medical profession and society at large as a threat to the social order (Gordon, 1976). Gynecologists, presenting themselves as the experts on women, abounded with advice, theories and practices to remedy the situation. Dr. Charles Meigs, for example, advised his medical students in 1848 (the year of the first woman's rights convention):

> [Woman's] intellectual and moral perceptivity and forces. . . are feminine as her organs are. Beyond all these, you shall have to explore the history of those functions and destines which her sexual nature enables her to fulfill and the strange and secret influences which her organs, by their nervous constitution, and the functions, by their relation to her whole life-force, whether in sickness or health, are capable of exerting, not on the body alone, but on the heart, the mind, and the very soul of woman. The medical practitioner has, then, much to study, as to the female, that is not purely medical—but psychological and moral rather: such researches will be a future obligation lying heavily on you. . .(quoted in Barker-Benfield, 1976:83).

The study of a woman's organs it was argued would offer insights into her psyche and being. In 1866, Dr. Ray stated:

> With woman it is but a step from extreme nervous susceptibility to downright hysteria, and from that to overt insanity. In the sexual evolution, in pregnancy, in the parturient period, in lactation, strange thoughts, extraordinary feelings, unseasonable appetites, criminal impulses, may haunt a mind at other times innocent and pure (quoted in Barker-Benfield, 1976:83).

Thus, women's physiology was not only the key to understanding the female but the seat of her insanity and crimes. What had been considered normal functions of womanhood—pregnancy, lactation—not only became diseases of the body but diseases of the mind. Surgical remedies became mechanisms for social control. Women were first defined as deviant by their behavior and then in turn this deviance was attributed to their biology, requiring medical intervention. The reproductive organs became the primary focus for this intervention, whether the problem was defined as physical, mental or moral. Removal of the uterus—"what she is in health, in character, in her charms, alike of body, mind and soul is because of her womb alone" (quoted in Barker-Benfield, 1976:88)— came to be viewed as an acceptable procedure for treating psychological, sexual and physiological disorders. [Among those disturbances seen as biological in origin were hysteria, ineptness as a wife or an interest in women's rights (Ehrenreich and English, 1979).] Castration and sexual surgery such as a clitoridectomy were diagnosed for such "disorders" as masturbation or a "heightened" interest in sex, or such "sins" as using contraceptives and abortion. Removal of the ovaries was thought to cure insanity and oversexuality—the two often being equated (Barker-Benfield, 1976). As women's health care increasingly revolved around these surgical procedures, women became accustomed to male doctors, particularly among the middle and upper classes. Concomitantly, the defining of women's reproductive cycles as diseases in need of medical management broadened the scope and increased the profits of physicians. Male doctors became accustomed to lucrative practices based on this new approach to female anatomy.

Midwives and lay healers were dealt the final death blow in 1910 when the Carnegie Foundation hired Abraham Flexner to inspect and report on all medical training centers. His report would inform Carnegie as to which schools were "reputable" and should receive funding and those which were "not reputable" and should not receive funding. Flexner met with AMA officials before making his inspections. Flexner approved the major, male-controlled "scientific" centers such as Johns Hopkins Medical School while rejecting the smaller, irregular schools which enrolled women, blacks and students from the working class. The lines were drawn on issues of sex, race and class, leaving the future of medical care to white, upper-class men. This led to a massive closing of schools which could not receive funding or licensing and whose faculty were suddenly looked upon as quacks. The removal of women as primary healers did not remove women entirely from health delivery; they remain to this day in underserved areas as midwives relegated to illegal status or demoted to the status of nurse, subservient to the male doctor.

This change in health care organization coincided with an emerging socialist and feminist movement in America between approximately 1910 and 1920. It is with this movement that the term "birth control" came into existence and arose as a central political issue. Birth control was understood as vital to the political emancipation of both men and women, as well as the "revolutionizing" of society in terms of power for the working class and for women. This was a working class movement concerned with class inequalities in the power structure. Margaret Sanger was at this time a socialist and concerned with the connections between birth control and liberation for women generally and, in particular, for people of the working class, both men and women. After 1920, however, the birth control movement and Sanger evolved in a less radical, more liberal and male-defined direction. The movement was reduced to "planned parenthood," focusing solely on the regulation of reproduction rather than the feminist and socialist goals of political and social equality. The next 30 years brought about sweeping changes in attitudes toward birth control, including its legalization and final takeover by the medical profession to regulate and control distribution and research (Gordon, 1976).

Reproduction has undergone conceptual and practical shifts in perspective. The diseasing of women's bodies has contributed to a lack of control over their lives. Reproduction and contraception during the late nineteenth and early twentieth centuries changed from social/organic, female-controlled normal functions to biological/technological, male-controlled disease processes. Women in the late twentieth century are concerned with many of the same problems with regard to control of their bodies despite changes in the parameters of these concerns due to both technological innovations and societal changes. The women's health movement today has become increasingly interested in unraveling the biological/

technical, male-controlled disease approach to reproduction. This research is important for analyzing what this approach has meant for women's health care and their life options.

III. CURRENT CONCERNS

To the degree that discrimination toward women is pervasive in our society, it is also deeply embedded in the field of medicine. While sexism existed long before the rise of our health care system, modern medicine has been a major reinforcer of these prejudices. It is the primary institution in this society for women to turn to for reproductive care. The result of this dominance is that every cycle that is normal and healthy in female development is made into a disease controlled by the medical establishment.

Birth control and contraception are researched, developed, controlled and distributed by the medical profession. Just as birth control is defined as a medical concern, a number of other natural processes have been reconceived as medical problems: childbirth is treated as a surgical procedure (Arms, 1975); menopause has become carcinogenic and hazardous to a woman's health in Western society, necessitating drugs and/or surgery, even though it is a universal process found even in cultures where there is no cancer[2] (Culpepper, 1978; Weideger, 1975); menstruation, historically defined as something "dirty" or "the curse," has more recently been treated by doctors as a slightly disgusting affliction which makes women more irrational (Delaney et al., 1976).[3] Premenstrual syndrome (PMS) is a newly defined "disease" which recreates an old dilemma for women. On the one hand, some women do suffer physiologically based discomfort with menstruation. It is an improvement to have this taken seriously instead of dismissed as a psychosomatic problem (read, "overemotional"). On the other hand, if a woman's very biological structure is defined as the source of violent, irrational behavior, social control of women, rather than autonomous equality, becomes the logical and oppressive conclusion. And last but not least, women's sexuality, which has historically been labeled deviant, was traditionally cast into a heterosexual framework revolving around men's needs. In Victorian society, "ladies" were supposed to be frigid, passive recipients of male passion. Now, women are told to be multiorgasmic despite controversies as to where and how these orgasms occur—controversies, until recently, entered into exclusively by men (Bullough and Bullough, 1977).

The "diseasing of reproduction" creates fears in women which in turn produces dependence on the medical profession and the authority of the doctor. A process evolves which keeps women obsessed with their bodies, necessitating constant checkups and perpetuating their reliance on experts. Women become concerned with every change in their bodies because their bodies have become alienated, disease-producing agents out of their control. Women's bodies, regardless of class or status, become objects of fear and dread negating the possibility of subjective awareness within women and solidarity among women based on shared reproductive interests.[4]

Mary Howell, former Associate Dean of Harvard Medical School, has conducted research which documents the degrading attitudes toward women prevalent in medical school training—both toward female medical students and female patients (Howell, 1973). In addition, Fidell points out that

> If during medical training, many physicians get into the habit of referring to women under fifty as 'douch bags' and patients over fifty as 'the crock' (as it is done in one leading medical school), it is hard to see how the problems of women could be taken seriously (quoted in Ruzek, 1978:84).

Scully and Bart's research supports the above information in a study of gynecological text books used in medical schools. They found disrespectful attitudes toward women, dated and sexist information about female sexuality, as well as the defining of women's bodies in terms of their relationships to men (Scully and Bart, 1973). Scully (1980) also found this direction reflected in the training of gynecological residents.

A further aspect of sexism in health care is the image of women portrayed in drug company advertising and promotion. Women are represented as suffering primarily from psychosomatic rather than organic problems. Traditional sex roles are reinforced in these advertisements through males portraying the doctor, females the nurse and patient. The female patient is generally a housewife suffering from anxiety or other disabilities which prove bothersome to husbands and require tranquilizing medication (Prather and Fidell, 1973, 1975). The drug industry invests over three-fourths of a billion dollars each year on advertisements to about 250,000 doctors. These dollars are not spent needlessly. Doctors do use these products and prescribe them, primarily to women patients, resulting in overuse of drugs by patients and large profits for drug companies (Ruzek, 1978).

Many women are becoming angry and frustrated with traditional medical practice. Medical childbirth practices, the predominant and most accepted form of childbirth in America today, are being questioned. Many women are choosing alternatives such as homebirths and midwives over hospital births and doctors. This has become a large enough movement for hospitals to respond with alternative birth centers and nurse-midwives in order to meet women's needs and to keep childbirth under the control of medicine (Ryan, 1978). Surgery on women in the form of hysterectomies, mastectomies and caesarean sections have reached "epidemic proportion." Despite the fact that these surgeries can be useful, they are often unnecessary and can have little impact in effecting a cure (Daly, 1978; Corea, 1977). Gynecologists describe the normal uterus as "a possible breeding ground for cancer" and as a "potentially lethal organ" as reasons in many cases for its removal (Scheifelbein, 1980; Larned, 1974). Dr. Robert Wilson in his book *Feminine Forever* further rationalizes hysterectomies:

> A woman who has had her uterus removed but retains her ovaries thus appears fortunate indeed... She is truly an emancipated woman... If your uterus has been removed, estrogen therapy will provide all its benefits without the annoyance of menstrual bleeding. You are a lucky woman (Wilson, 1966:138-9).

What is not stated here is that the death rate for hysterectomy is higher than the death rate for uterine/cervical cancer—a statistic which casts a dubious light on the preventive potency for hysterectomies (Daly, 1978).

Estrogen replacement therapy, a menopausal or post-hysterectomy hormonal treatment, has also been widely criticized as a cancer-causing procedure and is a highly controversial issue both within and beyond the medical profession (Seaman and Seaman, 1977). Hormones such as estrogen are also found in the birth control pill. This form of birth control, at one time hailed as the most wonderful of wonder drugs is being shown to have far-reaching complications. The intrauterine device (IUD), which has never been properly tested or understood, has been found to cause sterility, severe uterine and tubal infections and even, in some cases, death (Corea, 1977). The amount of cancer caused in the children of the women who were prescribed the hormone diethylstilbestrol (DES) in the 1940s and 1950s is coming to the attention of the public in leaps and bounds (Corea, 1977). Over the past 10 years there have been numerous congressional hearings on DES, unnecessary hysterectomies, birth control methods and the use of hormone therapy, as well as the role that drug companies and the medical profession have played in these treatments.

In recent research on gynecologists talking with women, analyses of tapes show that the power gap between doctor and patient discussed in feminist scholarship can be observed at the level of actual interactions. Doctors control the speech patterns, the flow of talk and the topics discussed. For example, Fisher (1982) has shown that, in a clinic for indigent patients where residents need training, women receive either a soft or hard sell for hysterectomies. Women with the same problems in the private sector of the hospital, where there are neither residents nor indigent patients, receive office procedures rather than surgery. She traces the development of these decisions in the talk between doctor and patient. Similarly, doctors often ignore or dominate women's experiential interpretations of their contraceptive needs. The medical approach is a technical one. Social, contextual information concerning women's daily lives is generally defined as irrelevant to health care decision making. But women conceptualize their bodies and reproduction as broader than just their biology. The institutional power of the doctor and the passivity of the patient role contribute to a truncation of women's contributions in the medical interaction. This control, analyzable at the level of medical institutions and observable in the doctor-patient discourse, can have serious consequences for women's reproductive regulation and thus their life options (Todd, 1983).

The foregoing examples of the treatment of women's bodies are and have been of great concern to the women's health movement. Imbedded in these concerns are theoretical assumptions and explanations as to the causes of the problems women face in their reproductive lives. These explanations can be viewed through three major theoretical frameworks which have been developed in the recent wave of feminist literature (Fee, 1973):

First, the traditional Marxist approach, while acknowledging the importance of patriarchy, examines the inequality of access to health care in our class system and the tremendous profits to be made from the diseasing of reproduction, stemming from an exploitative capitalist economic order.

Second, the radical feminist perspective, while acknowledging the importance of the profit motive, stresses an analysis of patriarchal cultural values toward and institutional definitions of reproduction—values and definitions created by men at the expense of women and by means of their oppression.

The third position, the socialist feminist framework, attempts to combine an analysis of the oppressive qualities of patriarchal society and the exploitation resulting from capitalism to arrive at explications of the means of reproduction in modern society.

A fourth and complementary area in need of theoretical development is the cultural rise of the scientific world view. Historically, conceptual shifts in world view arose in the sixteenth and seventeenth centuries, introducing what has been regarded by scholars as the rise of a scientific explanatory system. This system was incorporated into Western society's institutions in the nineteenth and twentieth centuries. One aspect of this institutionalization, the notion that the conscious mind can be understood as separate from the mechanical body, has influenced medical theory and practice. The medical model assumes a health care delivery service based on the illness of individuals or individual organs. The assumptions behind this model are particularly problematic when treating reproductive cycles which are normal, social and biological activities in women's lives. Merchant (1980), in her historical work on the rise of science, discusses how the image of nature changed from female to male, active to passive, holistic to mechanical parts, contextual to context-free, and subjective to objective—all based on external forces and "laws" beyond human control. These shifts in perspective toward nature are also reflected in understandings of human beings. In particular this world view allows for a male definition of reproduction: a conception of women as passive, divided into mechanical bodily parts. The contextual aspects of woman's reproductive life and her subjective understandings are negated in favor of objective technical medical control.

Within the very fabric of these ideas of nature, society and human beings came a legitimation for medical science that the new medical men needed. While the medical takeover of normal, healthy reproductive functions in women can be understood through a political/economic and patriarchal lens—doctors did gain power, status and profit through sexist definitions of women—neither of these points provide the rationale that science gives for the diseasing of reproduction.[5]

The defining of reproduction in a scientific, physiological mode has important consequences for social theory as well as for women's lives. When a society ideologically considers reproduction to be a biological issue, there is no need to incorporate it into a theory of that society. The means of reproduction, thus sex roles and "the woman question," can be overlooked and/or dismissed as irrelevant to social and political concerns.

IV. CONCLUSIONS

Much work, both of a scholarly and political nature, has been done to reverse the image of the female body as structurally diseased and deviant. The incorporation of a conceptual analysis of the rise of a scientific world view and its effects on medical definitions of disease into the theoretical socialist feminist framework could prove important for developing clearer social understandings for the treatment of women's bodies. This is an important focus of inquiry in that women are in a complicated double bind in the reconceptualization of the means of reproduction.

Women from all strata of society are increasingly, with varying degrees of success, striving to be recognized outside of traditional roles which define them in terms of their anatomy. This is a particularly crucial time for women to refuse and refute the "anatomy-as-destiny" legacy. With forces such as sociobiology offering a genetic rationale for women's traditional reproductive functions and the rise of political right representing roadblocks to women's control of their lives, clarity in women's understandings of their bodies is a necessity. This necessity requires careful theoretical analyses as well as practical change.

While the anatomy-as-destiny argument must be understood as a derogatory theory of women, it is also important to change the legacy of negative definitions of that anatomy. On the one hand, women are defined in the lofty terms of perpetuators of the race—motherhood and apple pie; on the other hand, their very bodies and reproductive functions are denigrated as diseased and deviant. Both of these versions are detrimental to the liberation of women in society. A woman's psyche does not reside in her uterus, but neither is her uterus a bad place. An analysis of the female body is needed which incorporates a definition of the body's processes within a broader definition of women's possibilities. To simply deny female physiology in response to the anatomy-as-destiny argument is to leave unquestioned, and thus implicitly accepted, a history which defines this anatomy as deviant. The implications for this denial are serious.

Examples of the consequences of stigmatizing the female anatomy are rampant in women's health care. We live in a society which places heavy emphasis on the female breast—its size, its shape, its age. At the same time radical mastectomy is the predominant operation for breast cancer in the United States despite the fact that this cure is considered no more effective than less extreme methods used in Britain and in some U.S. health centers (Crile, 1974). Hysterectomies are done with great frequency and often unnecessarily (Scheifelbein, 1980). The uterus is first defined as providing a woman's only function in life and then it is dispensed with as if it were a problematic, diseased organ any woman would be better off without (Fisher, 1982).

Women are caught in a double bind: On the one hand, the very definition of being a woman is objectified into sexual and/or reproductive bodily parts; on the other hand, those same parts are seen as unnecessary, often inconvenient and diseased, to be lopped off or cut out without regard. Both positions are detrimental to a woman's definition of self and her potential in society. It becomes crucially important that while striving for freedom from a life defined by reproductive responsibility women also seek social understandings which allow that anatomy is never destiny but neither is it deviant.

ACKNOWLEDGMENTS

An earlier version of this paper was first presented to the 1981 meeting of the Western Society of Criminology, San Deigo, California. I am grateful to Rae Lesser Blumberg and Janet Schmidt for their encouragement of this work, and to Steven Spitzer and Rochelle Kern for their editorial comments.

NOTES

1. Flexner did in fact get rid of many "quacks." However, by strictly defining medical care in terms of "regular" doctors, many qualified healers also disappeared.

2. It is interesting to note that while reproductive cycles are normal and healthy aspects of women's lives, medical intervention can turn them into iatrogenic diseases, primarily drug related.

3. One gynecological text asserts that "if menstruation can be abolished. . . it would be a blessing to not only the woman but her husband" (quoted in Scheifelbein, 1980).

4. The women's health movement has made strides in providing alternative reproductive care. While this more progressive approach has flourished in some areas of the country, the medical model predominates in treatment for the majority of women.

5. See Ehrenreich and English (1979) for their work on science as a legitimating ideology for the treatment of women by experts in general and doctors in particular. They assert that science had, it itself, been an inherently good, "revolutionary force" distorted by charlatans. This leaves "Science" as such, on its own terms, a pure, objective entity. However, a broader analysis of the conceptual scheme of the rise of a scientific world views shows how these new concepts complemented changing social values and the rise of technical medicine (Todd, 1981).

REFERENCES

Arms, Suzanne
  1975 Immaculate Deception. Boston: Houghton Mifflin.
Barker-Benfield, G.J.
  1976 The Horrors of the Half-Known Life. New York: Harper and Row.
Bullough, Vern and Bonnie Bullough
  1977 Sin, Sickness and Sanity: A History of Sexual Attitudes. New York: New American
       Library.
Corea, Gena
  1977 The Hidden Malpractice: How American Medicine Treats Women as Patients and Profes-
       sionals. New York: William Morrow.
Crile, George, Jr.
  1974 What Women Should Know about the Breast Cancer Controversy. New York: Pocket
       Books.
Culpepper, Emily
  1978 "Exploring menstrual attitudes." In M.S. Hennifin, et al. (eds.), Women Look at Biology
       Looking at Women. Cambridge Massachusetts: Schenckman.
Daly, Mary
  1978 Gyn/Ecology: The Metaethics of Radical Feminism. Boston: Beacon Press.
Delaney, Janice, Mary Jane Lupton and Emily Toth
  1976 The Curse: A Cultural History of Menstruation. New York: New American Library.
Ehrenreich, Barbara and Deirdre English
  1979 For Her Own Good: 150 Years of the Expert's Advice to Women. Garden City, New
       York: Anchor Books.
Fee, Elizabeth
  1973 "Women and health care: a comparison of theories." In Vincente Navarro (ed.), Health
       and Medical Care in the United States: A Critical Analysis. Farmingdale, New York:
       Baywood.
Fisher, Sue
  1981 "The decision-making context: how doctor and patient communicate." In Robert J. DiPietro
       (ed.), Linquistics and the Professions. Norwood, New Jersey: Ablex.
Gordon, Linda
  1976 Woman's Body, Woman's Right. New York: Penguin Books.
Howell, Mary
  1973 Why Would a "Girl" Go Into Medicine: A Guide for Women. Old Westbury, New York:
       The Feminist Press. Published under pseudonym Margaret Campbell, M.D.
Larned, Deborah
  1974 "The greening of the womb." New Times (December 27).
Merchant, Carolyn
  1980 The Death of Nature: Women, Ecology, and the Scientific Revolution. San Francisco:
       Harper and Row.
Prather, Jane and Linda Fidell
  1973 "Medical advertising—pressures for prescribing psychoactive drugs to women." Paper
       presented at the 68th Annual Meeting of the American Sociological Association, (Septem-
       ber), New York. Mimeographed.
Prather, Jane and Linda Fidell
  1975 "Sex differences in the content and style of medical advertisements." Social Science and
       Medicine 9 23-26.

Rich, Adrienne
  1976 Of Women Born: Motherhood as Experience and Institution. New York: W.W. Norton.
Ruzek, Sheryl Burt
  1978 The Women's Health Movement, Feminist Alternatives to Medical Control. New York: Praeger.
Rayan, Catherine M.
  1978 "An applicaton of social movements theory to a study of midwifery." Unpublished paper, University of California, San Deigo.
Scheifelbein, Susan
  1980 "The female patient: heeded? hustled? healed? Saturday Review, (March 29).
Scully, Diana
  1980 Men Who Control Women's Health: The Miseducation of Obstetrician-Gynecologists. Boston: Houghton-Mifflin.
Scully, Diana and Pauline Bart
  1973 "A funny thing happened on the way to the orifice: women in gynecology textbooks." American Journal of Sociology 78:1045-50.
Seaman, Barbara and Gideon Seaman
  1977 Women and the Crisis in Sex Hormones. New York: Rawson Associates. Public Interest. New Haven: Yale University Press.
Stevens, Rosemary
  1971 American Medicine and the Public Interest. New Haven: Yale University Press.
Todd, Alexandra Dundas
  1981 "The medicalization of reproduction: scientific medicine and the diseasing of the healthy woman". Unpublished doctoral dissertation. Department of Sociology, University of California, San Diego.
Todd, Alexandra Dundas
  1983 "A diagnosis of doctor patient discourse in the prescription of contraception." In Sue Fisher and Alexandra Todd (eds.), The Social Organization of Doctor/Patient Communication. Washington, D.C.: Center for Applied Linguistics.
Weideger, Paula
  1975 Menstruation and Menopause. New York: Dell.
Wilson, Robert A., M.D.
  1966 Feminine Forever. New York: M. Evans.
Wertz, Richard W. and Dorothy C.
  1977 Lying In: A History of Childbirth in America. New York: MacMillan.

PART II

LAW AND JUSTICE IN CONTEMPORARY AMERICA

IMPLEMENTING PUBLIC LAW 94-142, THE EDUCATION FOR ALL HANDICAPPED CHILDREN ACT, IN AN ILLINOIS SCHOOL DISTRICT

F. James Davis and Barbara Sherman Heyl

I. INTRODUCTION

The most comprehensive federal statute affecting special education is the Education for All Handicapped Children Act of 1975 (Public Law 94-142). Its provisions are supported significantly by Section 504 of the Rehabilitation Act of 1973. Both are essentially civil rights laws. Section 504 states that handicapped people shall not be discriminated against by reason of their handicaps. Public Law 94-142 mandates that public schools provide free appropriate education for all handicapped children. These laws were the culmination of several years of legislative and judicial developments at both the state and federal levels that were dubbed "the quiet revolution" (Diamond, 1973; Weintraub and Abeson, 1974). The federal government had done little to assist education of the handicapped until 1966, when Congress added Title VI to the Elementary and Secondary Education Act (Public Law 89-750). The Bureau of Education for the

Research in Law, Deviance and Social Control, Volume 5, pages 99-139

Handicapped (BEH) of the U.S. Office of Education was established by Title VI, to provide leadership for the emerging field of special education.

Once P.L. 94-142 was passed, the BEH was charged by Congress with responsibility for monitoring the implementation of the law. It funded a number of studies to determine how the states and local districts were responding to the law. Then in the spring of 1978 the BEH staff decided that, although data on the positions taken by professional educators were important, the law was intended to have its major impact on the individual children in need of special educational services. The need, then, was for data on the educational experiences of individual children as related to P.L. 94-142 and for feedback from the parents of these children. The BEH funded five contract projects designed to focus on a small number of children for a five-year period to determine what impact implementation of P.L. 94-142 may have had on these children and their families in local school districts. The data in this paper are from one of these studies, covering four years of field research on one school district in Illinois including intensive case data on twelve children, representing all classifications of special education in the district except the profoundly mentally retarded.

The sociology of law was one perspective used to guide the study, supplemented by four other sociological models: the labeling of deviant behavior, minority-dominant relations, symbolic interactionism, and family adaptation. Central to the study of law in society are the conflicts and accommodations among groups with different amounts of power as they attempt to advance their own interests (Pound, 1942:65-86; Turk, 1966; Quinney, 1969:20-30; Chambliss and Seidman, 1971:63-73; Hills, 1971:191-95; Akers and Hawkins, 1975:5-15; Davis, 1962:69-71; 1978:135-39). A group considers its interests served by legal norms that are perceived to be congruent with its major values (Pound, 1923:141-65; 1942:108-118; Chambliss and Seidman, 1971:51-52), and also with its existential or "legislative fact" beliefs (Patterson, 1963:30-35; Henshel and Silverman, 1975:Ch.1; Davis, 1975:52-54; 1978:131-35). Interest group cross-pressures influence the legislation, judical interpretation and administration of legal norms. The ultimate effects of a state or federal law depend on the operation of interest groups at the points of local impact. Groups active in supporting or opposing the passage and implementation of P.L. 94-142 include special and regular educators, parents of "special" and "normal" children, and administrators of local, state and federal educational agencies.

II. THE EDUCATION FOR ALL HANDICAPPED CHILDREN ACT OF 1975

A. Interest Groups and Passage of the Act

Postwar concern for the physically handicapped spawned the vocational rehabilitation movement, designed to facilitate employability and economic independence (Usdane, 1966; Sussman, 1966; Albrecht, 1976b). Oriented largely toward a medical model, the resulting programs of rehabilitation and interest group organizations have emphasized clinical treatment and job training that is specific to particular handicapping conditions (Myers, 1966:37; Scott, 1966:134-38; Wessen, 1966:164-78). Although physically handicapped groups and agencies were to influence passage of the Rehabilitation Act of 1973 (P.L. 93-122), the key impetus for establishing the rights of the handicapped in public schools came from organizations for the mentally retarded.

National awareness of handicapped groups was expanded by the founding of the National Association for Retarded Citizens (NARC) in 1950, which initiated publicity, parent organizations, demonstration projects and legislation for retarded children. In 1962 the report by President Kennedy's Panel on Mental Retardation produced action in all the states to develop comprehensive programs. In 1968 the International League of Societies of the Mentally Handicapped adopted a declaration of the human rights of the mentally retarded that was substantially adopted in 1971 by the General Assembly of the United Nations. Lawsuits and other actions on behalf of the retarded culminated in the key federal court decisions and legislation of the 1970s on the educational rights of all handicapped children (Lippman and Goldberg, 1973:Ch. 3; Turnbull and Turnbull, 1978:19).

Misuse of the Educable Mentally Retarded label was alleged in a class action in 1970 on behalf of nine Mexican-American children who had scored low on an IQ test printed in English [*Diana v. State Board of Education*, Civ. C 70-37-RFP (N.D. Cal., Jan. 7, 1970, and June 18, 1972)]. The Federal District Court for Northern California ordered that the children be retested in their primary language. NARC and its state affiliates publicized this and other successes, and supported further litigation and political action. Interest in the mislabeling of bilingual and poor black children became widespread in ethnic organizations, among special and general educators, and in the U.S. Office of Education (Hobbs, 1975). Research by sociologists lent support to this concern (Mercer, 1973).

The NARC became particularly active after the victory in 1972 in the landmark case in Federal District Court in Pennsylvania (Lippman and Goldberg, 1973:Chs. 4-7). This case was initiated by the Pennsylvania Association for Retarded Children (PARC) in response to experiences of the mentally retarded residents of Pennhurst State School and Hospital. PARC joined 13 selected sets of parents in a class action against the Commonwealth of Pennsylvania. Classifying this as a civil rights case, the court cited the 1954 U.S. Supreme Court case of *Brown v. Board of Education of Topeka, Kansas* (347 U.S. 483) as a controlling precedent. In effect, this extended from racial groups to the handicapped the Constitutional requirement of equal access of all "classes" (categories) of persons to the public schools. The court ordered Pennsylvania to locate all its handicapped children from ages 6 to 21 and to provide public education for all of them [*Pennsylvania Association for Retarded Children v. Commonwealth of*

Pennsylvania, 334 F. Supp. 1257 (E.D. Pa. 1971) and 343 F. Supp. 279 (E.D. Pa. 1972)]. Special educators were among the key witnesses on which the court relied.

The PARC case was affirmed and its scope rapidly enlarged by state and federal courts and legislatures (Lippman and Goldberg, 1973:Ch. 7; Turnbull and Turnbull, 1978:35-83). The basic right of the handicapped to educational opportunity was extended to include handicapped categories other than the mentally retarded in a class action in another Federal District Court case—*Mills et al. v. Board of Education of the District of Columbia et al.* [348 F. Supp. 866 (D.D.C. 1972)]. The Congress cited the *PARC, Mills,* and *Brown* cases in its summary of the need for passing P.L. 94-142 and noted that the educational rights of handicapped children had been supported in more than 36 state court decisions (*U.S. Code Congressional and Administrative News*, 1975:1430-31).

Organizations for handicaps other than mental retardation, including those for physical disabilities, also exerted public pressure in the early 1970s. Coalitions of various handicapped groups apparently had considerable influence. The coalition of the Disabled in Action was effective in state legislatures, and passage of the Rehabilitation Act of 1973 was encouraged by a much publicized wheel chair sit-in at the Lincoln Memorial in Washington, D.C. In 1974 the American Coalition of Citizens with Disabilities was formed. This group helped get P.L. 94-142 passed and then exerted pressures on the U.S. Office of Education to adopt firm guidelines for implementation. Both special and general educational associations exerted public influence. In 1971 the Council for Exceptional Children, a professional organization of special educators, adopted a declaration of the right of handicapped children to education and also formulated a model state statute.

The Congress summarized the interest groups from many states that had appeared at hearings for P.L. 94-142, emphasizing the testimony given by Pennsylvania officials on the implementation of the *PARC* decision. It acknowledged the role of Associations for Retarded Children, of major professional associations of both general and special educators, and of the BEH and other federal and state agencies of education. Also cited were organizations representing handicapped persons, parents and consumers (*U.S. Code Congressional and Administrative News*. 1975:1430).

B. Key Provisions of the Act

The Act is impressive in its intent, "very broad, both in vision and in scope" (Large, 1980). It defines "handicapped children" to include those who are "mentally retarded, hard of hearing, deaf, speech-impaired, visually handicapped, seriously emotionally disturbed, orthopedically impaired, or other health-impaired children, or children with specific learning disabilities" [20 U.S.C.

1401 (1)]. Thus all these children are to receive a "free, appropriate public education." That is, the special instruction needed is to be provided by the public school sytems at no cost to the parents. The specific educational setting and goals are to be decided by the professionals who work with the child in a conference with parents and written into an Individualized Educational Program. In addition, the setting is to be in "the least restrictive environment" that meets the child's individual learning needs. Thus, school systems, founded on the concept of mass education and the necessity for grouping children—by age, by class, by "reading group levels" within the class—were being told to look at handicapped children *individually* and to address their specific, individual learning needs. In addition, the Act has still another unusual characteristic: it is unique among educational legislation in that it has no termination date. It stands as law until repealed by Congress. The major provisions of the Act can be described briefly as follows (see Turnbull and Turnbull, 1978:Ch. 3-8):

1. *Zero Reject.* *All* handicapped children are required to have full and free access to public education, regardless of the degree of the handicap. This right does not depend on the receipt of federal funds.

2. *Individualized Educational Programs* (IEP). An individual plan (including a statement of the child's present performance levels, instructional goals, details of and schedules for special education services to be provided) must be written every year and agreed on in a planning conference, for each child included in a program of special education.

3. *Least Restrictive Environment* (LRE). To thc maximum extent appropriate, handicapped children are to be educated with nonhandicapped children. The emphasis for implementation is on what is appropriate for each child, which precludes wholesale "mainstreaming" of handicapped children into regular classrooms. For one child the LRE may be the regular classroom; for another a special school. However, movement of a child in the more restrictive direction— out of a regular classroom, into a special room or school—obligates the local public school to provide justification that education in regular classes with the use of supplementary aids and services cannot be achieved satisfactorily.

4. *Protection in Evaluation Procedures* (PEP). All test scores and other filed material in the child's academic record are confidential and may be released only after administrative and signed parental permissions have been obtained.

5. *Parental Involvement* (PI). Parents must be given adequate notice of planning conferences, full information and encouragement to participate. Parents may request a different time, and they may waive their right to attend.

6. *Due Process.* Parents have the right to procedural due process. If they wish to appeal a placement decision they have the right to a hearing arranged by the school district, the outcome of which may be appealed in the courts.

III. IMPLEMENTING THE ACT: PROBLEMS AND ISSUES

A. A Challenge to the Existing Educational Structures

The law is a powerful statement of the right to equal educational opportunity for all handicapped children. With its passage Congress was recognizing, as it had with passage of previous civil rights laws, that segregating whole categories of individuals into special settings is discriminatory. The catchword for the desegregation of handicapped children was "mainstreaming," and it early became the focus of arguments about P.L. 94-142, even though the goal of "Least Restrictive Environment" was only one provision of the Act. As one major lobbyist for the Act, Edwin Martin, then Deputy Commissioner of the U.S. Office of Education, put it:

> Most of us support mainstreaming because we have seen segregated schools for black children, because we have seen institutions for the retarded, because we have seen Indian reservations, and because we are struck dumb by what has happened in segregated settings. Our support of mainstreaming, it seems to me, is based on our assumptions and values rather than on any research that indicates that mainstreaming is the best solution for all children (Martin, 1978: v-vi).

Thus, the law is based on a commitment to basic values very similar to those that gave rise to the racial school desegregation case of *Brown v. Board of Education*, 347 U.S. 483 (1954). But as a nation we can document the obstacles encountered during the nearly 30 years of efforts at realizing those values of equal educational opportunity for black students. We know now that compared to obtaining favorable court decisions and federal legislation, changing school and community practices can be a truly difficult proposition. And it is precisely a change in school and community practices that is required for the full implementation of P.L. 94-142.

In a major sense the law challenges the view held by the community and professional educators that handicapped children are significantly different from other children. Indeed, the increase of special education programs at the public school level and at the university levels for the training of "special" teachers consolidated the view that different theories, settings and teaching practices were essential if handicapped children were effectively to be taught (Sarason and Doris, 1978:8-9). With P.L. 94-142 even the special educators, long the major advocates for the rights of the handicapped to education, were being told to loosen their hold on the role of "expert" so as to allow regular educators and parents a genuine partnership role in educational planning for handicapped children, and to look vigilantly for an educational setting for each handicapped child that would be appropriate for that child's learning needs *and* be "the least restrictive environment.'' In fact, all educational personnel were challenged to reduce the separation between "regular" and "special" education wherever possible, keeping each child's individual learning needs paramount, however. If the school personnel were recommending a special education placement, the burden of proof fell on them to explain why a less restrictive environment was not also appropriate. It was perceived that paperwork and conference time would be dramatically increased and communcation with parents was to be significantly improved.

It is not surprising that much opposition to the law surfaced within the educational establishment:

> They were people engaged in public service, carrying out their tasks in ways that their professional training as well as long-standing custom had supported as right and effective. To be told, then, that their values were wrong, that they had been contributing to the evil, and that they would have to accommodate to new procedures and practices—it is no wonder that far from dissolving opposition, the adjudications may have had an opposite effect (Sarason and Doris, 1978:7).

Interestingly, the opposition from educators had to be carefully phrased. No educational group had opposed passage of the law. The later opposition from teacher's organizations made clear that these groups supported the spirit and intent of the law, objecting only to the problems and deficiencies encountered in its implementation [see statements from Albert Shanker, President of the American Federation of Teachers (1980), and Mary Rita Hanley, Past President of the Pennsylvania Association for Children with Learning Disabilities (1979)]. The concerns of the professional educators are important factors to be considered, since full implementation of the law rests primarily with the school personnel. The lobbyists for P.L. 94-142 acknowledged that in their efforts to build support they had often bypassed school personnel because "parents had been more successful in dealing with legislators than with the schools, which were often reluctant to change" (Martin, 1978:iii).

B. Mainstreaming and the Least Restrictive Environment

With the passage of the Act, the catchwords that had sparked previously heated controversy in the field of special education—*mainstreaming, least restrictive environment*, and *normalization*—now found attention in a much broader arena: that of the world of public education in practice (Dybward 1980). Since these words had played an important part in the legislative history of the Act, public school officials and teachers had to wonder just how the terms and their underlying values would be implemented. Teachers feared, for example, that large numbers of handicapped children would be dumped into their classrooms. These fears produced a fixation on the term "mainstreaming," with the lay definition of it as "the placing of children with special needs full-time into regular class-rooms." This definition is a serious oversimplification of the concept.

The year P.L. 94-142 was passed, the Council for Exceptional Children (1975:174) published a statement on mainstreaming that specified that the term encompassed a *range* of settings for children who needed more specialized help than the regular classroom could provide. Some agreement among professionals stipulates that a mainstreamed child must spend more than half the time in a regular classroom and that the regular teacher has the *primary* responsibility for the child's progress (Forness, 1979:508). However, one often hears that a child who spends the majority of his or her time in special education settings has been "mainstreamed" into physical education, art or recess periods. It should be noted that, for all the talk about mainstreaming, the term has little legal status, not even appearing in the Act itself. Instead, the Act mandates that handicapped children be educated in the Least Restrictive Environment. Emphasizing this point, the report to Congress submitted by the U.S. Department of Education (1981:9,11) following the second year of implementation of P.L. 94-142 stated that "LRE does not simply mean placing all handicapped children in regular classrooms," that a residential school may be the LRE and that "the determining factor is appropriateness."

The concerns of the regular educators remain at a high level for a variety of reasons. In many cases, they were not aware of or sympathetic towards these more flexible interpretations. A questionnaire study in the fall of 1978, the school year in which P.L. 94-142 went into effect, measured the level of awareness of and concerns about the law of a random sample of educators in the state of Kansas. The analysis indicated that "the majority of educators are relatively unaware of and generally in disagreement with the legislation" (Holloway and Kerr, 1979:246). It should be noted that only ten of the 635 respondents gave their current teaching assignment as "Special Education." Thus, these findings represent primarily the views of regular educators.

In a recent study of regular teachers in rural and small city school districts in central Wisconsin, the authors (Ringlaben and Price, 1981:302) draw the reader's attention to "the large percentage of teachers who believe they know very little about exceptional children and feel unprepared for mainstreaming." The authors point out that over half of the sample had received no in-service training and over 86% of the sample indicated no academic course work in the area of mainstreaming (Ringlaben and Price, 1981:302-304). Pratt and Watkins (1980) cite research that reveals that school principals, as well as regular teachers, often have negative attitudes toward special education. Sarason and Doris (1978:9) note:

The school principal, either by tradition or administrative regulations, came from 'regular' education and considered himself incompetent to advise or guide the special class teacher;

not infrequently, the principal saw the special class as either an unasked-for burden or a blemish on the school image.

Thus, the resistance toward mainstreaming and implementing the LRE provision can be at least partly explained by the fact that special education has been structurally and conceptually separated from regular education.

The professional training of teachers, whether for regular or special education, has emphasized that teaching handicapped children requires *special* training. The separation of regular and special education in the public schools has its origins in the separation at the university level. Or as Sarason and Doris (1978:8-9) present it: "The opposition to mainstreaming children was long contained in the political-administrative-social structure of departments and schools of education in our colleges and universities." In addition, the general population has supported the separation of "regular" and "special" teachers and of "regular" and "special" pupils. Thus, the law runs counter to instructional practice, as well as to educational and social opinion.

In addition, the actual implementation of the provision of the LRE is difficult. First, it requires the *availability* of a range of special educational environments— such that one of the settings "appropriate" for that child can be seen as a "least restrictive" alternative. Thus, local school districts must generate a variety of special learning settings and resources, with varying degrees of contact by the student with regular education (Polloway and Smith, 1980:300-301). In its report to Congress, the U.S. Department of Education (1981:9) indicated that, in the second year of implementation of P.L. 94-142, districts nationwide had been expanding existing services and adding new program alternatives. Commonly used options are those of the "instructional room" (where students spend more than 50% of their school day, also participating in "regular class" activities part of the day) and the "resource room" (for students who spend the majority of their school day in the regular classroom, but who come to the resource room to work one-to-one or in small groups with a special education teacher). Individual schedules can be devised that maximize the students' chances for learning in both the special and regular class settings (see development of IEP below). Secondly, implementing LRE is difficult because it requires the decision makers to assess how the new educational setting under consideration will affect the child. There are no reliable data available that correlate success in a particular setting with the myriad of variables that characterize that child. Keeping a child in a restrictive environment just because "S/he is doing so well there," is now unacceptable. That child might also do well in a less restrictive setting, and in this case keeping the child in the safe environment violates LRE. The move in the less restrictive direction is fraught with risk since such a move usually involves a reduction in special support services to the child, and the child may flounder. Implementing LRE requires a sensitive matching of the individual child to the least restrictive, appropriate setting.

C. The Individualized Educational Program

The requirement that an Individualized Educational Program (IEP) be written every year for every child receiving special educational services is a powerful statement that P.L. 94-142 is not "the mainstreaming law." The IEP provision operationalizes the requirement that professionals and parents consider seriously and plan for the *individual* learning needs of the child. If followed, this certainly precludes wholesale mainstreaming of handicapped children into regular classrooms, as noted previously. In addition, this planning for the needs of the individual child runs counter to the traditional practices in the public schools— that of planning for whole *groups* of children, such as by grade, by separate class or by reading group. In combination with LRE requirements, the development of an IEP is intended to facilitate agreement on the particular placement setting that is appropriate for *this* particular child. Once an appropriate setting is agreed upon, the local school system is mandated to provide it.

School systems, however, have vested interests in maintaining existing programs and avoiding the development of new ones, which will inevitably cost extra money. As Large (1980:247) notes, "While the IEP is supposed to stress the uniqueness of each child, the producer of the IEP—whether the teacher, administrator, or professional team—has an existing program to justify and an abundance of paperwork." In addition, the law mandates that the school provide an "appropriate" environment but does not define the term. Appropriate for whom—the individual child, the handicapped children in his or her special category, handicapped children generally, or the whole school system? Large (1980:264) responds:

> A strong case can be made from the language of the Act itself that Congress intended the concept [appropriate] to relate to what was best for each individual child. However, applications of the concept in local disputes between parents and school systems indicates that local agencies are defining the term to suit their own needs and existing programs rather than to fit the individual children.

Although school officials may not be showing innovation in programming for individual handicapped children, they are seeing to it that the IEP paperwork gets done. Conferences are held once a year; the child's educational progress is reviewed in front of parents, if they attend, and specific learning goals for the coming year are set down in writing. Much of this planning and writing falls on the special education teachers. This work is sandwiched into the already full school day. Price and Goodman (1980) conducted a time expenditure study of 75 teachers preparing IEP documents for a sample of 807 exceptional children. The amount of time varied significantly by type of handicapping condition, with the average time being six and one-half hours, which is approximately equivalent to one school day per child. Time spent preparing for the IEP conference, testing the child and assembling data, attending the conference and writing up the document were among those activities. In spite of the fact that several of these activities had to be accomplished during the school day (e.g., testing the child, attending the conference), the teachers reported that 32% of the work connected with the IEP was done on their personal time (hours of the day during which the teacher is not required to be in the school building) (Price and Goodman, 1980:448,450). The authors ask: "Can we depend on the unpaid contribution of teachers to accomplish a task required by law?" In addition, 8% of the time spent on IEPs came from the teacher's released time during the school day. If this extra work time is diminished for teachers in coming years, the time will have to be found elsewhere—either by taking more from personal time or by cutting into instructional time (Price and Goodman, 1980:452-53). With this situation, it is no wonder that teachers have negative feelings about the IEP requirement. Yet this provision is at the heart of the law's intent that handicapped children be taken seriously as individuals and educational plans be made accordingly.

D. Parental Participation and Due Process

Congress wrote into P.L. 94-142 an important set of rights for the parents of handicapped children. These rights are grounded in the basic principle that those affected by the policies and practices of a public agency have a right to participate in the shaping of those policies. In the case of disagreement with finalized policies, the affected citizens should have the right granted in the Constitution to due process procedures of appeal. These rights have not always been in public favor with respect to the education of handicapped children. The educational professionals have had particular power in this arena. Regarding due process, P.L. 94-142 grants to handicapped children this right which all others in the educational system—from teachers to nonhandicapped children—have long since had safeguarded in state statutes (Turnbull and Turnbull, 1979:180-81).

The Act specifically requires local schools to inform parents of their rights to examine their children's school records, to request a professional evaluation and to be present at all conferences at which placement decisions or reviews will be made. In fact, no preplacement evaluation or initial placement decision can be made without informed parental consent. The Act goes further than establishing parental rights to information and consent by attempting to secure a place for parents as partners in the decision-making team. For example, a recent "policy paper on the IEP," reviewing the Office of Special Education's (1980:23) interpretation of the IEP requirement, states: "the legislative history of the Act makes it clear that the parents of a handicapped child are to be involved throughout the entire process of developing, reviewing, and revising the child's IEP."

Implementing this intent of the law is a difficult task. In spite of the fact that local schools inform parents in writing, and in their own language, about approaching conferences and their purposes, nationally only about 50% of IEP meetings are attended by parents (U.S. Department of Education, 1981:12). In addition, several studies of conferences with parents in attendance indicate that parents often play a passive role (Goldstein et al., 1980:283-84; U.S. Department of Education, 1981:12). The parents are, for the most part, the receivers of information about their children's progress, learning difficulties and test scores. Some of the information comes to them in a form they cannot readily comprehend. In a survey of parental reactions to IEP conferences, the researchers found "a recurring criticism... that the types of communication, whether they were verbal or written, were loaded with technical jargon" (Lewis et al., 1981:23). In another study, Gilliam and Coleman (1981) asked 130 participants in 27 IEP conferences to rank-order the participants according to the "influence" and "contributions" made to the conference outcomes. The high rankings received by the specialists and the low rankings given to parents and school principals is explained in the following way:

> [A] possible explanation is that the most influential roles (special education teacher, psychologist, director [of special education]) are those members who offer hard data in terms of test scores, diagnostic reports, and cumulative records, and who are therefore able to contribute information based upon these data. Since parents are frequently left out of the assessment process, they have little hard data to contribute (Gilliam and Coleman. 1981:643).

Parents usually hear these "hard data" for the first time in the conferences and are therefore ill-prepared to respond to the facts and interpretations presented. Sometimes these new tests scores will reveal additional learning problems with which the professionals are familiar but which constitute new and disturbing news to the parents. It is clear that the technical tools for assessment of academic progress give power to the educators and weaken the ability of parents to influence conference decisions.

There are also data showing that school personnel do not feel that parents are well informed enough to make evaluations of their children's educational needs or of the "appropriateness" of a particular learning setting (Yoshida et al., 1978). In some cases, the IEP document has already been prepared and the purpose of the conference is simply to inform the parents and to obtain their approval (Goldstein et al., 1980:281-4). This practice is in clear violation of the Act's definition of an IEP as "a written statement *developed in any meeting* with the agency representative, the teacher, the parent, and the child, whenever appropriate" (Office of Special Education, 1980:23; emphasis in original).

The problem of ensuring a place for parents as equal, active partners in decision-making about the education of their handicapped children is a difficult one. Many parents of these children are coping with monumental tasks of family survival, are extremely grateful to the school system for giving special help to their children and are glad to leave all school-related decisions to the educators. Among parents who do attend the IEP conferences as primarily "passive" participants, researchers report as unanticipated findings the "overwhelmingly positive reaction to the conferences'' on the part of parents (Goldstein et al., 1980:284; Lewis et al., 1981).

But to those parents who do want to assert their place at the conference table, who want to be certain their views influence decisions or who want to appeal final decisions, P.L. 94-142 gives a clear and strong mandate. This may be another major source of school professionals' concerns about the Act. Since "practically everything a school might do concerning a handicapped child's education can be 'tested' or challenged in a due process hearing" (Turnbull and Turnbull, 1978:180), activist, fully-informed parents could see to it that the local school fulfills all the provisions of the Act. Thus, because the Act gives parents the rights to full information about the education of their children and a share in the decision making, as well as due process, parents can then safeguard all the *other* rights granted by P.L. 94-142. They can insist that the local school provide their children with free, appropriate education, with individualized educational programming, in the least restrictive environment! Any law which gives such broad mandates to a minority is destined to have a rocky political future and will certainly face obstacles in achieving full implementation.

IV. THE RESEARCH QUESTIONS

The initial aim was limited to studying the impact of all the major provisions of the act on a sample of families in the district, beginning with 1978/79, the first school year in which full implementation of the law was required. Processes were to be investigated by gathering intensive, longitudinal data on the children, their families, and the educators involved with those children. We made a detailed list of questions as to relationships between the independent variable (P.L. 94-142), 15 intervening variables (see Fig. 1) and the dependent variables (the educational, personal, social-participational and economic effects of the Act on the cases). These specific questions were grouped in relation to the general sociological questions guiding the study.

As the case-study design was activated, we began to accumulate extensive data on the views and actions of regular and special teachers, administrators at all levels and other district professionals. The study was thus broadened to encompass the impact of P.L. 94-142 on the occupants of roles in the provision of special education as well as on the recipients. The child-family cases became part of a larger study of the entire *district as a case* in the application of the Act. The central questions of the study were therefore not limited to the child and family experiences.

Question 1. What impact has P.L. 94-142 had on the schools and families in a district that already had a relatively progressive system of special education? Although the district under study (and the State of Illinois as a whole) already had comparatively advanced provisions for special education, it seemed reason-

Figure 1.   Variables Affecting the Implementation of the Law

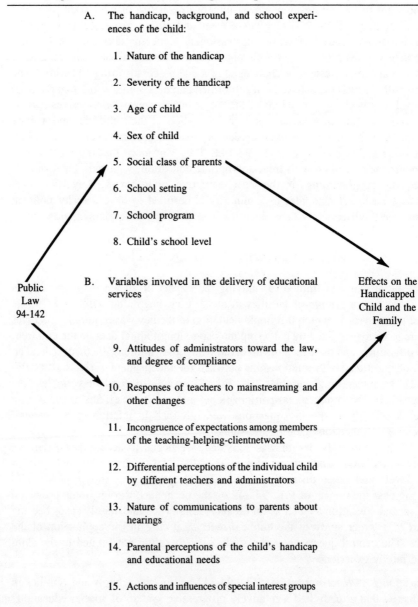

A. The handicap, background, and school experiences of the child:

    1. Nature of the handicap

    2. Severity of the handicap

    3. Age of child

    4. Sex of child

    5. Social class of parents

    6. School setting

    7. School program

    8. Child's school level

Public
Law
94-142

B. Variables involved in the delivery of educational services

Effects on the
Handicapped
Child and the
Family

    9. Attitudes of administrators toward the law, and degree of compliance

    10. Responses of teachers to mainstreaming and other changes

    11. Incongruence of expectations among members of the teaching-helping-clientnetwork

    12. Differential perceptions of the individual child by different teachers and administrators

    13. Nature of communications to parents about hearings

    14. Parental perceptions of the child's handicap and educational needs

    15. Actions and influences of special interest groups

able to expect a substantial impact. A heavy impact nationally was expected because of the strong intent of Congress to include all handicapped children and to ensure individualized handling of their education, backed by firm and detailed guidelines for implementation, promulgated by the U.S. Office of Education [then part of the Department of Health, Education and Welfare (HEW)]. The Act is also very comprehensive, requiring countless interpretations and application to the organizational structures of school districts. Action is required on matters not covered in many states, and provisions are often different from those of the states. Many interview questions and time comparisons were needed to help us separate the effects of P.L. 94-142 from those of state laws and regulations and preexisting district practices.

Question 2. How has application of the major provisions of P.L. 94-142 been influenced by interest groups within the district? Further, is the intent of Congress likely to be thwarted to the extent that the local alignment of interest groups differs from that which produced the federal statute? Many of the interest groups that influenced passage of P.L. 94-142 are found in the district, such as associations of both general and special educators and associations for the mentally retarded and other handicapped groups. It was assumed that parents of at least some handicapped school children might be influential locally, either in organizations or as individual families. It was also assumed that the relative power of different interest groups would be different from that at the national level, and that implementation of the law would depend heavily on the local power alignment. Local interest groups differ in their access to essential information, the extent to which their values and beliefs are supported in the community and the degree to which the provisions seem to affect their particular interests and needs.

Question 3. To what extent do the parents of handicapped children participate in procedures established by P.L. 94-142, either as partners in program planning or as adversaries when they feel it necessary to oppose professional educators? We assumed that at least some of the parents would be eager to take advantage of the expanded educational opportunities under the Act, to take time and energy to help ensure that the best possible education is provided to the child, and to exercise their right of appeal if necessary. Nationally, many parents had been heavily involved in the state and federal court cases and political actions leading to the passage of the Act. We assumed that parents in the district under study, which is a relatively affluent district and one with a reputation for leadership in special education, would be especially likely to participate in protecting the rights and advancing the interests of their children. However, we also expected parental participation to vary, especially by social class.

V. THE DATA BASE

This report is based on 445 interview and observational reports, and also on district statistical summaries and selected data from the sampled students' school files. A brief description of the selection and observation of the sample of cases will help to account for the total data base of the study. The aim of intensive, longitudinal observation was pursued by limiting the sample of cases to twelve. Because parental agreement to talk with us was necessary before a child's identity could be revealed, selections required cooperation from the district Director of Special Education. The 575 children in special education at the time were stratified by type of handicap and elementary grade level, and selections of identifying numbers were made from a table of random numbers. A probability sample helped to avoid having the sample handpicked for us and offered some assurance of a range of situations and variables. Estimates of sampling error were precluded by the small number of cases, of course, so the case conclusions may not be representative of the district.

We wanted to include at least one case from each of the district's six categories, omitting only the very few "profoundly retarded" cases (5 out of 575). Thus only four speech cases were sampled rather than the seven of twelve that would have been proportional to the 62% speech cases in the district. The relative frequencies were then used to determine the number sought in each remaining category.[1] In instances of dual classification, the major handicap was used for sampling. The result, shown in the 1978/79 column in Table 1, was one each in the categories of Trainable Mentally Handicapped (TMH), Behavior Disorder (BD), and Physically Handicapped (PH), two from Educable Mentally Handicapped (EMH), and three from Learning Disabilities (LD).

Eight were sampled from the primary grades (including kindergarten), and four from the intermediate (fourth through sixth grades), about the district proportions. By 1981/82, two (Mary and Lyle; see Table 1 for pseudonyms) remained at the primary level; seven were intermediate; and three (Kenneth, Kirk and Elena) had entered high school.

Five girls and seven boys were sampled. Neither the sex ratio of the 575 in special education nor the social class distribution of their families were known. Using occupation and education, we rated two of the selected families as "upper middle class," five as "lower middle class," three as "working class" and two as "lower class." Two of the families live in public housing. The occupation ranged from unemployed to officer worker, fireman, hairdresser, road construction worker, recruiting sergeant, factory foreman, excavating contractor, teacher, professor and printing entrepreneur. One family is Puerto Rican; one is black.

Nearly 400 of the reports on interviews and observations are contained in the 12 case files, although much of this content is concerned with views and actions of teachers, administrators or other professionals, not just with responses of the

Table 1. Changes in Classification and Program of
12 Illinois Cases: 1978-1982[a]

Pseudonym of child	1978-79	1979/80	1980/81	1981/82
Mary	EMH(2)	None(5)	None(5)	EMH(2)
	Same	Less	Same	More
Kenneth	EMH(3)	EMH(3)	EMH(3)	EMH(3)
	Same	Same	Same	Same
Robin	*TMH-Sp(1)	TMH-Sp(1)	TMH-Sp(1)	TMH-Sp(1)
	Same	Same	Same	Same
Vern	*LD-Sp(4)	LD-Sp(3)	LD-Sp(3)	LD-Sp(4)
	Same	More	Same	Less
Ian	LD(4)	LD(4)	LD(4)	LD(4)
	More	Same	Same	Same
Kirk	*LD-BD(4)	LD-BD(3)	LD-BD(4)	None(5)
	Same	More	Less	Less
Vicki	*BD-Sp(1)	BD-Sp(1)	BD-Sp(1)	EMH(2)
	Same	Same	Same	Less
Craig	Sp(4)	Sp(4)	Sp(4)	None(5)
	Same	Same	Same	Less
Norman	Sp(4)	Sp(4)	Sp(4)	Sp(4)
	More	Same	Same	Same
Tracy	Sp(4)	LD-Sp(4)	LD-Sp(4)	LD-Sp(4)
	More	More	Same	More
Lyle	Sp(4)	Sp(4)	Sp(4)	Sp(4)
	More	Same	Same	Same
Elena	**PH(3)	PH(3)	PH(3)	PH(3)
	Same	Same	Same	Same

[a] Key:

EMH	=	Educable Mentally Handicapped	(1) Special School
TMH	=	Trainable Mentally Handicapped	(2) Separate class entirely
LD	=	Learning Disability	(3) Separate class predominantly
BD	=	Behavior Disorder	(4) Regular class predominantly
SP	=	Speech	(5) Regular class entirely
PH	=	Physical Handicap	

*Secondary classification is indicated after the hyphen.
**Hearing impaired

More	=	more restrictive than in prior year
Some	=	no change from prior year
Less	=	less restrictive than in previous year

child and family. The 45 or more reports that are not tied to particular cases, together with a great many of the case reports, have illuminated the impact of P.L. 94-142 on the district as a whole. Almost 300 of the 445 reports were made during the first two years of the study, when we had full federal funding from the (then) Bureau of Education for the Handicapped. With university help the field work continued for a third year on a reduced basis, and it had to be curtailed still further during the fourth year. The data base can be understood more fully in relation to our field research procedures, described next.

VI. FIELD METHODS

From the outset our pursuit of the case data often provided opportunities to observe, or to converse about, various aspects of the provision of special educational services in the school or the district as a whole. Such information was fully recorded, and special interviews with administrators, teachers, therapists, social workers or others were often requested in order to follow up on promising leads. We could hardly have devised a better way of gaining access to the complex organizational structure of the district. We moved among different levels of administration, from school to school, among regular and special teachers and other professionals, into individualized program planning (IEP) conferences, and into homes. A brief description will indicate how the field procedures used to gather the child-family case data facilitated the study of the district as a case in formal social organization.

Observations of the 12 children were conducted at school, mainly by graduate assistants. The child was observed at different times of the day and in varied activities, including lunch and free play. Observers were instructed to pay particular attention to problems and progress in learning, patterns of interaction with teachers and peers, self-esteem and style of managing the problems of the handicap. The handling and responses of children other than the ones being observed were also recorded as far as possible. Spontaneous interviews with teachers were included in the observational reports. The principal investigators conducted interviews with key teachers and administrators as needed, usually about learning progress, planning conferences and program placements.

Each of the two principal investigators was responsible for regular interviews in six of the homes. Conversations were centered on key questions about the family's experiences with special education, mainly about recent events at school, and usually lasted about an hour. Questions were asked, but interviewees were urged to define their experiences in their own words and to emphasize what was important to them. Note taking was minimized, and tape recorders were not used during the interviews. Observations of pertinent behavior were included in the interview reports. Data gathered from families, as well as from school personnel and official records, were all obtained with parental permission and kept confidential. Pseudonyms have been used in all reports, and the district has been identified only as one in Illinois.

Data from the child's school and central district files were used to provide checks on interview and observational data. We had access to test scores, Individualized Educational Programs (IEPs), psychological evaluations, professional recommendations for program placements, program changes and recorded progress. Interviews with administrators and teachers, especially special educators, were used to help interpret the file data.

Both for the child-family cases and the broader study, we made use of triangulation. Frequent comparisons of different sources of data were made to provide checks on validity, and also to facilitate pursuit of data needed to resolve ambiguities or contradictions, to fill gaps, to clarify continuities or sudden changes, or to show causal connections. Such triangulation during the data-gathering phase enhances the power of field research to reveal unexpected events and connections, subjective meaning of actions, and complex relationships (Denzin, 1978:Ch. 10). Triangulation was also valuable during the analysis state, after the data in the field reports were coded, transcribed onto data worksheets and tabulated.

VII. FINDINGS

In answer to the *first general question* of the study, much evidence has been found to support the conclusion that P.L. 94-142 has had a substantial impact on an already progressive district. The changes in the fall of 1978 were less dramatic than they might have been because the district had begun two years earlier to reorganize and plan for full implementation. Significant additions of special education services and necessary changes in coordination were made in the fall of 1976, and some of the children in the case sample were already in programs that were started or modified at that time. The provision of special facilities for TMH children, and for the profoundly and multiply handicapped, indicate that the Zero Reject provision was being heeded by 1978. Provisions were in place for due process appeal hearings in the district, and many hearings have been held, none of them involving our 12 cases.

One change has been to bring the long-established program in speech therapy under the supervision of the district Director of Special Education, a major shift because in 1978/79 three-fifths of all children on the Director's list were speech cases. Therapists have continued to test and make their own decisions about the need for help, so that speech cases have been excluded from the formal Individualized Educational Program (IEP) conference process. However, therapists have to fill out the IEP forms and by district policy are being asked to screen all new children in the school, so that the testing and paperwork often delay therapy until the fourth week or so of the school term. One usually calm speech therapist told us in 1981 that P.L. 94-142 is "the most stupid law ever passed."

The Act evidently has increased the workload of teachers and administrators considerably. The scheduling and conducting of IEP conferences occupies a large amount of staff time during each spring term, and some special conferences have to be held in the fall. Usually from six to ten professionals are present at a half-hour conference, the aim of which is to determine the child's program placement for the following year. Several times IEP conferences for children in our sample ran well over the half-hour allotment, and since all conferences were scheduled back-to-back, professionals and parents felt the time squeeze. If speech cases were included in the IEP process, the already heavy impact on the workload of the staff would be more than doubled. In addition, the Act has brought a major increase in requests for professional evaluation (testing and diagnosis) of learning problems. Parents or professionals can make such requests, and no initial placement in special education or a major change in program can be made without a full evaluation. The Director for the state-run Special Education Cooperative that serviced the district with all its special education diagnostic work and evaluations during the first year of our study noted the following: "The main problem in handling all the cases is the shortage of school psychologists. Since [P.L.] 94-142, referrals have more than doubled. The universities cannot generate enough school psychologists to do the needed work."

Administrators and teachers in the district seem well aware of the mandates of the Act, although many oversimplify its intent by calling it the "mainstreaming law." Some of the regular classroom teachers complained about being expected to handle learning problems for which they were not trained. Complaints as well as praise contributed evidence of the impact of the Act on the district. Special education teachers, except for speech therapists, generally were the strongest and most dedicated supporters of the Act.

In *Ian's case*, the district Director of Special Education and both principals involved were favorable to the law's provision for Learning Disability (LD) service for a parochial school, although the mother reported an uphill struggle to get the LD testing accomplished at the end of Ian's first-grade year, 1977/78. Puzzled by his "slow learning," his working-class parents have helped him with reading and arithmetic, hired summer tutors, and the mother has been a strong advocate of his rights. Since 1978 Ian has spent a small part of each day in the LD resource room in the public school across the street from his parochial school (refer back to Table 1). He has been teased by his regular classmates for being a "dummy," but his family is much more aware of stigma in relation to Ian's younger brother, who has cerebral palsy.

Tracy's case provides evidence of a lack of sympathy for P.L. 94-142 by at least some general educators. Tracy was in speech therapy during 1978/79 when she was falling behind in the first grade, and her mother made repeated requests for testing for LD problems. Tracy's three older siblings all had been diagnosed as having learning disabilities in their elementary school years. Both the principal and the regular classroom teacher resisted, preferring the traditional procedure of retaining Tracy in the first grade for another year without special help to promotion and part-time help in an LD resource room. The principal supported the teacher's argument that special evaluations should be minimized in the first grade, thus protecting small children from stigma and restrictive placements. The LD teacher preferred a preventive view that children should be referred for testing at the earliest sign of special learning problems. Strong action by the mother resulted in testing, the discovery of LD problems, and adoption of the LD teacher's recommendation of promotion and LD resource room help. The amount of LD resource room help was increased in 1979/80, and again in 1981/ 82, and increased still more for 1982/83 by transferring Tracy to an LD instructional room in another school. Tracy's experience illustrates our conclusion from the cases that special education teachers prevail in program placements in conflicts with administrators and regular classroom teachers.

Issues have repeatedly arisen in the district over efforts to implement the provisions of P.L. 94-142, as amply illustrated in our cases. *Vern's case* illustrates the potential for successful application of the principles of IEP and LRE. His achievement had been well below grade level, and his IEP for 1978/79 called for him to repeat first grade, have speech therapy and get LD resource room help. The cross-pressures concerning Vern during that year are evident in the words of three key participants. The teacher with whom he was repeating first grade blamed his difficulties mainly on the culture of poverty, saying:

> He does have some perceptual problems, and some problems of coordination too. He has reversals and other perceptual difficulties, so he needs his glasses. . . . Well, I think he could overcome these problems if he had a different home background. They just do things when they feel like it, apparently. So Vern hasn't learned to take responsibility for anything, and that is why he doesn't have his glasses on so much of the time. . . .

Vern's mother strongly resented this regular classroom teacher and felt that the brief sessions in the LD room were not helping enough. In the approximate words of the LD teacher:

> Mrs. C. recently came to school and tried to persuade us that Vern should be put into an EMH program next fall, rather than in the self-contained LD room I have recommended. The EMH room has a small number of pupils per teacher, and intensive individual instruction, I explained to Mrs. C. that Vern's IQ is within the normal range, and that what he needs is help with his perceptual problems and, to the extent possible, with coordination. The EMH program would put a heavy stigma on Vern, more than the LD program does.

Vern had an older brother in an EMH room, and the individual attention there prompted his mother to suggest the same for him. Instead, Vern went into the LD instructional room for two years, where he received much individual attention and support. His academic achievement, class participation, interaction with peers, and self-confidence all greatly improved. Even three operations on his nearly-blind "lazy eye" did not slow his improvement. In 1981/82 he was mainstreamed into a regular fourth-grade classroom, getting only speech therapy thereafter. Vern's father attibuted much of the improvement to the boy's regular attendance at after-school tutoring sessions in reading at the housing project.

Kirk had part-time help in combined LD-BD resources rooms throughout his elementary schooling, and the dual placement helped to avoid clear explanations of his learning problems. Behavior problems were noted repeatedly, interpreted by the father as evidence that Kirk had inherited his "bad temper." This father believes that parents know their child better than any teacher ever can. The teachers have often rejected the parental suggestion that Kirk has a speech defect. In 1978/79 Kirk had an especially patient sixth-grade teacher. During that same year Kirk's LD-BD resource room teacher described a conversation that became a turning point:

> Several weeks ago he asked me. 'Why am I in this room? It is because I am a dummy?' I told him no, that his IQ is within the normal range, and that there is no reason why he can't do average work and keep himself under control. He seemed amazed and pleased by this, and I think this has had a lot to do with the fact that his reading and other work have shown so much improvement recently. . . . I have spent more time counseling Kirk than helping him with reading or other subjects. I finally concluded that he has no LD problems, or only minor ones, and that his main problems are emotional. He gets frustrated when he can't do his school work right, and he is distractable. When things don't go right, he just can't keep his mind on his work, and he just falls apart if he has to take a test or complete some assignment then. I think it is his self-concept that has been the problem.

This special teacher recommended a self-contained LD-BD room for Kirk upon his entry into junior high school, but that he be gradually mainstreamed, as ready. At the end of his seventh-grade year, the teacher of his room said Kirk had needed the special help, but that he was ready for the approach built into the system in the eighth grade and in high school. She explained:

> The gradual move toward mainstreaming is right for Kirk from here on. He should be moved out of the LD designated classes next year, especially in math, whenever he is ready for it. He needs support, but I think by the time he gets to high school the 'success program' will be about all the support he needs. That program gives them counseling and some support. You see, they have different ability levels in our high school, so they can place the student at the right level for each subject.

Kirk was ready just in time for the system-mandated shift in the LRE direction. The IEP process apparently was used with dedication and skill for Kirk as well as for Vern, both of whom were moved in the more restrictive direction for a time before being mainstreamed.

Certainly there has been no wholesale movement in the mainstreaming direction in our cases, as further illustrated in the *case of Elena*. Since age three she had been in programs either for the hearing impaired or the deaf. The teacher who had had Elena for three years in a self-contained room for the hearing impaired resisted Elena's strong desire to be mainstreamed in junior high saying:

Elena is very bright and has excellent work habits, but she has a serious hearing impairment. She would not have kept up if she had not had so much special help, especially since her hearing aid hasn't worked right much of this year. A lot of my work with her has been on a one-to-one basis. I though seriously about mainstreaming her, but I know she would not do very well with only itinerant special help. Right now she hates to leave all her friends at school here, and they will go to the regular junior high school. Her brother is in the experimental junior high's program for the hearing impaired and deaf, and he doesn't like it. Maybe Elena will like it after she gets there. She makes friends. She may also change her mind about going to college, and the special program is in a school with an academic orientation. She could be a good teacher, and I have suggested her teaching P.E. [She is a runner, on the track team.] I would like to see her mainstreamed, but I think it would be wrong for her.

Elena's teacher's dilemma involved conflicting values: a choice betwen academic achievement and the avoidance of the stigma of a physical handicap. Elena wanted to avoid sign language and other stigmata of a program that includes deaf children. However, she made the best of the special placement, is now (1981/82) in the special program in the experimental high school, and indeed talks about going to college and becoming a P.E. teacher.

Mary's case is the only one during our study in which mainstreaming was later reversed. (See Table 1 for the changes in 1979 and 1981). While in kindergarten in 1977/78 she was tested, diagnosed as "high EMH," and placed in a self-contained room devoted to preparing both EMH and LD children for first grade. In 1979 her mother demanded Mary's removal from this room, saying she was "not dumb and never needed any special education in the first place." Tests showed that Mary had made some progress in the special setting, and the professionals at the IEP conference knew of the (absent) parents' demand for mainstreaming. After the resulting placement in a regular first grade, the mother refused permission even for Mary to have speech therapy, saying it was "just her two missing front teeth." Some surgery to counter the effects of repeated infections then greatly improved Mary's hearing, and the parents believed the source of Mary's learning problems had been removed. Unfortunately, Mary still could not do regular first-grade work, and she began worrying that other children were talking about her. According to her teacher:

> She is a frustrated little girl, and she worries about not being able to do the work. She is also an angry little girl. She hits other children. Things are not good at home....Her self-concept has definitely gone down during the year. It's a problem for her because this class has a wide range of abilities....Mary is at the bottom....But she is good at handwriting and art....She participates well in class, but in the last weeks Mary [has] simply [sat] back at her desk and not come up to the rug to share in the discussion....Lately she has fewer and fewer days when she tries.

Mary's mother had faced up to the lack of progress at least by early March of 1980, saying desperately:

> I don't feel like she is learning anything at all. I work with her night after night, but she doesn't even know words like *the, is, it,* and *are*....She will just not be ready for second grade. She must need some more special help. I didn't think special education helped her much, but I may have been wrong, because this year she is making no progress. She really

needs some skills she simply doesn't have....I don't think it's the teacher's fault. I don't know who to blame, and I don't know what to do.

The family then moved to California, where the mother refused to agree to have Mary retained in the first grade another year, because she would then be "too old when she graduates from high school." Mary's difficulties in the California school resulted in retesting and the decision to put her into a self-contained EMH room, this time with full parental support. Mary now seems to have the least restrictive environment (LRE) in which she can learn effectively, a situation denied her during two critical early years in her education. The district in Illinois may have been in violation of the law when it failed to provide any special support to Mary or to her first-grade teacher as part of the transition from the instructional room in 1978/79 to the regular classroom across town in 1979/80. No IEP was written in spring 1979 to set instructional goals for the coming year because, according to the instructional room teacher, Mary was being main-streamed out of special education, and IEPs are written only for children's receiving special services. In Mary's case, full mainstreaming was clearly pre-mature—and may never be appropriate.

The Director believes wholesale mainstreaming has been avoided in the district as a whole, as it has been in our case. He substantiated that a major impact of the first years of implementing the Act in the district was a significant increase in referrals. Indeed the proportion of children receiving special educational serv-ices climbed to 20% of the total school population during the first three years of P.L. 94-142. This is in contrast to the approximately 12% for the previous three years. The 94-142 funds for special education are generated for each child receiving such services, and the district received full 94-142 funds for all children, even though the Act stipulates a maximum of 12% for the state as a whole. The district responded to the financial incentive as well as to the legal requirement to locate all children in need of special services.

Looking at the district as a whole, movement was, then, in the opposite direction from mainstreaming during those first years of 94-142. More children were in special environments than previously. Interestingly, as the funding levels for 94-142 did not increase each year as originally planned—and indeed talk of federal support for education became ominous as the budget cuts became the watchword of President Reagan's administration—personnel in the local school administration began to question their financial ability to continue supporting their unusually high proportions of special education students. The present district director noted that, "Now, before anyone gets referred [to special education], we have to meet with the teacher and principal and review the whole situation and be sure that all other alternatives have been exhausted!" In 1981/82 the proportion of special education students was down slightly, to 16%.

Although the explanations maybe unrelated, the movement of our cases mirrors the early trend toward more special placements (see Table 1, showing a total of seven moves in the more restrictive direction, and one move in the less restrictive direction during 1978/79 and 1979/80) and the trend away from special placements this past year (see Table 1, showing no movement in 1980/81 in any direction except for Kirk in the less restrictive direction, but 1981/82 saw four placements in the less restrictive direction and only one, Mary, in the more restrictive direction). The trends fit the prediction made by Sarason and Doris (1978:17):

> If the trend for increased numbers of special classes were to continue, both the state and federal budgets would have to expand considerably. In a sense, the process came full circle: Local school districts would not increase the numbers of special classes unless a good part of the costs came from the state or federal government, and now these governments are concerned that they may not be able to stand the increasing costs. Not surprisingly, economics has been and continues to be a potential factor.

Clearly, in summary for the first general question, P.L. 94-142 has had a major impact on special education in an already progressive school district. The series have been reorganized, new ones provided, and efforts to implement the provisions of the Act have resulted in larger numbers of children served (until the onset of federal budget cutting) and increased workloads, professional issues, problems of communication, and some apparent successes and failures with individual children. The IEP conference process has apparently been guided carefully by the special educators. On the other hand, recent budget restrictions have resulted in an informal but effective policy of accepting fewer referrals and limiting program options.

Affirmative evidence has also been found for our *second general question*, as to whether or not the interest groups in the district have influenced the application of P.L. 94-142. However, the local alignment of interest groups is different from that which affected the passage of the Act. Especially missing, for the most part, is direct influence by local voluntary associations of educators and of the handicapped. One exception is an association of parents of children with LD problems, a group that at least provides LD information and mutual support.

The strong legislative role played by groups such as the National Association for Retarded Citizens and by state and national associations of both general and special educators is not apparent at the level of district application. At the least, however, we may assume that educational associations have been important in communicating to individual educators about the requirements and implementation of the Act. The major official interest groups—the federal BEH and its successors, and state educational agencies—are visibly represented by the school district administration, especially by the Office of the Director of Special Education. The district administrators seem to have been trying to balance the Act's strong civil rights requirements for individualized educational services against the educational budget cuts.

Four groups guarding their perceived professional interests as the law is administered are special educators, therapists, regular classroom teachers and administrators. Differences among these groups over applications of the law are prominent in the cases cited above. These interest blocs appear within each school and in the district at large. Some of the special educators and therapists work in more than one school.

Speech therapists have retained a strong sense of identity and special interests, and resent the paperwork and being supervised by the district Director. Further, speech cases generate more than half of the federal funds coming into the district for added services, yet none of this money has been used to hire extra therapists to help with the added task each year of screening all new children for speech problems. The Director's answer has been that extra therapists for temporary work are not available. In addition, apparently none of the federal money has been used for participation by therapists in the IEP conference process, when placements in adddition to speech are being considered. One of the reasons for including speech in the Act was to encourage the use of speech therapy as a means of helping to find other learning problems, as it did in Tracy's case, discussed earlier. It is small wonder that speech therapists in the district remain a strong interest group and that they consider themselves victims under P.L. 94-142.

Only a few of the families in our case study have been very active in protecting their interests, and usually as individual families rather than as members of organizations. In the only case in which a parental association has been mentioned (Tracy's, noted above), the influence has been great. Tracy's mother was invited to a meeting of parents of LD children several years ago when one of her older children was having LD difficulties. She was invited by the school principal, who later became Superintendent of the District. Tracy's mother told us:

> It was really an eye-opener. A Mrs. B. was Chairperson of the group, and neighbor of Dr. T, who spoke to the parents. He had a long tale of the frustration they had in getting their own son's problems diagnosed. It was a very moving statement. He has us all in tears about all that they went through with their boy.

Tracy's mother kept in touch with the (now) Superintendent, occasionally calling him about learning problems. Her threat to call him was probably the decisive factor in her success in getting Tracy tested for LD problems in the face of opposition from the principal and classroom teacher. Although this contact was unusually fortunate, the experience suggests that parent groups and other voluntary organizations for the handicapped have considerable potential for influencing school and district policies. So far, however, this influence has been more latent than manifest in the district studied.

The system of special education in the district at any given time represents the tentative outcome of the give-and-take among the interest groups. This "negotiated order" (Day and Day, 1977; Strauss, 1978) varies with family class position, the training and experience of teachers and administrators, budgetary contingencies and other situational factors. The negotiated order is especially subject to change when there is even a temporary shift in the balance of power among the interest groups. The alleged lack of sufficient specialized personnel, such as school psychologists enhances the power of the professionals; it blunts parental initiatives for reclassification and for changes in the child's program. The families studied have generally not exercised much power to protect their perceived interests. Some have, however, as explained below.

The *third general question* of the study is: To what extent do the parents of handicapped children participate in procedures established by P.L. 94-142, either as partners in program planning or as adversaries of professional educators? Our finding is that, in any given year, 8 of the 12 families have not participated much as partners in decision making, nor have they adopted an adversarial role against the professionals. Those who have been most assertive, advocating the child's interests in confrontation with teachers and administrators, have so far filed no appeals for due process hearings. Some other parents in the district have filed appeals, and the Director believes the potential threat of parental appeals and lawsuits influences district policies.

The families of Ian, Tracy and Robin, classified throughout our study as three of the most assertive ones, have been concerned mainly with IEP planning and decision making. Ian's mother, referring both to Ian (see above) and his more severely handicapped younger brother, explained her involvement to us this way: "I am going to see that they get all the help they can get. . . . Maybe I am a little over-protective, but you must understand they're all I've got, and all I'll ever have." Tracy's mother (above) after overcoming strong professional opposition to LD testing in 1979, commented that, "Sometimes you've really got to be stubborn, just got to insist."

In *Robin's case*, her strong advocate has been her foster mother, a teacher's wife who has also been caring for some other rather severely handicapped children. Robin was nearly 12 years old when we met her in 1978/79, but she was working at the second-grade level, in a special school for Trainable Mentally Handicapped (TMH) children. Part of her prior schooling had been in a program for the Educable Mentally Handicapped (EMH), and she has been a "star" in the TMH school. Her test scores fall on the margin between EMH and TMH. She is primarily mentally retarded, with a damaged ear drum and other physical complications, and she has needed much speech therapy.

Five years earlier Robin had received an EMH placement and had not been able to cope with it, partly at least because of family upheaval and some major surgery. At the May 1979 IEP conference, her foster mother asked for an evaluation and discussion of an EMH placement, but testing was delayed until fall and the staff discouraged a program shift. They thought Robin's looks, her speech and her bossy habits would make her extremely conspicuous in an EMH room, where she would be at the bottom rather than the top. The foster mother did not appeal this decision, but wished she knew fully what her rights were, saying:

> They all said to me, 'Why she's doings so beautifully in TMH!' Yes, but maybe she would do well in another program too. Doesn't she deserve the chance to try it? We thought the law mandated the least restrictive environment for each child, yet it doesn't seem to work that way.

In the fall this foster mother had to become assertive again, even calling the district Superintendent and demanding action, before retesting occurred and a special IEP conference was finally held in December 1979. Testing again showed Robin to be a borderline case, and the parental proposal was given full consideration. The decision was against the change to EMH, and the foster mother berated herself for not pushing years earlier toward the more challenging environment she felt Robin needed but which the girl could not now handle. Now Robin will stay in the TMH program until she is 18, in a class where the teacher often does not call on her because she knows all the answers. For her best subjects she has recently been moved into a room with other more advanced students and is being challenged again. The decision was against taking the risks of transfer to a program that might not be restrictive enough, risks that proved disastrous in the case of Mary's move from EMH to a regular classroom. To an assertive parent, the professional caution needed to determine the appropriate LRE in such cases is very frustrating and the classification of "retarded" is hard to accept as a permanent label.

The fourth assertive fammily 1978/79, although very anxious about the possible stigma of having *Craig's minor speech problems* associated with the district's programs for handicapped children, was concerned mainly about his progress in reading in the first grade. He should have speech therapy, they said, "as long as he needs it." The bright professor's child was not working very hard, and his mother was upset because he was not in the advanced reading group. This mother put much pressure on the child and his teacher. However, in 1979/80 she became much less involved, at the same time Mary's mother became more assertive after the move to California (see above), thus replacing Craig's family as one of the four assertive ones.

The second pattern of parental response is the expressive style, observed (in any given year) in four of the families in our case sample. This style involves little participation but strong criticism of the educators' handling of the child, much of it expressed privately rather than to teachers or administrators. It involves much avoidance of the special education network, selective noncompliance and occasional expressive confrontations. Parents in this pattern rarely go to IEP conferences, often mislaying the notices and claiming they were not received. The behavior is very defensive, and school personnel tend to be blamed for the child's learning difficulties. This was the style of Mary's mother until she learned more about P.L. 94-142, moved to California, and began to demand testing and otherwise to assert her parental rights. In the same year Craig's mother (just discussed) shifted from an assertive to a more expressive stance.

The three families in the expressive mode throughout our study have been those of Vern, Kirk and Elena (all considered earlier). Sometimes we have heard such declarations as "Tomorrow I am going to that school and tell them that, etc."—a stated intention rarely carried out. When there is some assertiveness within this framework, it tends to take the form of noncooperation, such as refusing to sign permission forms for testing or program placements. Elena's Puerto Rican father occasionally talks with teachers; but, instead of discussing the family's anxieties about the girl's special learning problems, he expresses strong concerns about the secular influences on Elena at school. The main school contact Kirk's father has had for many years was a telephone call in which he "told off" the principal for sending a note to the parents to get the boy's behavioral problems straightened out. Such parental hit-and-run tactics suggest feelings of powerlessness about the child's education.

The third style of family response in our cases is passive compliance—involving very little participation and little or no criticism. Four of the families—those of Vicki, Kenneth, Lyle and Norman—have fit this passive mode throughout our study (refer back to Table 1). This style seems to be based either on the belief that there is little the family needs to do or that it is powerless and therefore cannot do anything.

Vicki was classed as a case of Behavior Disorder (BD) during the first three years of our study and also received speech therapy. She came to professional attention at age four when her older brother was diagnosed as TMH. Until 1981 she was in a private school (at district expense) for children from ages three to eleven with behavior problems, a school in which her (divorced) mother had received part of her education. In four and one-half years (from 1977 to 1981) in this school, with much individual attention and a system of rewards, her tantrums and other behavioral symptoms became much less severe. Her learning, at age ten, had progressed only to the latter half of the second grade.

Vicki's move to a foster home in 1980 caused the postponement of action to transfer her to a public school setting. The foster home was very supportive, and Vicki seemed relieved to be away from her critical, demanding mother. Action was finally taken in 1981 to remove her from the special school, and she was tested and moved to a self-contained EMH room in a public school near the foster home. Vicki's mother has resisted giving up permanent custody of the girl, but she has played a very passive role in the IEP decisions, even in this major change from the BD to the EMH classification. When this mother gets to a conference, she is quiet and compliant. Ill informed, struggling to earn a meager living and to take care of the one child left at home, and feeling powerless, she is awed by the professionals around the conference table and accepts their proposals.

The *case of Kenneth* also appears to reflect feelings of parental powerlessness. This large, black family lives in a too-small public housing unit. Kenneth's intelligence test scores have been on the margin between low normal and retarded. When tested at age five, he was diagnosed as having "a moderate degree of emotional disturbance, causing pseudo-retardation," and placed in a kindergarten for emotionally disturbed children. When he was seven, Kenneth's tests showed low normal potential, and he went into a regular first grade. At age nine he was having serious learning problems, was tested again and found "mildly retarded." At this point the mother requested that he be moved into an EMH program, a placement that she thought had been helpful to Kenneth's older brother. Kenneth participated eagerly and was near the top of his EMH classes in elementary school, although his sixth grade teacher thought his clowning stance covered up feelings of inadequacy. He liked sports and arithmetic, but his academic achievements have fallen several years below grade level for his age. In junior high he became a major disciplinary problem at school, even stealing and getting into fights.

When Kenneth was in elementary school, his parents rarely attended IEP conferences. They complied with professional decisions and seemed careful to avoid any criticism of the teachers and administrators. Moreover, in statements like the following, Kenneth's stepfather expressed gratitude when the boy was in sixth grade: "Kenneth has been a little slow at school, especially in reading, but these special teachers have helped him make progress. We are really grateful for all the special help he gets." However, when confronted with Kenneth's behavioral problems in junior high school, his stepfather became aware that the boy's achievements were well below the grade level for his age. He said:

> I thought Kenneth was getting help to *catch up* to the other kids his age, but he is in junior high and he can't read as well as our little second-grade girl can. He just doesn't know the words, or anything. I just don't think the teachers have been doing their job.

Apparently, although this was the second child they had had in the EMH track, these parents did not know its full meaning until recently. The mother's rare act of participation, her request for EMH, had been uninformed. The parents were unaware that Kenneth would be expected to arrive only at about the fourth-to sixth-grade level of achievement by the time he completed the high school EMH program. For a time this stepfather became critical, in the expressive style. Once he had absorbed the new information fully, however, the stepfather returned to his style of passive compliance, saying, "They are doing the best they can for Kenneth, and we will just have to hope for the best."

In the *cases of Lyle and Norman*, their middle-class parents have seemed informed and cooperative. Although both boys are in their fourth year of speech therapy, the families assume the help will not be needed much longer. These families have not avoided contacts with teachers, but have trusted the speech therapists and have believed there is little if anything for the parents to do. *Norman's* parents, recently divorced, have shown little concern over the boy's speech problems. The boy's older sister also has had mild speech difficulties. The parents believe chronic ear infections may have affected Norman's speech development. Norman is self-contained and often quiet, but responsive and fairly active, and both his teachers and his parents have thought of him as a very normal boy.

Lyle's speech difficulties are greater than Norman's, and he is a highly active, aggressive boy. However, Lyle is so bright and charming, and has done such outstanding school work, that his parents believe all they need to do about his speech is to be patient and trust the therapy. Their only serious concern seems to be a fear that someone might think Lyle's speech problems are symptoms of mental deficiency. For Lyle's parents, the feared label seems to be "learning disability," just as it is "handicapped" for Craig's and Norman's parents and "special education" for Tracy's mother—all of them fearing the same thing, the stigma of mental retardation. In the following statement, Tracy's mother explained her fear of "special education":

> That hurt me more than anything, when she [the first-grade teacher] said Tracy is 'trainable.' I know she did not mean to hurt me, but, oh, that shook me. It was like she had just given up on Tracy, and the principal wanted to go along, and put her into that narrow little niche—hold her back, and see her as of low intelligence, and they tried to make me see it this way. Yes, I felt so powerless and angry and abandoned, and hurt, and frustrated.

At the 1982 IEP conference this mother, who had demanded LD help and did not consider it a category of special education, feared that moving Tracy to a more self-contained LD room (on the other side of town) might lead to an EMH room and finally to the dreaded TMH placement.

We have attempted to determine what factors have accounted for the style of family response in our cases. Typically, only one parent has participated in the school contacts, regardless of how well the two parents agree on the learning problems of the child. In eight of our cases the main family representative has been the mother; in three, the father; and in only one case has it been about equal. All the most assertive parents have been mothers. Two of the three male representatives have exhibited the style of expressive criticism, and one that of passive compliance. The style of family involvement does not seem to be affected by the gender of the handicapped child.

We had assumed that parents of children with the most serious handicaps would be most strongly motivated to get involved in the educational processes. Initial inspection of Table 2 indicates a small association in the opposite direction from that expected. However, a disproportionate number of the serious cases were in working- and lower-class families, so it is necessary to control for social class. When this is done, the relationship between severity of handicap and family assertiveness is direct and moderately large. Thus, middle-class parents

Table 2.   Presence of Designated Categories for
Four Variables in Cases Representing Three Levels of
Parental Assertiveness for Four School Years, 1978-1982

Pseudonym of Child	Level of Parental Assertiveness[a]	"Severe" or "Moderate to Severe" Handicap	Middle class status[b]	Handicapped sibling(s)	One spouse at Home[c]
Robin	I	×	×	×	×
Ian	I			×	×
Craig[d]	I		×		×
Tracy	I	×	×	×	×
Mary[d]	II		×		
Vern	II	×		×	×
Kirk	II	×	×		
Elena	II	×		×	×
Kenneth	III	×		×	
Vicki	III	×		×	
Norman	III		×		
Lyle	III		×		×

[a] I = Active advocates of children's educational interests. II = Somewhat involved, somewhat critical and watchful, more inclined to avoidance than to firm and persistent participation. III = Compliance with the system, with little or no criticism.

[b] Either upper middle or lower class. No × in this column means working or lower class.

[c] One spouse spends the major part of his or her workday in the home.

[d] For Craig and Mary, there were the levels assigned in 1978/79; for 1979/80, 1980/81, and 1981/82, the level for Craig was II, and for Mary it was I.

seem very likely, and those with lower status very unlikely, to be assertive in advocating the interests of the more severely handicapped children.

This finding was consistent with our original hypothesis about social class, i.e., that higher status would be associated with assertiveness for the cases as a whole. Table 2 shows a rather marked relationship between social class and level of parental assertiveness. Despite having a disproportionate share of the more severe cases, working- and especially lower-class families were less likely to be active advocates of the interests of their handicapped children. If severity of handicap is controlled for, the positive association between class and assertiveness is increased for the more severe cases but the relationship is negative for the less severe ones. Thus, middle-class parents have been more likely to be active on behalf of children with more severe handicaps, but not for those with less serious problems.

As we have seen, the middle-class parents of Norman and Lyle have believed there is no reason for them to assert themselves concerning the therapy for speech problems they considered temporary and not very serious. Kirk's father, whom we have rated as middle class, has been an expressive critic rather than an advocate. This may be a result of his working-class background, a status not far removed from his current position of factory foreman. Tracy's mother, although also having moved upward in social status, has become a strong advocate in spite of the difficulty for her. In the following, she reveals some of her feelings: "Oh, it is terribly intimidating to go to these conferences. Those people with all that education, and then me, with my high school diploma! I really do feel at a disadvantage." Ian's mother has expressed similar feelings, and done battle in spite of them, as Mary's mother finally did after moving to California. Evidently Vicki's mother, and the parents of Kenneth, Vern and possibly Elena, have not been able to overcome such feelings of inadequacy and powerlessness and to participate as P.L. 94-142 provides for. The parents are badly outnumbered in the conferences by professionals who are well prepared and who have often agreed on the outcome ahead of time.

From Table 2 it appears that having at least one other handicapped child is as important as middle-class status in determining family involvement, and that having one spouse not employed outside the home is also important. Families with experience with another handicapped child are more likely to be informed and to feel secure enough to participate on the planning "team"—even to challenge its decisions if necessary. They are also more likely to have made significant adaptations to the handicapped status, including its stigma (Farber, 1976:462). Yet unless at least one parent can find the time to get to meetings and to make telephone calls at crucial times, full participation in the IEP process is very difficult to manage. In our cases, all the parental advocates were mothers not working outside in 1978/79, and this has been true of three of the four mothers during the next three years (with Mary's mother in the assertive group instead of Craig's).

Ian's mother is the most unusual parent in the cases, in that she has been the advocate and also the sole support for the family during periods when her husband has been disabled. A majority of her income-earning work is done in the home. She is also the only strongly assertive parent whom we have considered working class rather than middle class. Often she has said, "I just don't have the education I need to help my own children." Much of her knowledge about special education, as well as her motivation to be an advocate, seems to derive from having two handicapped children. Commenting about the stigma they have encountered with their more profoundly handicapped child, she said: "People just don't know what we go through."

Vern's mother remarked on how having more than one handicapped child helped the family to adapt to the stigma:

We had trouble with that when Timmy [the older boy] was first having difficulty. I just didn't want to accept the idea that he wasn't quite right. Then, after a while, I told myself he needed extra help and that nothing was more important than that. Just about anybody can

need some special help sometimes. Then when Vern came along we didn't hesitate about it.
We want him to have all the special help he can get.

However, having the two handicapped children was not sufficient to produce
advocacy in this case, and Vern's parents have been closer to the expressive
style. So what combination of variables is most likely to produce advocacy? In
only two of the cases, those of Robin and Tracy, were all four of the factors in
Table 2 present. Apparently all four variables are not essential to strong family
assertiveness; two seem sufficient in the case of Ian and also for Craig (in 1978/
79) and only one for Mary (from 1979 to 1982). It might be argued that there
were two variables in Mary's case, because her mother perceived the learning
problems as much more severe after Mary was moved into a regular classroom
in the fall of 1979.

Except for Ian's family, social class appears to be essential to assertiveness.
In the expressively critical category (the middle group of Table 2), the only one
of the four factors missing in the cases of Vern and Elena is middle-class status.
Kirk's family is shown as middle class, for economic reasons, but as foreman
of a work crew the father retains a working-class outlook. Probably the generally
passive parents of Kenneth and Vicki, whose handicaps are relatively severe,
would be more assertive if they had the knowledge and confidence of the middle
class.

The families studied seem to have to be vigorous and determined in order to
be taken seriously as part of the "planning team." Perhaps it is not an over-
statement to suggest that the district schools want to limit the role of parents in
IEP conferences to providing information and observing, as reported in a statewide study in Connecticut (Yoshida et al., 1977). When asked if it might be
possible to telephone parents to confirm the dates of IEP conferences, Ian's
(parochial) school principal gave this answer.

Do you know how much work that would be for the District? Please don't ask them to do
that. With so many families having two parents working, we often cannot reach the parents
when we need to when a child is sick, even when we have three different telephone numbers. . . . Sometimes, of course, it's a relief when they parents don't show up. Not in Ian's
case, of course, but sometimes parents get so defensive when the are faced with statements
about all the limitations the professionals see in *their* child.

It should not be surprising that teachers and administrators find it hard to accept
parents as equal partners in making what have been regarded as complex professional decisions, or that the parents have difficulty performing, either as team
members or as adversaries. The educators in the district seem generally more
aware of the civil rights nature of P.L. 94-142 than are the parents of handicapped
children, and there is considerable fear among the educators of the potential of
more fully informed and assertive parents. There are barriers to communication
between school professionals and the parents, and to cooperation in IEP planning,

especially for lower-status families. Both professional acceptance of parents on the team and active parental participation in decision making are directly related to the class position of the family.

VIII. CONCLUSION

The impact of the Education for All Handicapped Children Act (P.L. 94-142) on the school district studied has been substantial, even though the district and the State of Illinois as a whole already had relatively advanced provisions for special education. Our conclusions are based on a study begun in 1978/79, the year the Act went into full effect. The study was started as a longitudinal case analysis of 12 handicapped children but was broadened to include other data about the district as a case in implementing the law.

The Zero Reject provision of the Act was in operation by 1978. Programs for the mentally retarded and the multiply handicapped have been added; speech therapists have been screening all new children in the schools; and other efforts have been made to provide a range of services and settings with different degrees of restrictiveness. Provisions have been made for due process hearings, and they have been used. Our case data provided evidence of action and issues, within the district on four of the key provisions of the Act: Individualized Educational Program (IEP), Least Restrictive Environment (LRE), Protection in Evaluation Procedures (PEP), and Parental Involvement (PI).

Workloads in the schools of the district have been affected heavily by P.L. 94-142. IEPs mean much paperwork, and the initial placement and annual review conferences for each child receiving special services each year require considerable time by special education teachers, regular teachers, school administrators, district administrators, school psychologists and school social workers. Much of this time is evidently uncompensated overtime work. Speech therapists, carrying the entire diagnostic and IEP burden for the speech problems, have perhaps had the worst of it. Some federal money comes into the district to cover at least part of the added expense resulting from the Act—a flat sum for each child receiving special services, including speech therapy. State and district funds pay for most of the cost of special education (Shanker, 1980:55-56), P.L. 94-142 is not a funding act; it is a basic civil rights provision for equal educational opportunity for handicapped children. The Congress intended for the basic provisions of this Act to be followed whether any federal funds were appropriated for it or not. Even so, school districts must balance the costs of this far-reaching law against the educational opportunities of all other children.

Special education was already established as a set of special services before the Rehabilitation Act of 1973, and P.L. 94-142 were passed. The intent of Congress to desegregate special education was clear in the Zero Reject and LRE provisions of P.L. 94-142, which led to the misconception that large numbers of handicapped children would be dumped into regular classrooms, and to the common reference to the Act as "the mainstreaming law." Even a great many general educators, and some special ones, have shared this anxiety. In the district studied, wholesale mainstreaming clearly has not occurred since the Act went into effect. There has been some movement of children into more restrictive as well as into less restrictive settings during the four years. In three of our cases mainstreaming has occurred, later to be reversed in one instance. It is our conclusion that the IEP process is being used very carefully in the district. The special education teachers have not at all been inclined to push handicapped children into regular classrooms, but rather seem dedicated to promoting the most appropriate individualized learning environments.

District implementation of the complex statute has brought several governmental and professional interest groups into contact over the key issues and tasks, and also into contact with the families of handicapped children. The relative power of the interest groups in the district appears to be different from the national alignment that influenced passage of the Act. Conspicuously absent has been evidence of influence by a local or state affiliate of the nationally influential National Association for Retarded Citizens, or by other similar organizations. The only family that has told us about an organization for parents of handicapped school children was strongly influenced by that contact (an LD group), suggesting the potential of such groups for raising family awareness of their civil rights under P.L. 94-142 and for building the confidence needed to protect the family's interests.

We found three styles of family response to special education in the district—assertive, expressive and passive. In any given year we found four of our families in the group, so that only one-third of them were active advocates for the educational interests of their children. None of these has filed an appeal for a due process hearing, although hearings have been held in the district. The most assertive parents have all been mothers. The expressive families are critical of the IEP decisions and the teaching, sometimes vacillating between explosive confrontation and compliance, but they participate very little. The passive families comply, without criticism, with professional decisions.

The hypothesis that family assertiveness depends on the severity of the learning handicap has been supported for middle-class parents but not for those with lower-class status. Having middle-class status seems essential to assertiveness in most case, especially when the handicap is severe. Also important are having one or more other handicapped children and having at least one spouse not working outside the home. Parents with less education and lower community status are apparently more likely than are middle-class parents to be uninformed and to feel powerless about school issues.

P.L. 94-142 requires school professionals to accept their clients' parents as members of the planning team and to encourage them to participate fully. It also gives parents adversarial rights against the team. Both the team and adversarial roles are difficult, for educators and for parents. With the exception of one heroic working-class mother, it appears from the families studied that it is necessary to have middle-class status and to have one spouse at home in order to be taken seriously in planning and decision making, as well as to be strongly assertive. And even our most assertive families took action without being sure of their precise rights or how to proceed. If the balance of interest group influence in the district is to reflect the degree of parental involvement required by the Act, parents of handicapped school children apparently will need a great deal more information about their rights under the law, and sustained encouragement to defend them. This is an outcome not desired by many educators, even some of the special ones.

School districts encounter opposition from vested interest groups as they move to provide a range of special learning environments, adequate diagnostic services and IEP decision-making procedures. They also face claims that expensive special programs jeopardize the educational rights of all other children (Large, 1980:241-42). Two of the ways in which the district studied has tried to balance these rights are (1) to assign children to existing programs rather than trying each year to create the best setting for individual needs, and (2) to maintain some control over the number of referrals to special education. Threatened budget cuts have already brought about the placing of ceilings on referrals and have discouraged the addition of program options. Budget cutting may be expected to curtail referrals further, to reduce the range of program options, to minimize attempts to keep parents informed and participating, and otherwise to reduce district efforts to implement the Act. These reductions will likely make it necessary to handle greater numbers of handicapped children in regular classrooms. Ironically, this means that more mainstreaming may come about as a result of reduced efforts to realize P.L. 94-142 than from efforts toward full implementation. But, unfortunately, it will be the old version of mainstreaming—that of having children with learning handicaps in regular classrooms, without special help (Sarason and Doris, 1978:16-17).

There are signs of further national curtailment of funding and implementation of P.L. 94-142, even the possibility of repeal. In early 1982, in a spirit of crisis, a movement was organized to save special education in Illinois. The Reagan administration has proposed to reduce the funds for Illinois from $74.1 million in 1981/82 to $57.2 million in 1982/83, and then to replace this with a block grant of only $43.2 million in 1983/84. The State of Illinois, rather than moving to add funds to compensate for the loss of federal support, is making cuts of its own, both in special and general education. Federal court interpretations appear to be shifting to narrower views of the educational rights of the handicapped, suggesting that a great many speech, LD and other "mild" cases may be eliminated from special education. This squares with the goal of sharply reversing federal involvement in education, health and welfare (Sarason and Doris, 1978:5). Thus the Reagan policy initiatives have mounted a major challenge to implementing the still new civil rights of handicapped children and their families. The district studied is trimming its sails and continuing its special services at the maximum level possible each year, but it is also anticipating the possibility of drastic cutbacks in its system of special education. This severe outcome has been at least postponed with the passage in mid-1983 by the Illinois legislature of modest increases in state taxes and funds for education.

ACKNOWLEDGMENTS

The project was funded chiefly with federal funds from the Bureau of Education for the Handicapped under Contract No. 300780461. This paper does not necessarily reflect the views or policies of the U.S. Office of Education, nor does mention of trade names, commercial products, or organizations imply endorsement by the U.S. government. We also wish to thank Illinois State University for significant support. We are grateful to the children studied, their families, the district Director of Special Education, and all the teachers, administrators and other professionals who generously cooperated with our study over a four-year period.

NOTE

1.   It should be noted that, contrary to the perception of the general population, the category of the physically handicapped is a very low frequency category. This classification includes the deaf and hearing impaired, the blind and visually impaired, the orthopedically handicapped, and others considered to be health impaired—and still results in the smallest category—only 10 cases of the total of 575 students in special education in the district, or 1.7% in October 1978. The Trainable Mentally Handicapped, defined as those who are retarded but who can profit from programs training them in self-care and simple job skills, accounted for 16, or 2.8% of the total. Behavior Disordered children numbered 20, or 3.5%. The Educable Mentally handicapped are defined as children whose mental capacity is mildly or moderately impaired, and included 54 children, or 9.4%. The largest category below Speech, with its 62% is that of Learning Disabilities, with 116 students, or 20.2% of the district total. To count in the LD category under P.L. 94-142, the child must exhibit a "specific" learning disability by exhibiting one or more deficits in essential learning processes, such as perception, conceptualization, memory or motor function.

REFERENCES

Akers, Ronald L. and Richard Hawkins (eds.)
    1975   Law and Control in Society. Englewood Cliffs, N.J.: Prentice-Hall.
Albrecht, Gary L. (ed)
    1976a   The Sociology of Physical Disability and Rehabilitation. Pittsburgh: University of Pittsburgh Press.
    1976b   "Social policy and the management of human resources." Chapter 11 in The Sociology of Physical Disability and Rehabilitation. Pittsburgh: University of Pittsburgh Press.
Chambliss, William J. and Robert B. Seidman
    1971   Law, Order and Power, Reading, Mass.: Addison-Wesley.

Davis, F. James
  1962   "Law and social organization," Part I in F. James Davis, Henry H. Foster, Jr., C. Ray
         Jeffery, and E. Eugene David, Society and The Law. New York: The Free Press.
  1975   "Beliefs, values, power and public definition of deviance." Pp. 50-59 in F. James Davis
         and Richard Stivers (eds.), The Collective Definition of Deviance, New York: The Free
         Press.
  1978   "Toward a theory of law in society." Sociological Focus 11(2):127-41.
Day, Robert and JoAnne V. Day
  1977   "A review of the current state of negotiated order theory: an appreciation and a critique."
         Sociological Quarterly 18 (1):126-42.
Denzin, Norman
  1978   The Research Act: A Theoretical Introduction to Sociological Research Methods. 2nd ed.
         New York: McGraw-Hill.
Dimond, Paul R.
  1973   "The constitutional right to education: the quiet revolution." The Hasting Law Journal
         24 (May):1087-1127.
Dybward, Gunnar
  1980   "Avoiding misconceptions of mainstreaming, the least restrictive environment, and nor-
         malization." Exceptional Children 47 (Oct): 85-88.
Farber, Bernard
  1976   "Family processes." Chapter 14 in William M. Cruickshank (ed.), Cerebral Palsy: A
         Developmental Disability. 3rd rev. ed. Syracuse, N.Y.: Syracuse University Press.
Forness, Steven R.
  1979   "Clinical criteria for mainstreaming mildly handicapped children." Psychology in the
         Schools 16 (Oct.):508-514.
Gilliam, James E. and Margarert C. Coleman
  1981   "Who influences IEP committee decisions?" Exceptional Children 47 (May):642-644.
Goldstein, Sue, Bonnie Strickland, Ann P. Turnbull and Lynn Curry
  1979   "An observational analysis of the IEP conference." Exceptional Children 46 (Jan.):278-
         286.
Hanley, Mary Rita
  1979   "Adrift in the mainstream?" Exceptional Parent 9 (August): E3-E6.
Henshel, Richard L. and Robert A. Silverman
  1975   Perception in Criminology. New York: Columbia University Press.
Hills, Stuart L.
  1971   Crime, Power and Morality. Scranton, Pa.: Chandler.
Hobbs, Nicholas (ed.)
  1975   Issues in the Classification of Children, 2 vols. San Francisco: Jossey-Bass, Inc.
Holloway, William H. and Michael E. Kerr
  1979   "A state-wide profile of the P.L. 94-142 related concerns of educators: implications for
         planning and changing." Planning and Changing 10 (Winter):246-256.
Large, Donald W.
  1980   "Special problems of the deaf under the Education for All Handicapped Children Act of
         1975." Washington University Law Quarterly 58 (2):213-275.
Lewis, Christine L. Judith P. Busch, Barton B. Proger and Phillip J. Juska
  1981   "Parents' perspectives concerning the IEP process." Education Unlimited 3 (May/June):18-
         23.
Lippman, Leopold D. and I. Ignacy Goldberg
  1973   Right to Education: Anatomy of the Pennsylvania Case and Its Implications for Exceptional
         Students. New York: Teachers College Press.
Martin, Edwin
  1978   "Preface." Pp. iii-vi in Maynard C. Reynolds (ed.) Emerging Structures. Reston, Virginia:
         Council for Exceptional Children.

Mercer, Jane R.
1973   Labeling the Mentally Retarded. Berkeley: University of California Press.
Myers, Jerome K.
1966   "Consequences and prognoses of disability." Chapter 2 in Marvin B. Sussman (ed.),
       Sociology and Rehabilitation. Washington, D.C.: American Sociological Association.
Office of Special Education
1980   "Excerpts from the office of special education's policy paper on the IEP." Exceptional
       Parent 10 (Aug.):20-23.
Patterson, Edwin W.
1963   Law in a Scientific Age. New York: Columbia University Press.
Polloway, Edward and David Smith
1980   "P.L. 94-142 and educational placement decisions." Journal for Special Educators 16
       (Spring):298-301.
Pound, Roscoe
1923   Interpretations of Legal History. New York: Macmillan.
1942   Social Control Through Law. New Haven: Yale University Press.
Pratt, Evelyn and J. Foster Watkins
1980   "Mainstreaming—a concept in need of operational clarification." Capstone Journal of
       Education 1 (1):5-15.
Price, Marianne and Libby Goodman
1980   "Individualized education programs: a cost study." Exceptional Children 46 (6):446-454.
Quinney, Richard
1969   Crime and Justice in Society. Boston: Little Brown.
Ringlaben, Ravic P. and Jay R. Price
1981   "Regular classroom teachers' perceptions of mainstreaming effects." Exceptional Children
       47 (4):302-304.
Sarason, Seymour and John Doris
1978   "Mainstreaming: dilemmas, opposition, opportunities." Pp. 3-39 in Maynard C. Reynolds
       (ed.), Futures of Education for Exceptional Students: Emerging Structures. Reston, Virgina:
       Council for Exceptional Children.
Scott, Robert A.
1966   "Comments about interpersonal processes of rehabilitation."Chapter 7 in Marvin B. Suss-
       man (ed.), Sociology and Rehabilitation. Washington, D.C.: American Sociological
       Association.
1969   The Making of Blind Men. New York: Russell Sage Foundation.
Shanker, Albert
1980   "Public law 94-142: prospects and problems." Exceptional Parent 10 (Aug):51-56.
Strauss, Anselm
1978   Negotiations: Varieties, Contexts, Processes, and Social Order. San Francisco: Jossey-
       Bass, Inc.
Sussman, Marvin B. (ed.)
1966   Sociology and Rehabilitation. Washington, D.C.: American Sociological Association.
Turk, Austin, T.
1966   "Conflict and criminality." American Sociological Review 31 (June):338-52.
Turnbull, H. Rutherford and Ann Turnbull
1978   Free Appropriate Public Education: Law and Implementation. Denver: Love.
U.S. Code Congressional and Administrative News
1975   94th Congress, First Session, 1975, Vol. 2: Legislative History, P.L. 94-142.
U.S. Department of Education
1981   "Second annual report to Congress on the implementation of Public Law 94-142: The
       Education for All Handicapped Children Act—U.S. Department of Education." Excep-
       tional Parent 2 (April):9-14.

Usdane, William M.
   1966   "Introduction." Marvin B. Sussman (ed.), Sociology and Rehabilitation. Washington,
          D.C.: American Sociological Association.
Weintraub, Frederick J. and Alan Abeson
   1974   "New educational policies for the handicapped: the quiet revolution." Phi Delta Kappan
          55:526-529;569.
Wessen, Albert F.
   1966   "The rehabilitation apparatus and organization theory." Chapter 9 in Marvin B. Sussman
          (ed.), Sociology and Rehabilitation. Washington, D.C.: American Sociological Association.
Yoshida, Roland K., Kathleen S. Fenton, James P. Maxwell and Martin J. Kaufman
   1977   Parental Involvement in the Special Education Pupil Planning Process: The School's Per-
          spective. Washington, D.C.: State Program Studies Branch, Division of Innovation and
          Development, Bureau of Education for the Handicapped, U.S. Office of Education.
Yoshida, Roland K., Kathleen S. Fenton, Martin J. Kaufman and James P. Maxwell
   1978   "Parental involvement in the special education pupil planning process: the school's per-
          spective." Exceptional Children 44 (April):531-534.

URBAN REDEVELOPMENT AND PUBLIC DRUNKENNESS IN FRESNO:
A CALIFORNIA MOVE TOWARD RECRIMINALIZATION

Richard Speiglman and Friedner D. Wittman

INTRODUCTION

Over the years community development and land use strategies have forced marginal groups to leave the community, or have segregated them in public housing, or have occasionally integrated them into the dominant social structure by dispersing them into the local economy (Comerio, 1982). Alcohol abuse has figured prominently in the rhetoric and tactics used in putting these strategies into action, to justify extraordinary efforts to deal with marginal individuals or, from a different but complementary perspective, to resolve land use conflicts. Certain abusers of alcohol found to be concentrated in particular geographic areas have been contained or dispersed—those who are drunk in public and those who lack "class," along with those found in their company or who appear like them. They have been handled using the argument that the "disease" controlling them renders them unable to manage their own affairs. This argument allows social

Research in Law, Deviance and Social Control, Volume 5, pages 141-170
Copyright © 1983 by JAI Press, Inc.
All rights of reproduction in any form reserved
ISBN: 0-89232-334-5

welfare and social control agencies, under rubrics of treatment and punishment, to intervene in the visible alcoholic's affairs nominally for the inebriate's own good.

During the 1981 California legislative session, Fresno Assemblyman Jim Costa introduced legislation creating an equivalence between punitive and rehabilitative treatment of public drunks. The new provision reflected the view that with the appropriate choice before them, convicted inebriates who had been choosing periodic dry-outs in the county jail over invitations into treatment would now see it in their interest to accept treatment voluntarily. Becoming law in California in January 1982, this statute provides counties with a sentencing structure previously considered sufficiently dubious that earlier attempts at similar legislation failed to attract serious support.

The matter came to the legislature through the Assembly Criminal Justice Committee at the request of the Fresno County legislator. Why would we find a change in policy coming out of Fresno in 1981? What explains the timing and the location of support for this legislation? Reflection on these questions involves a discussion of land use, business patterns, farm labor, immigration, and racial attitudes in the Central Valley.

The sociology of law must be able to analyze legal categories systematically, to observe changes in these categories, and to explain the relationship between legalistic developments and broader social change. This paper explores the origin of a new California statute—one elaborating sanctions for recidivist acts of public drunkenness.

Hall (1952) stands as one of the first innovative students of the law, its origin, and the social structure. Since his work, Chambliss has noted (1964:67), "there has been a severe shortage of sociologically relevant analyses of the relationship between particular laws and the social setting in which these laws emerge, are interpreted, and take form." The field, Chambliss continues, requires just such analyses. Galliher (1980) has continued this critique in a review of this still-sparse literature, lamenting the lack of integration among the various academic fields which are brought into studies of the law and commenting that there is no systematic, integrated research tradition which has resulted. He distinguishes between analyses that focus on structural explanations for legal change and those that rely on triggering events to explain the origin of the legislation in question. Each approach, he concludes, has its strengths and weaknesss. Finally, Galliher (1980) criticizes the absence of analyscs of laws which deal with economic matters.

Chambliss (1964:76-77) concludes his article on vagrancy law saying: "when changed social conditions create a perceived need for legal changes...these alterations will be effected through the revision and refocusing of existing statutes...The analysis of the vagrancy statutes (and Hall's analysis of theft as well) has demonstrated the importance of 'vested interest' groups in the emergence and/or alteration of laws."

Comment on the enactment and enforcement of laws prohibiting public drunkenness—even if conducted in a manner to explore both structural and triggering explanations—would seem to represent a trivial undertaking. In fact, the conjuncture of the homeless-transient-inebriety issues offers the opportunity for study of policies toward and consequent influences on marginal populations, for these groups are thought to retard the development of business and to constrain rises in property value.[1] As Molotch (1976:310) observes, "The city is, for those who count, a growth machine," and those who count tend to make their influence heard in the lawmaking process. Conversely, when growth fails to materialize, a scapegoat may be sought. Public inebriates both signify an excuse for faltered growth and offer a possible strategy for overcoming this failure.

Our argument goes as follows: (1) policy concerning control of a marginal and deviant population—homeless and inebriate people constitute such a group—is not preordained; (2) the selection of specific strategies of control reflects particular concerns and political constraints both at the local level and within broader political and economic contours; (3) in this case moves, first, to legitimize longer jail terms for public inebriates and, second, to motivate them into long-term treatment developed in the specific historical context of the jurisdiction in which the policy was drawn up.

This contribution to the study of the recriminalization of inebriety focuses on Fresno, first, because of that county's dramatic arrest rate for public inebriates and, second, because new California legislation originated from that jurisdiction.

Our paper reviews the development of public drunkenness law generally and recalls its specific manifestations within California. We then document the concrete situation in Fresno, including actions taken by policy-influentials and policymakers in that county. Finally, we assess difficulties in the implementation of the new law and draw conclusions on the meaning of recriminalization.

II. DECRIMINALIZATION OF PUBLIC DRUNKENNESS

In part the recent history of control of public inebriates has revolved around civil rights issues. Partly out of humanitarianism and partly from practical concerns such as fiscal problems and law suits, control and service activities have been transferred to agencies thought better able to handle public drunks. The decriminalization period can be dated to the first diversion programs instituted with suspended sentences in the 1950s (see Room, 1978). Following years saw the beginning of a movement to decriminalize as some judges, in an unorganized and sporadic manner, refused to process drunks in court. Subsequently, formal court decisions and then legislation reinforced this approach.

The constitutional basis for a U.S. Supreme Court decision on the matter was laid in 1962 in *Robinson v. California*. Here the court held that punishment for the condition of being addicted to narcotics was unconstitutional. The 1966 U.S.

Court of Appeals *Easter v. District of Columbia* and *Driver v. Hinnant* decisions held, in the former case, that public drunks should be diverted to short-term emergency detoxification, diagnosis and referral. *Driver* went on to find that a conviction for public inebriety constitutes cruel and unusual punishment because alcoholism is an illness and because of the consequent involuntary nature of a public inebriate's drunken state.

Nationally, a groundswell of support for decriminalization became evident. Three major commissions, in the years 1966 and 1967, found the criminal law to be an ineffective, inhumane and costly approach to the control of public drunkenness.[2] The subsequent U.S. Supreme Court decision in *Powell v. Texas* (1968) failed to institutionalize such radical steps on the pragmatic basis that visible alternatives were lacking. Nevertheless, the *Powell* opinions, which were sharply divided, all observed that the criminal process is an inappropriate mechanism for handling drunks.

By 1968 congressional interest in the topic was evident. Enacted that year, the District of Columbia Alcoholic Rehabilitation Act of 1967 concluded that criminal justice handling of chronic alcoholics was not only ineffective but aggravative and generally bad policy. Instead, a public health approach to treatment of alcoholism was said to permit prevention, earlier detection, and effective treatment and to relieve police and other criminal justice agencies of a major burden impeding their important work. A joint policy statement from the American Medical Association (AMA) and American Bar Association (ABA) in 1969 reinforced this approach as it called on states to recognize alcoholism as an illness and to stop treating public inebriates as criminal offenders. Congress, in 1970, enacted the Comprehensive Alcohol Abuse and Alcoholism Prevention, Treatment, and Rehabilitation Act, thereby creating the National Institute on Alcohol Abuse and Alcoholism and requiring states seeking treatment grants to prioritize the decriminalization of treatment for public inebriates. The following year a call for state decriminalization of public drunkenness and continuity of care provision for all alcoholics came from the National Conference of Commissioners on Uniform State Laws. All public drunkenness was to be handled outside the court system. Congressional action in 1974 required implementation of the Uniform Act from states qualifying for certain grant funds. By 1980, as political and economic pressures for decriminalization increased, 34 states qualified for grants by adopting legislation interpreted as decriminalization.

III. CALIFORNIA DRUNKENNESS LAW

Under federal standards California was not considered to have decriminalized. Governor Edmund G. (Jerry) Brown Jr. vetoed statewide legislative action in this regard in 1975, leaving California counties the option to use medical detoxification in decriminalizing public drunkenness.

Since 1872 California statutes have incorporated legislation criminalizing public drunkenness under Section 647 of the California Penal Code, which concerns itself with "disorderly conduct."[3] Under this heading one finds subsections proscribing solicitation [647(a),(b),(d)], lewd conduct [647(a)], prostitution [647(b)], begging [647(c)], loitering [647 (d),(e)], and drunkenness [647(f)]— generally forms of behavior which would be legal in private. Presently, the section on drunkenness reads as follows:

> Every person who commits any of the following acts is guilty of disorderly conduct, a misdemeanor:
>
> . . . .
>
> (f)Who is found in any public place under the influence of intoxicating liquor, any drug, toluene, any substance defined as a poison in Schedule D of Section 4160 of the Business and Professions Code, or any combination of any intoxicating liquor, drug, toluene, or any such poison, in such a condition that he is unable to exercise care for his own safety or the safety of others, or by reason of his being under the influence of intoxicating liquor, any drug, toluene, any substance defined as a poison in Schedule D of Section 4160 of the Business and Professions Code, or any combination of any intoxicating liquor, drug, toluene, or any such poison, interferes with or obstructs or prevents the free use of any street, sidewalk, or other public way.

As early as 1957 the Legislature evidenced concern that discretion be available at the correctional stage for release of drunks. The "kick-out" procedure, as it was known, was incorporated into Penal Code Section 849(b)(2):

> Any peace officer may release from custody, instead of taking such person before a magistrate, any person arrested without a warrant whenever:
>
> (2) The person arrested was arrested for intoxication only, and no further proceedings are desirable.

As Stevens (1981) observes, this statute gives a police officer the discretion to arrest or ignore drunks, and the jailer the discretion to keep and file complaints or release those booked. At least one unwritten purpose of giving the jailers and police such broad discretion is to provide a means for them to cope with overcrowded jails.

Another refinement provided additional flexibility for both police and jail staff. Section 64(ff), enacted in 1971, encouraged the use of protective civil custody in lieu of arrest for those violating 647(f).[4] This statute, a remnant of California's frustrated move toward decriminalization, suggests the split between idea and reality. Although the law permits local officials to seek treatment in lieu of criminal punishment, it has not mandated the construction of any civil custody facilities or provided funding to the counties for expenses involved. As a result, most counties, which are increasingly hard pressed financially, have no such facility to this day. It was not until 1973, in fact, that California authorized regulations for the construction of 647(ff) facilities (Stevens, 1981).[5]

Although giving lip service to decriminalization by encouraging 72-hour civil commitment of public drunks under Section 647(ff), California Penal Code Section 647(f) nevertheless permits local jurisdictions to arrest persons for being drunk in public. While some state policy influentials, and certainly many nationally, have pushed for decriminalization, local jurisdictions have successfully resisted the implemetation of policies and court decisions in this area. Historically most California jurisdictions have arrested and detained in jail those charged with public drunkenness, making little use of the decriminalization provision. The practical issue in most places has been whether these jail stays be punitive (harsh experiences and more than a few hours in length), or simply lifesaving (dry-out period only).

A lower court, in the *Sundance v. Municipal Court of Los Angeles* decision, has been responsible for making detention of inebriates more costly and unpopular, once again underlining the unacceptable nature of options at the local level. The Los Angeles court required beds in drunk tanks, safe and healthy paddy-wagons, medical screening of inebriates on intake and hourly thereafter, preservation of police evidence, and the cessation of mass arraignments, and also that trials be given to 647(f) cases—with the right to utilize as a defense the argument that a chronic, homeless alcoholic has no option but to drink in public ("Minutes," 1979).

This decision has had a profound impact on strategic planning and policymaking as well as legal thinking in the alcohol field. The "Memorandum Opinion," in part, concluded:

> The court finds, by reason of a combination of factors, that current investigative, accusational, prosecuting, and judicial policies, practices, and procedures involved in the handling of 647(f) cases result in a widespread denial of due process of law. It should be made clear that the deprivation of due process is not caused by evil intent, incompetent performance, or method designed to deprive 647(f) defendants of their rights. Rather, it has come about because of a widely held but perhaps unperceived and unarticulated notion of police, prosecutors, and courts that the purpose of charging defendants with a crime under 647(f) is to give the defendant some assitance against the effect of his illness, and not to bring down society's wrath by criminal prosecution. Since historically criminal prosecution has been the only viable way of getting a public inebriate off the street and sobered up, the methods used to do that have been forced into the mold of a criminal prosecution without the reality thereof.... If it can be said, as it can, that criminal prosecution with all due process safeguards makes no social sense for alcoholics, then non-criminal remedies such as diversion must be attempted.... It is concluded that diversion of 647(f) arrestees to detoxification results in both a social advantage and an economic saving (*Sundance et al. v. Municipal Court of Los Angeles Judicial District et al.*, 1977;33,41,77).

The *Sundance* court, however, found it could not carry this last finding into a judgment, declaring the policy choice to be a legislative, not a judicial, one.

Fearing similar decisions in their locales, some criminal justice officials have generally stopped criminal prosecutions under 647(f). Instead, with "kick-out" authority granted under Penal Code Section 849(b)(2), those picked up under drunkenness charges remain jailed only until sober, usually no longer than six to eight hours. They are then released, with no formal charges filed against them. While those charged with inebriety may be booked into jail, they rarely face arraignment or any subsequent judicial process or, as some might note, standard due process proceeding.

Nationally, decriminalization promised to solve the problem of public drunkenness, or at least minimally to take it out of the hands of police agencies and place it more appropriately with treatment officials. Preferably, police were only to deliver drunks to detoxification facilities, with even that responsibility better relegated to a nonpolice service agency. *Sundance* made clear to Fresno County that, without considerable expenditures in providing due process and medical supervision, there was no constitutional basis for holding drunks against their will longer than required for sobering up. The reality, in many places, and particularly in California (Fresno included), was that decriminalization meant only shorter periods in jail rather than avoidance of the criminal justice system altogether. As a result, observers say, things generally got worse. The "revolving door" policy of arrests turned into a "spinning door" of jail dry-out periods. Further, the number of *visible* public inebriates increased, thereby making the use of criminal justice alternatives increasingly probable.[6]

What were the consequences of these policies for the population of public inebriates? The evidence from California indicates that while there had been a rapid decline in California public drunkenness arrests in the late 1960s and early 1970s, this trend reversed itself by 1974, when arrests rose once again (Reynolds, 1977). By 1980, although arrest *rates* remained down, the *number* of statewide drunk arrests approached those for 1971 (California, Department of Justice, Bureau of Criminal Statistics, 1980; Collins, 1980; Cameron, 1980). With hard times in the past few years, the numbers—or at least public attention to them— have begun to rise. Newspaper clippings from Martinez to San Francisco and Santa Barbara attest to renewed public concern with drunks.[7]

In California, with policy concerning the control and treatment of public inebriates largely localized, a variety of policies are possible. However, counties regularly express their dismay at the costs involved, and the lack of useful options to them. Among the options, they may choose to ignore public inebriates, though at potentially great human cost to the drunks themselves, economic cost to private interests, and political cost to elected officials. Drunks may thereby be permitted to disrupt the flow of business, to induce complaints from citizens or businesses, or to succumb to the elements, be they natural or social, and suffer severe illness and death.[8] Second, jurisdictions may arrest and detain inebriates, but at substantial economic costs by filling up the jails and opening themselves to lawsuits contesting unconstitutional processing of drunks and lack of medical treatment for them. Third, counties may decide to utilize medical model civil detoxification centers under a state statute which encourages this alternative. But this too ends up costing a great deal of money—medical personnel are required to be on duty at all times—and results in the removal of drunks from the streets for a period of only 72 hours, an inadequate amount of time according to some decision makers. Perhaps as a result, in spite of talk about decriminalization both across the country and within California by county option, very little use is made of the diversion provision. Instead, counties tend to formulate mixed strategies in their public drunkenness policy.

Precisely how do communities come to terms with the uninviting choices? Fresno's inventive solution and its potentially significant impact on the state as a whole requires comment. In describing this history our work concerns itself with community development patterns, with sentiment toward public inebriates, and with practices in handling community development. The intersection of particular concerns and attitudes, with political and economic developments, results in specific policy changes—in particular, in new public drunkenness law. This fresh effort at control of drunkenness also offers the opportunity for an examination of alcohol policies more generally.

IV. PENAL CODE SECTION 647d

On January 1, 1982, California Assembly Bill 1091, "Inebriates—Recovery Programs," joined the statutes prohibiting disorderly conduct as California Penal Code Section 647d without Governor Jerry Brown's signature.[9] The bill created an equivalence between 60 days of mandatory treatment for alcoholism and 90 days of jail time upon a third public intoxication conviction within 12 months.

Nominally, the bill appears to offer inebriates a choice between rehabilitation treatment and jail time. The bill seeks to encourage inebriates into treatment by the device of requiring less treatment than jail time (indicating some concern for whether the inebriate might otherwise choose jail over rehabilitation). While having a statewide effect, the bill's legislative history shows clearly that it was directed at conditions in Fresno, California; in effect, the bill is an attempt to use legal means to remove inebriates from a downtown shopping area in this middle-size city. The bill's originators appear to have both rehabilitation and commercial objectives in mind. Confusion over forced action in the former area to obtain positive results in the latter has complicated matters to the point that what began as essentially uncontested legislation now promotes conflict among merchants, criminal justice administrators, alcohol treatment officials and civil libertarians.[10] One year after the bill's enactment, Fresno County remains unable to implement its own legislation.

The following discussion covers four areas: First, we describe the community development situation in Fresno, California, which provided the context for origination of the Costa bill. Second, we review the actions taken by several groups in Fresno to deal with public inebriates within the community development context and accounts for current frustrations in terms of community development issues, complicated by the presence of the public inebriates in Fresno's central business district. Third, we outline the post-Costa situation. Finally, we discuss comments on policy decisions at hand prior to the recriminalization of public drunkenness, in particular those requiring further analysis.

A. Community Development and Public Inebriates in Downtown Fresno

Fresno, a ciy of 218,000 inhabitants in a county of 515,000, sits in the central part of the San Joaquin Valley, California's richest agricultural region. As the agricultural industry has prospered so has Fresno, which for a century has functoned as a service center to the agricultural community within a 100-mile radius. While per capita personal income in Fresno County was within the bottom one-fifth for all California counties in 1959, by 1978 county incomes rose to the state's top one-third (County Supervisors' Association of California, 1981:45,47). Fresno County stands out as a leading producer for many commodities.[11] With the city dominating the economy and politics of central California, Fresno's daily newspaper—the *Bee*—reflects this status as the major print medium for the counties between Sacramento and Bakersfield. In its location, Fresno county takes on a special status of neutral territory in California's north-south battles, and Fresno remains the one city of any size associated with neither regional group. Because of this and the geographic convenience it offers, Fresno attracts many statewide meetings and conventions. Fresno has grown steadily in population since World War II; as the population has grown, and as Fresno's role as a service center to agriculture has expanded, the city has grown physically.

Fresno shares the California valley syndrome of small cities with large skid rows, a condition probably linked with farming economies, their requirements for mobile labor pool, and good weather.[12]

Fresno's original core contains the complex of city and county government buildings in the heart of the downtown area, close by the north-south rail and highway transportation system that services the entire valley and state; see the accompanying map (Figure 1).

Between the government complex and the transportation arteries is located Fresno's original business district, an area of about 20 blocks. This central business district contains a mixture of retail shopping, including one large department store, several variety stores, and a number of speciality shops and restaurants; office buildings emphasizing insurance, legal and banking services; a few apartment houses serving predominantly low-income groups; and some hotels and motels for business travelers and tourists. A few blocks away from the central district stands Fresno's convention center, built in the mid-1960s.

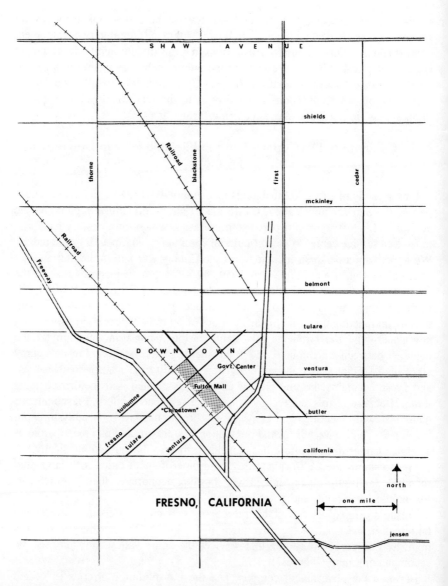

Figure 1.

Immediately to the west of downtown is a low-income residential area known as "Chinatown" which includes a mix of Asian, Mexican-American, white and a few black residents.

In the mid-1960s, Fresno planned for its future downtown growth by creating a "mall" area in the central business district. The Fulton Mall, as the area is now known, was created by closing off about a dozen streets in the area, remodeling them to create pedestrian walkways. Though these malls are now widely present in communities throughout the country, at its creation the Fulton Mall was hailed as an innovation in downtown renewal.

The economic objective underlying the Fulton Mall renewal was its resuscitation as a major retail shopping area for Fresnans. But, instead, development of retail shopping and many professional services shifted to the northern fringe of the city. Beginning with the opening of a suburban shopping center in 1972, Shaw Avenue, a major artery at the northern edge of the city, developed rapidly as a location for retail and professional services. The physical remodeling of the Fulton Mall had little offsetting effect. The Mall remains a commercial power in Fresno, but it has not experienced the growth originally intended for it and in fact has probably declined in its share of the total retail market. Certainly the establishment of new retail establishments, and expansion of existing businesses, have been disappointing. Until the last two or three years, growth activity on the Mall has been virtually nil, with many stores and offices vacant, particularly toward the nothern end of the Mall. Merchants, complaining about the situation, demanded that the streets by swept of litter—both human bodies and wastepaper. As they explained it:

> One of the problems facing the downtown area is that of the public inebriate. The presence of the public inebriate in the downtown area adds to the perception of threat or danger and affects the desire to shop and conduct business in the downtown central business district (Fresno County and City Chamber of Commerce. March 18, 1981).

In the last few years, the Mall has obtained a new lease on life. Although it has not proved capable of pulling retail shoppers away from Shaw Avenue, the Mall has attracted new interest as a setting for office uses. In 1977, the Fresno County Department of Health committed itself to locate most of its operations, involving a staff of about 500 people, in remodeled facilities at the least successful north end of the Mall. Still in progress as a two-stage project, about 300 staff have moved to the Mall already, with the remainder to follow within the year Concomitantly, the Mall is the subject of new construction and remodeling with the emphasis on new offices, particularly for legal, banking, insurance and professional services. The Mall is picking up for the first time since the original planning some 15 years ago.

The Mall currently attracts some middle-class shoppers but appears to serve primarily poorer workers, many of whom live in the nearby lower-income residential areas, including "Chinatown." The Mall has also long been associated with the presence of panhandlers and public inebriates. Retailers on the Mall are particularly concerned that the presence of skid-row types discourages the maintenance of their businesses and constrains future growth. Potential developers also have insisted that the area be cleaned up, one developer demanding the removal of a cheap hotel before proceeding with his project. The strength of new development on the Mall depends heavily upon the confidence of investors. "Cleaning up the Mall" has become a necessary token of good faith and competence in the City of Fresno's contribution to development activities.

As the Shaw Avenue commercial development took hold in the mid-1970s, Fulton Mall merchants made strong efforts to "clean up" the appearance of the Mall to make it competitively attractive to middle class shoppers. A major part of this clean-up effort involved work with the local police to keep public inebriates away from the Mall. Public inebriates were taken by the police to the Fresno County Branch Jail, a minimum-security jail farm outside of the city which, using prisoner labor, launders for county facilities, grows food and does some maintenance work.[13]

It has never been clear that all of the persons on the mall creating the "bad image" of concern to Mall merchants are public inebraites.[14] With no test of intoxication given, the arrest power results in general sweeps of the Mall of any "undesirable" three times daily, at 6 A.M., 6 P.M., and midnight. Following the 6 A.M. roundup, the early morning routine includes a second sweep, this time by street cleaners, leaving the shining Mall to await the day's first workers and shoppers.

Who, in fact, are the people on the Mall who are of concern to the merchants? What do they do that is offensive? How many of them are there? At present answers to these questions are based largely on impressions. Systematic studies and observations of life on the Mall have not been done, as both police and treatment officials note.

Arrest statistics provide some information. Even these data are quite imperfect for research and policymaking purposes, however, since the Penal Code section under which arrests are made involves not just public inebriety but a variety of other behaviors as well. People are arrested under this charge to break up barroom and marital disputes as well as to complete a wide spectrum of police-citizen interactions. Despite these problems, though, the arrest statistics offer an image of the population at issue.

In Fresno County, those arrested over the past years have been widely distributed by age, with most arrests among 19- to 24-year-olds (some 800-1000 of each age group each year), the number declining for those in their late 20s and into their 30s and 40s (to about 200 arrests per cohort per year), rising slightly for those in their 50s. Almost all are men, with women comprising in 1979 only 5.8% of the county arrests.

The data indicate that, while whites contribute only about half the drunk arrests

expected from their population size, Hispanics are arrested two-thirds again as
frequently as their proportion of the population would predict. Blacks are arrested
about one-quarter more than their share of the population.[15] The evidence is
strong that men of Mexican descent are arrested for public drunkenness in Fresno
County far out of proportion to their part of the population.

Briefly, merchants are concerned with both appearance and with behavior.
Appearance issues have to do with the kinds of clothes people wear, cleanliness,
grooming and ethnicity. Behavioral problems have to do with loitering, rifling
trash cans or panhandling. Drinking in public on or about the Mall itself is minor
in comparison to these other issues. However, evidence that this is not a minor
problem is contained in the fact that Fresno County exhibits the highest per
capita drunkenness arrest rate for California counties over 200,000 in population.
Its 41.7 arrests per thousand in 1980 almost doubled the arrest rate of its closest
competitor—Kern county's 23.9 arrests per thousand. Estimates are that at least
one-quarter of the county's drunkenness arrests result from only the few blocks
bounded by the Mall.

The people involved include both residents of nearby low-income housing, in
two or three apartment facilities, and transients. The population, both elderly
persons and young/middle-aged men, includes many who are itinerant or seasonal
workers or who work at spot jobs. While the Sheriff comments that many are
"railroad bums," other informants suggest most are not, instead being individuals who receive veterans' benefits or public assistance, including both welfare
and Social Security payments. It is not clear how many of them are "skid-row
alcoholics" in the conventional uses of the term implying people whose lives
are centered around drinking. Differing life-styles seem as much involved as do
careers of public intoxication. The "problem" population is not homogeneous,
nor are its members entirely without resources or organization.

How many people are there in this population? Estimates range from about
50 to 75, in the City of Fresno, to 3,000 in the county as a whole. City observers
note that this figure is probably down dramatically from a decade ago, when
closer to two or three hundred public inebriates resided in Fresno. Nevertheless,
symbolically public inebriates remain a big problem. Presently, in their three
regular sweeps, the Fresno police arrest and book up to 40 persons per day into
the county jail about two blocks from the Mall, releasing them six to eight hours
later with no charges pending. Those persons actually arrested and booked from
throughout the county for charges related to being drunk in public numbered
19,668 in 1980. Some unknown proportion of this figure represents multiple
arrests of the same individuals.

Perhaps as a result of this daily routine, in the State of California, Fresno's
arrests for public drunkenness were surpassed only by Los Angeles County's
59,428 and Orange County's 19,785. With 2.18% of the state's people in 1980,
Fresno recorded 8.53% of all California drunkenness arrests in that year, or
almost four times the statewide arrest rate.[16]

B. Policymaking in Fresno

How Fresno's policy makers chose the Costa bill as their solution to Fresno's problems remains to be explained. One simple analysis, including that of a legal adviser to California's Governor Brown, summarizes the bill as the product of merchants' desires to increase their abilities to keep habitual drunks off the streets. According to the Fresno County and City Chamber of Commerce, downtown Fresno's problem with public inebriates results from the practice of short-term jailing. Following arrest and a few hours in jail, they go out and start drinking again, reports the Chamber's spokesperson. They lie around the court house park area and the Mall, presenting an image which is not good. And many of them are victims of crime themselves.

AB 1091, the Chamber said, resulted from people's perception that crime was a lot worse than it really was, especially in the downtown area. This view follows from loitering and other behavior connected with the presence of public inebriates. Several officials we interviewed cited a Chamber of Commerce study said to indicate that many of these people were repeat offenders, that the criminal justice system was already congested and not helping the drunks, that they are victims themselves, and that their alcoholism is not presently being helped. The belief was prevalent that public inebriates constitute a tremendous strain on local resources (law enforcement, health, emergency), attract crime, and disrupt the downtown shopping mall.

Why are voluntary programs insufficient in Fresno? At the current time, said the Chamber staff person, the alcohol programs locally are pretty much on a voluntary basis. Public inebriates and transients are more those who have chosen that life-style and don't want rehabilitation or treatment, so the programs fail to help them, she concluded. It is for this reason that "constructive coercion" comes into play.[17]

With the *Sundance* decision, Fresno County judges declined to hear drunkenness cases, and efforts to keep public inebriates at the jail farm were seriously limited. Mall merchants, as a result, sought new approaches to deal with public inebriates. The Chamber convinced that they could at one and the same time help drunks and the image problems in the downtown area, thereby encouraging shopping by those who want to do business there—organized a Crime Task Force. There was a legal decision ("called 'Sundance' or something like that," said a Chamber of Commerce spokesperson) "which says that a sentence to treatment is not equal protection, so we came up with a new section of the code providing that a local entity with such a facility could refer people to that program." No one would be "sentenced" to treatment.

The Crime Task Force of the Fresno City and County Chamber of Commerce committed itself to finding a mechanism that would permit full criminal justice processing for public drunkenness offenders. In existence since December 1980, the Task Force was described as a very dedicated group which met intensely every other Friday morning at 7:30 for the first six months. It was supposed to end July 1, 1981, but the Chamber decided it would go on through the end of the year. In May 1982, the Task Force continued to meet.

The Task Force included membership from the mayor's office, local law enforcement officials (Chief of Police, District Attorney, Sheriff, Public Defender, Presiding Judge of the Municipal Court), members of the City Council and Board of Supervisors, representatives from the Fresno merchant community, particularly the director of the Downtown Association of Fresno (a private non-profit organization supported by voluntary assessment from merchants in the downtown Fresno area), a criminologist from the local state university campus, and the director of the alcoholism treatment program that had worked with inebriates at the Jail.[18] The plan which attracted central interest was put forward by a member of the university criminology faculty. State Assemblyman Jim Costa also attended Task Force meetings and eventually carried the bill to Sacramento.

The group approached its task with the dual objectives of providing treatment services to public inebriates and cleaning up the central business district (primarily the Mall). As new legislation would be necessary to counteract the *Sundance* decision, the legislation would provide for treatment following arrest, permitting the offender to choose between jail time as a prisoner in the Branch Jail and treatment under an alcoholic rehabilitation program segregated from other activities at the jail but using its facilities. It was hoped that this approach would address the concerns of *Sundance*, provide treatment for skid-row alcoholics, and clean up the Mall (and other commercial retail areas).

The AB 1091 approach will save money in the long run, reported Assemblyman Costa's assistant, in that it will be cheaper than arresting these people every other day and providing for their detoxification and protective custody. The revolving door, in the words of the assistant to the chairperson of the California Senate's Judiciary Committee, just is not working out.

The Chamber's Task Force staffer said her group discovered that since there is a sort of social structure among the public inebriates, word spreads about their treatment in various places. The Task Force believes the word will get around that repeat offenders will be sentenced to rehabilitation and treatment, so those who don't want it will go somewhere else. Thereby the bill will discourage public inebriates from hanging out on the downtown mall. A legislative aide and others concerned with this problem hope the inebriates will go to the next county down the road before their third conviction.

A second orientation focused on the small but significant value to be reaped from coerced treatment. One County Sheriff's official stated, "Treatment has to be given to them whether they want it or not." Stressing the significance of the police powers he said, "these people have to be approached at a particular time with treatment."

A Crime Task Force Memo (Fresno County and City Chamber of Commerce, March 18, 1981) stresses the significance of the coercive influence:

It is recommended that the Fresno County and City Chamber of Commerce:

1) Support the attached proposal for a one year pilot project for the treatment and rehabilitation of public inebriates, including private sector support for one-third of the cost of such a program, with the City and County each assuming a third of the cost; and
2) Support legislation introduced by Assemblyman Jim Costa which would amend existing law to allow longer sentencing of public inebriates.

Under this rationale, it is only the coercive mechanism of stiffer sentences (the 90 jail days) which makes 60 days of treatment tempting. The Crime Task Force Memo spells this out, noting that "In order to refer public inebriates for treatment and rehabilitation service, legislation is necessary in order to allow longer periods of sentencing of the public inebriate." In short, to make treatment work, the threat of a more substantial punishment is required.

Costa brought the problem to the Assembly Criminal Justice Committee, saying that he wanted to do something about public inebriates. Jeff Ruch, working for the Committee, relates how he drafted the bill at Costa's request. The object, Ruch says, was to get a long-term (defined as at least one month) civil commitment for this population. The criminal law was to be used as a handle to get that commitment, providing the coercive mechanism in this design. The Penal Code route was taken because otherwise the number of hearings required to get long-term *civil* commitment would be self-defeating. "I am not convinced the concept will make a lot of sense" Ruch said, although "the law regarding sentencing of repeat-offending prostitutes was used as a model for this legislation, and there are other examples of the use of cumulative sentencing structures as well." At the time, of passage, standards form treatment were unclear, to be left up to Costa's office with the help and agreement of the State Department of Alcohol and Drugs.

We were told that initially there was some concern by Legal Aid people in the county. They wondered if the Costa bill would result in fair treatment for those charged under its provisions. The Fresno Public Defender was very valuable here, the Costa bill's supporters, claimed, in saying that the legislation provided for more humane treatment for those suffering from this "alcohol problem." Current facilities were inadequate; police power couldn't be utilized; and the provision of new voluntary services would be much more expensive, requiring capital expenditures, while the AB 1091 program would provide for an inexpensive alternative. The Task Force determined that it could treat 20-40 public inebriates for an additional financing of $30,000.

The bill at base appears to be a merchant-inspired effort to clean up the downtown mall, combining support for treatment with the desire to move the problem to the next county. This strategy comes out clearly in Crime Task Force documents "A Program for the Public Inebriate," the central document in the Chamber of Commerce approach, plans for the dispersal of Fresno drunks elsewhere:

> There is some chance that, once the proposed programs is implemented, some of this group may find Fresno a less desireable place and move elsewhere. . . .
> The possibility that the group might decrease in size suggests that any program developed to meet this need should be flexible so that the size and cost of the program can be adjusted downwards as the need decreased, if it does (Dean, n.d.).

Political and economic realities shaped the features of the bill. The alcohol literature suggests that 60 days is not really enough to deal with this sort of problem. The Chamber staffer said that, although they knew this, the Task Force didn't think they could get more than 60 days in the legislation: "We want to solve the problem and nobody really is doing anything about it. We want to help the publc inebriate, the image they are presenting, and the merchants."

On September 14, 1981, when the bill was back in the Assembly for concurrence with Senate amendments, Costa's assistant said that she did not anticipate any problem getting the bill through. In fact, there was very little attention to the legislation at all, it seems. One legislator with whom we spoke who in fact voted for the bill in the Assembly Criminal Justice Committee—had no recollection of the measure and only upon our description of the bill did he comment that, in fact, he might really oppose the legislation. In all, AB 1091 went through the legislature with insignificant opposition. It passed the Senate 21-1 and the Assembly 70-2. Governor Jerry Brown allowed AB 1091 to become law without his signature—evidence, said a member of his Cabinet, that the bill didn't have a great deal of Brown's support. The Governor acquiesced to its passage, however, despite unanimous opposition to the bill from the County Alcohol Program Administrators Association of California (opposition which developed when word of the measure "leaked" out) and a recommendation for veto from Brown's own Department of Alcohol and Drug Programs.

Opposition to the bill during hearings also came from the American Civil Liberties Union and the California Attorneys for Criminal Justice (Los Angeles). The District Attorney's association took no position, while the Fresno and California Public Defenders supported the bill, as did the California Peace Officers' Association and the Peace Officers' Research Association of California, said our informants.

But full public debate on the matter clearly was avoided. Two of the bills' supporters inquired with some degree of concern as to how we had heard of the legislation. Costa's office said that they had not planned any press coverage until the bill was passed and signed by the Governor: clearly a questionable process, and one suggesting a certain amount of insecurity among its supporters.[19]

C. The Aftermath of Costa

At the time the legislation was passed we were told that it looked as though only Fresno Country would be involved in the program. It was the only county with funds available to provide the treatment mandated for the program. How did Fresno happen to have the money for this special program but not for sufficient detoxification facilities? Notwithstanding some offers of private funding from local merchants, the Fresno program for drunks is a bare-bones treatment mechanism, funded well below the level required for a full-service detoxification facility.

The Costa Bill became effective on January 1, 1982; nevertheless, plans for its implementation in Fresno remain up in the air at this writing. Some $30,000 in financial support has been obtained from three sources, with guarantees only for the first year of operation, and that to provide only one new staff person and no new treatment facilities. Fresno County, the City of Fresno, and the local Fresno business community will each contribute $10,000 to the treatment program, if the County Board of Supervisors decides to go ahead with implementation of the law. Since that state government offers no financial support, counties have the opion of implementing or disregarding the law. At this point, however, it is uncertain whether Fresno County will implement the legislation it was instrumental in obtaining. Several obstacles still stand in the way.

First, it is not yet clear who will conduct the treatment program.

Second, where will the treatment take place, at the Branch Jail or elsewhere? Although the Costa bill seems to provide for treatment outside the justice system, the Crime Task Force is moving toward adopting a plan that places treatment within the jail itself. While discussion during the development of the legislation emphasized the use of volunteer counseling assistance, this does not seem to be developing. Instead, the Fresno Comprehensive Alcoholism Program (CAP), which under an earlier director had been providing services at the Branch Jail prior to the *Sundance* decision, has been approached to provide counseling. The CAP administers both a social setting detoxification program (with 11 beds for men, 5 for women) and a 65-bed residential facility for long-term (six months to one year) recovery treatment. Both settings are open-door, located in the city of Fresno proper. The CAP's new director is prepared to work with clients from the Mall (some of the current clients already come from that area) and is willing to work more closely with the police; however, the director at this point considers the Branch Jail location out of the question for any CAP involvement for ethical reasons. She is not willing to treat drunks in the coercive jail setting.

Third, enormous logistical problems are involved. Presently the system is limited to arrest, booking, a six-hour accommodation in Fresno County Jail, and release. Few records are kept by police or jail, and presently prosecutorial, defense, and court personnel remain uninvolved. To begin the further processing of people now being detained, as well be required to obtain the necessary convictions for implementation of Penal Code Section 647d, would place a major strain on the entire criminal justice system. Police would be required to keep better records, store evidence, and appear in court to give testimony. Prosecutors would suddenly have to take on the cases of offenders they now ignore completely, as would defense attorneys. Courts would be filled with drunkenness offenders for arraignments, preliminary hearings, and trials; and the jail would bulge further at its seams with drunks kept days rather than hours in anticipation of hearings and trials. In this regard, we were told that the Sheriff's concern rises daily as his jail gains more inhabitants sentenced under the new, harsher drinking driver penalties. He is already over capacity and faces possible trouble with the state for failing to following guidelines on jail capacity.

Fourth, questions exist about the constitutionality of the Costa bill, particularly with selective implementation and with referrals going to an understaffed treatment program. Raised are problems of due process, equal protection, and cruel and unusual punishment. The County Alcoholism Director has already been told by Sundance himself—now a legal worker pushing for the protection of skid-row inhabitants' constitutional rights—that a legal challenge to the new law is highly likely. County judges have been refusing to hear drunk cases at all, and the County Alcoholism Director has serious doubts about the wisdom and efficacy of the law. He points out that his responsibilities for cleaning up the Mall (and any other areas) are restricted to dealing with "alcoholics." The Director is well aware of the problems involved in distinguishing "alcoholics" from others on the Mall. As matters stand right now, he is going to recommend *against* implementation of the county option before the Board of Supervisors.

This law is proving extremely difficult to implement. It is not at all clear that it will provide the basis for a remedy to the problems for which it was written. While the bill's originators and strongest advocates continue to express concern about its implementation, service providers in the alcoholism field are reluctant to support it, and its consequences for civil rights have alarmed several observers. The practical details of its implementation suggest the imposition of enormous burdens on already overloaded correctional and treatment services. Originally intended to remove public inebriates from central business district commercial areas, the bill now threatens to become a dead letter.

D. Recriminalization

The Fresno situation is instructive in two ways to students of alcohol problems. First, it invites a view of alcohol problems as components in the context of community problems, rather than as free-standing problems in their own right. Second, it provides some lessons for the planning of alcohol treatment and prevention programs.

The foregoing discussion makes clear that under closer examination the problem of "winos on the Mall" becomes a problem of community development

with an alcohol component. Broadly conceptualized, the community development problem becomes one of standards of living, of business concerns, of fiscal
problems and jail overcrowding, of class and race differences, and power dif-
ferentials. In this light, the Mall situation may be seen as a conflict between two
groups over urban land use. The "winos" are in fact part of a larger group of
low-income, lower-class individuals who either live in the area, and have as
much right to be there as anyone else, or are passing through in an itinerant life-
style.[20] The Mall's location near the jail, near transportation, and in the center
of town, where panhandling is easiest in a concentrated population, makes the
location attractive to itinerants. The merchants, developers, out-of-area shoppers,
and office users constitute the second group with claims on the Mall. As it turns
out, ostensibly the law protects the rights of both groups to be in the area. The
move by the merchant/developer/out-of-area group to use the law to force out
the poor/unattached/itinerant group under the general rubric of cleaning the area
of winos is an attempt that flies in the face of pre-Costa legislative trends and
creates enormous practical problems as well. The problem, then, remains what
to do about competing land uses in which alcohol is implicated.

    With the problem viewed from this perspective, one is led to ask more about
the presenting problems themselves: What, precisely, are the appearances and
behaviors (and the perceptions of them) that constitute "the problems?" How
closely tied in reality are these problems to the economic concerns of the merchant
group? The history of the Mall, and its recent developments, indicate that the
difficulty in attracting shoppers is due primarily to the growth of Shaw Avenue
as the prime retail area in Fresno. In fact, the Mall has begun to develop, but
more along the lines of office and government-convention uses than commercial
retail uses. The public inebriate population, while something of a drag on development, has not been an obstacle to it. Instead, where the market for new
development exists, the city has taken vigorous steps to resolve appearance
issues, such as in its agreement to tear down an old hotel near a new office
complex.

    From a social and humanitarian perspective, the problems of the public ine-
briate group are not well dealt with through the legislative means that have been
devised. The problems of adequate incomes, places to live and to socialize, jobs,
and health services are not solved by convicting someone of drunkenness three
times, then putting him or her into a minimally developed service program for
two months. The Chamber of Commerce committee, including representatives
from the city's treatment programs, has attempted to be conscientious in acknowledging these problems. The fact remains, however, that the extent of
services offered is likely to make very little dent in the problems. The "best"
that can be anticipated, lacking a commitment to provide food and shelter to all
residents requesting it, remains, tragically, the anachronism of general deter-
rence—in this case, pushing residents out of the county. On the contrary, the
attraction of more marginals who appear to take advantage of housing and other

support in the guise of treatment, however meager those may be, appears as the other, politically threatening result from the proposed innovation.

From a purely practical perspective, the problem of the inebriate group's presence is solving itself. The city's chief of Housing and Community Development observes that the group is considerably smaller now than it was several years ago and is decreasing.[21] If the current wave of development continues on its present course, the Mall's vitality is likely to increase to an admirably healthy level. The real problems of area decline are being experienced just to the west of the Mall, in "Chinatown." The city planner regards Chinatown, which is also a part of downtown Fresno, as the area that needs help now.

Even if the situation were static, the conflict over land use would still need to be resolved. Community planning activities, including housing, employment, and social services, would be required for a serious attack on the conflict. Legalistic means alone would be insufficient. This observation raises the importance of community planning for the reduction of community problems with alcohol components in them.

Traditionally, community planning activities have emphasized development activities, often at the expense of lower-status social and economic groups. In several cities, drunks provided rationales for moving large numbers of people out of the way of progress.[22] Alcohol problems in community planning tend to be seen as problems particularly of the lower-status groups. Alcoholism is abstracted out of the local setting as device for "cleaning up skid row," even though most skid-row dwellers are not particularly beset with alcohol problems and even though the "alcoholism" is often more a matter of drinking style than of personal problems with alcohol.

Professional planners and treatment providers by and large seem to be uncomfortable with this use of alcohol in community planning, as evidenced in interviews with the planner and the treatment providers in Fresno. Yet the politics of having to do the best they can within the use of alcohol issues as an exclusionary device for low-status groups.

An alternative approach adopts an inclusive rather than an exclusive approach. It would recognize the contradictions inherent in attempting to clean up the Mall through coercive treatment mechanisms. The inclusive approach would plan for services and settings for the public inebriates, and would involve working directly with them. Several examples of such efforts are available.[23] Examples of more comprehensive planning with low-status groups are also abundantly available.[24] The particular advantage of such an approach for Fresno would be that it would allow attention to the problems of Chinatown, also in danger of being treated in an exclusionary way that minimizes its connection to downtown Fresno. Within this broader planning framework, a number of alcohol-related issues can be dealt with (e.g., problem bars in Chinatown), and alcoholism treatment services, of the type provided by the CAP, can remain as services used only by voluntary clients.

Our observations and analysis stand in striking contrast to typical discussions of public inebriety and other social problems. Studies in the literature of skid row document the accumulation of marginal individuals into cities. These studies find individuals to be marginal in a variety of ways: marginal to the labor market and labor supply; marginal to production; and—some would argue—marginal to most cultural activities and even alienated from their abilities to take care of themselves. As Archard (1979) observes, however, typical studies of vagrants go little further than the enumeration of the most obvious aspect of the problem. As he puts it (1979:13):

> The predominant thrust of virtually all the literature on vagrancy separates the problem, and policy directed at it, from the wider society in which it is located. It denies the historical specificity of the problem, particularly the way in which the extent and form of vagrancy varies during different historical stages in the development of society. In addition most analyses avoid making any connections with the unequal distribution of political, economic and social power in our society as a relevant backcloth to understanding the issue and thereby acting towards it.

Rarely does the social science literature—and even more rarely does the governmental literature—address the context (economic factors, culture, psychology, historical specificity, and power relations) in which vagrancy appears and becomes problematic. The literature reflects a social scientific propensity toward microscopic focus and reformism. Missing have been broader perspectives on the social policy makers in a context of the human behavior as well as the broad array of historical, social, political, and economic factors intertwined in "social problems." It is in this regard that the present paper attempts to look beyond the "problems" of public drunks, beyond the individualistic humanism in their treatment, to a clearer understanding of the particularities of social policy and legalistic manneuvers.

V. CONCLUSION

This research supports the view that urban renewal activities and the related consignment of problem labels can be seen as the product of conflict between business interests and those who traditionally use the inner city areas, the socially marginal. In the case of Fresno, the threat of Mall or redevelopment failure contributes to pressures to place blame and to "do something." The Fresno case appears to be one in which business interests worked to define the situation of sluggish development of the Mall at least in part as an alcohol-related problem and successfully recruited public officials to concur and cooperate, first, in the definition and, second, in some action. The alcohol rubric provided ways of blaming problems of the Mall on deviant and marginal populations, and permitted the joint application of crime-oriented and treatment-oriented solutions, different though they may be, together and individually to deal with difficult conditions that are at base more a matter of urban structure than personal behavior. Both the Governor and the State Legislature also participated without much reservation in using alcohol as an instrument to attach problems and threats of failure to the city's weakest and most marginal groups.

So far the attempt to use the new law as the means for action has failed largely for two reasons: (1) even the punitive option requires fiscal expenditures which in this period governmental jursidictions are hard-pressed to supply, and (2) the protections created for public inebriates in the 1960s and nearly 1970s have left a residue of Constitutional protection which cannot easily be undone even though popular sentiment has shifted toward severe measures that equate treatment with punishment. The use of legal machinery to solve a land use dispute over social and economic claims proved to be a defective strategy in light of these factors.

ACKNOWLEDGMENTS

This is a revised version of a paper presented at the Annual Meeting, Society for the Study of Social Problems, San Francisco, California, September 1982. Preparation of this paper was supported in part by a National Alcohol Research Center Grant (AA-05595), a Graduate Research Training Grant on Alcohol Studies (AA-07240), and a Prevention Demonstration Research Grant (AA-05622), all from the National Institute on Alcohol Abuse and Alcoholism to the Alcohol Research Group.

The authors acknowledge the invaluable help of informants in Fresno and in other county and state offices. Our work gained additionally from the assistance of several colleauges who provided critical comments at several stages of our work. We especially thank James F. Mosher, Robin Room, and other associates at the Alcohol Research Group; Paul Takagi at the University of California, Berkeley; and members of the Sociology Colloquium at the University of California, Santa Cruz—who all made particular contributions to the analytical and editorial development of this paper.

NOTES

1. Inebriates do not constitute the only such group to which attention has been given. From New York to Oakland, there has been community conflict over hookers; zoning and housing battles rage over who rightfully belongs in the Columbia, Woodlawn, or Yerba Buena areas; and debates continue over the problem of transients in most California communities. Local crime commissions recently created in San Francisco, San Diego, and Oakland also influence such legislative moves. In some respects, our focus on *drunkenness* as the essential problem ingredient reflects somewhat arbitrary presumptions. As we note below, studies conducted on the actual role alcohol plays in skid row indicate that a minority of those arrested can be said to suffer from alcoholism.

2. See United States, President's Commission on Crime in the District of Columbia (1966), United States President's Commission on Law Enforcement and Administration of Justice (1967), and Cooperative Commission on the Study of Alcoholism (1967).

3. Penal Code 647(11) read at that time; "Every common drunkard...is a vagrant and is punishable by a fine not exceeding five hundred dollars ($500) or by imprisonment in the county

jail not exceeding six months or by both such fine and imprisonment'' (West, 1872, cited in Stevens, 1981 note 57).

4. Section 647(ff) reads as follows:

When a person has violated subdivision (f) of this section, a peace officer, if he is reasonably able to do so, shall place the person, or cause him to be placed, in civil protective custody. Such person shall be taken to a facility, designated pursuant to Section 5170 of the Welfare and Institutions Code, for the 72-hour treatment and evaluation of inebriates. A peace officer may place a person in civil protective custody with that kind and degree of force which would be lawful were he effecting an arrest for a misdemeanor without a warrant. No person who has been placed in civil protective custody shall thereafter be subject to any criminal prosecution or juvenile court proceeding based on the facts giving rise to such placement. This subdivision shall not apply to the following persons;

(1) Any person who is under the influence of any drug, or under the combined influence of intoxicating liquor and any drug.
(2) Any person who a peace officer has probable cause to believe has committed any felony, or who has committed any misdemeanor in addition to subdivsion (f) of this section.
(3)Any person who a peace officer in good faith believes will attempt escape or will be unreasonably difficult for medical personnel to control.

5. As decided by appellate courts, jurisdictions are not constrained to use *only* civil commitment. Nor does an individual suffer discrimination if the area in which the arrest takes place has no civil commitment facility at all. See *Johnson v. Muncipal Court*, Oakland Piedmont Judicial Dist. 70 Cal.App.3d 761(1977); *People v. Superior Court for County of Monterey*, 29 Cal.App.3d 397(1973); *People v. McNaught*, 31Cal.App.3d 605(1973).

6. The lack of enthusiasm on the part of treaters may reflect a more general disinterest among treatment personnel for the public inebriate (see Roizen and Weisner, n.d.). Additional evidence that public inebriates are being pushed *out* of the treatment slots elsewhere in California appears in work in progress at the Alcohol Research Group (see Speiglman and Weisner, 1982). Although Scrimgeour and Palmer (1976) noted that the health care system was not seeing the number of public inebriates formerly handled by the criminal justice system, they failed to conclude that a crisis was building. Kurtz and Regier foresaw this outcome in 1975, writing (p. 1437), "The need for peace keeping in the community will continue, and if alcohologists and their treatment programs fail to assume responsibility for keeping the peace by removing Skid Rowers from unwanted places, merchants and citizens will insist on a return to police control."

7. See *Los Angeles Times*, November 29, 1981, on the San Francisco Yerba Buena area; *Contra Costa Times*, November 11 and December 1 and 6, 1981, concerning Martinez; and *Santa Barbara News and Review*, February 12 and August 6, 1981. Addressing the issue of timing, we might reflection attention given to public inebriety as opposed to other social problems, alcoholism included. Between 1974 and 1980, what little growth there was in public concern over alcohol problems as major societal problems was in the area of "bums and derelicts on the streets," according to survey results analyzed by Cameron (1981).

8. In a recent statewide meeting on the problem of dealing with public inebriates, a representative of the police department of Los Angeles pointed out that since its local decriminalization move with the decision in the *Sundance* case more drunks die in a week on the streets than would have died in a year in jail, that the number of violent crimes increased by 70 percent, and that these social victims have become homicide victims as well. See Barrows (1979) and "Minutes," Public Inebriate Round Table Discussion (1979).

9. The Statute, "Disorderly conduct; Repetitive offenses; Alcohol treatment and recovery program," reads as follows:

Section 1. Section 647d is added to the Penal Code, to read:

647d. (a) Notwithstanding any other provision of law, subdivision (b) shall become operative in a county only if the board of supervisors adopts the provisions of subdivision (b) by ordinance after a finding that sufficient alcohol treatment and recovery facilities exist or will exist to accommodate the persons described in that subdivision.

(b) In any accusatory pleading charging a violation of subdivision (f) of Section 647, if the defendant has been previously convicted two or more times of a violation of subdivision (f) of Section 647 within the previous 12 months, each such previous conviction shall be charged in the accusatory pleading. If two or more of the previous convictions are found to be true by the jury, upon a jury trial, or by the court, upon a court trial, or are admitted by the defendant, the defendant shall be imprisoned in the county jail for a period of not less than 90 days. The trial court may grant probation or suspend the execution of sentence imposed upon the defendant if the court, as a condition of the probation or suspension, orders the defendant to spend 60 days in an alcohol treatment and recovery program in a facility which, as a minimum, meets the standards described in the guidelines for alcoholic recovery home programs issued by the Division of Alcohol Programs of the Department of Alcohol and Drug Abuse.

(c) The provisions of Section 4019 shall apply to the conditional attendance of an alcohol treatment and recovery program described in subdivision (b).

10. Literature assessing the ambiguities of the treatment-punishment interface raises many important issues. A central reference is Piven and Cloward (1971). See also references in Speiglman (1976) and Speiglman and Weisner (1982).

11. These include the following in which California output is first in the nation: alfalfa seed, almonds (shelled), cotton, figs, garlic, grapes, lettuce, melons, nectarines, onions, peaches, plums, pomegranates, safflower, and tomatoes (County Supervisors' Association of California, 1981, pp. 147-151).

12. For a particularly candid description of the problems experienced by city leaders in another country, see Stockton, California, Mayor's Urban Blight Committee (1955).

13. In this period a forerunner of one aspesct of the Costa bill was in use—a so-called hot card system. Under this arrangement, there was a card on file for each person with drunk arrests. According to the Sheriff, "It would accompany him to court. The first arrest, and the judge would kick him out. The second, and he would suspend the sentence. And the third, and he'd go to jail."

14. Evidence suggests that only some skid rowers and vagrants even drink and that far fewer could be considered suffering from alcoholism. See "Public Inebriety and Skidrow: Preliminary Formulations toward an Executive Initiative" (1980); Tidmarsh and Wood (1972); Wallace (1968); and San Francisco Blue Ribbon Committee on Public Inebriates (1981).

15. This information is from an analysis undertaken by Speiglman (1982) based on U.S. Census data and figures available through the Bureau of Criminal Statistics of the State of California. The only other data available were contained in a brief Sheriff's Department study in August 1981, which found that the 1572 males arrested for drunkenness were distributed as follows in a county registering a population which was, in 1980, about 37% Hispanic, 6% black, 3% Asian, 1% American Indian, and 53% other white:

Whites	24%
Hispanics	66%
Blacks	7%
Asians	0%
American Indians	2%

16. Monkkonen (1981) discusses implications of variation among jurisdictions' public drunkenness arrests.

17. The history of this category can be traced through works by Dana (1964), Roman and Trice (1967), Smart (1974), and Ward (1982).

18. The Downtown Association of Fresno includes the Mall but covers the entire downtown Fresno area as well.

19. In this regard at least one complaint was registered, in a letter from Leon Furra, Chairman of Los Angeles County's Commission on Alcoholism. The letter to Costa and other legislators noted that opposition to the bill had come from health and law enforcement services of Los Angeles as well as a unanimous Board of Supervisors who voted to decline to implement the statute. Furra wrote (December 15, 1981): "The County of Los Angeles Commission on Alcoholism was taken unawares by this legislation at our October meeting. It slipped by other very capable monitors of alcoholism legislation with whom we have spoken about the bill."

20. A *Fresno Bee* editorial (Feburary 9, 1982) addresses this very point, noting: "Downtown businessmen have long worried about the drunks who loiter on the malls and in Courthouse Park. This is, in a sense, their turf—the area near the county jail, where they now are warehoused overnight and released the next morning."

21. This trend, of course, may alter radically if the domestic economy continues its downslide. Reasonably it is a view of this future, as much as present reality, which drives officials to begin policy changes now.

22. In this regard, in addition to events in Fresno, note San Francisco's Yueba Buena area. Also, the redevelopment of the west end of Sacramento's downtown involved the destruction of old buildings and other facilities formerly serving as resources to its skid-row inhabitants. In 1960, as a result, arrests for drunkenness in Sacramento doubled from the level of one and two decades earlier as skid rowers, displaced from their previous habitat, suddenly became visible to business people and shoppers (Lockhart and Desrys, 1975).

23. In Albuquerque, New Mexico, Ken Wells of Alcohol Research and Training moved the ART's program site three times in two years to position the program in the midst of Albuquerque's skid row. From this base, the ART developed jobs, housing, and medical service agreements and worked closely with police to develop supports for skid-row dwellers who formerly had been routinely jailed and hospitalized in a revolving-door system. This program lasted from 1969 through 1972, as a pilot project later to be taken over by the local mental health center. The mental health center discontinued use of the skid row facility, requiring local inhabitants to seek services outside of the area at the mental health facility located a mile away. Jail/hospital placements soon increased to former levels.

In Ogden, Utah, the Weber County Mental Health Center developed a program on skid row that included residential and job services, working closely with local police and health services to minimize use of the jail/hospital settings in favor of the skid row settings. The program developed its own economy (including its own currency) within the surrounding community, created its own organization capable of receiving funds (Problems Anonymous Action Group, or PAAG), and through PAAG has become its own landlord. This program, begun about 1970, is still in operation.

In San Francisco, the Blue Ribbon Committee on Public Inebriates has recommended housing and social services for the 5000-plus group of marginal skid-row dwellers in the South of Market area who come in contact with police and the city's alcoholism services. The committee has taken the approach that provision of basic living supports must be seen as a first step to overcoming the expensive and frustrating use of the police/courts and hospital services of the county. The county's Alcohol Programs Director is currently developing a combination of private (corporate) and public agency support to establish these minimal living resources.

24. Perlman (1976) and Comerio (1982) at the University of California's College of Environmental Design provide two resources.

REFERENCES

American Medical Association and American Bar Association.
1969 "Joint policy statement."
Archard, Peter
1979 "Vagrancy—a literature review." In Tim Cook (ed.), Vagrancy, Some New Perspectives. London: Academic Press.
Barrows, David
1979 "Minutes, public inebriate roundtable discussion." (personal notes).
California, Department of Alcohol and Drug Programs.
1980 "Memo, 'public inebriate forum: issues and directions.' "
California, Department of Justice, Bureau of Criminal Statistics.
1979 "Criminal justice profile—1979: Fresno County." Sacramento: n.d.
California, Department of Justice, Bureau of Criminal Statistics.
1979 "Criminal justice profile—1979: statewide." Sacramento: n.d.
California, Department of Justice, Bureau of Criminal Statistics.
1980 "Criminal justice profile—1980: Fresno County." Sacramento: n.d.
California, Department of Justice, Bureau of Criminal Statistics.
1980 "Criminal justice profile—1980: statewide." Sacramento: n.d.
California, Penal Code, Section 647.
California, Penal Code, Section 849(b)(2).
Cameron, Tracy
1980 "Tables on alcohol-related problems, California 1950-1975." Berkeley: Social Research Group.
Cameron, Tracy
1981 "Alcoholism and alcohol problems: public opinion in California, 1974-1980, final report." Berkeley: Social Research Group, (February).
Chambliss, William J.
1964 "A sociological analysis of the law of vagrancy." Social Problems, Vol. 12: 67-77.
Collins, Gary
1980 "Tables on alcohol-related problems in California: an update of selected tables 1976-1979." Berkeley: Social Research Group, (August).
Comerio, Mary
1982 "Pruitt Igoe and other stories." Architectural Education, reprinted in Berkeley Graduate, (Feburary).
Contra Costa Times
1981 (November II)
Contra Costa Times
1981 (December 1).
Contra Costa Times
1981 (December 6).
Cooperative Commission on the Study of Alcoholism
1967 Alcohol Problems: a report to the nation. Prepared by T. F. A. Plaut. New York: Oxford University Press.
County Supervisors Association of California
1981 County Fact Book, n.d.
Daiber, Olga
1979 "Memo to 'county alcoholism administrators, state alcoholism advisory board, interested individuals' " concerning "Public inebriate roundtable discussion," (October 19).

168   RICHARD SPEIGLMAN and FRIEDNER D. WITTMAN

168   RICHARD SPEIGLMAN and FRIEDNER D. WITTMAN

168   RICHARD SPEIGLMAN and FRIEDNER D. WITTMAN

168   RICHARD SPEIGLMAN and FRIEDNER D. WITTMAN

Dana, A.
1964   "The constructive element of coercion," paper delivered before the Alcoholism Workshop, 17th Annual Meeting, Florida Psychological Association, (April) Noted in David A. Ward (1982).
Dean Charles W. "A program for the public inebriate," for the Task Force on Crime of the Fresno County Chamber of Commerce, n.d.
Driver v. Hinnant
1966   356 F.2d 761 (4th Cir.).
Easter v. District of Columbia
1966   361 F.2d 50 (D.C. Cir.)
Fresno Bee
1982   (February 9).
Fresno County and City Chamber of Commerce
1981   "Memo to board of directors from crime task force: recommended solutions to public inebriate problem," (March 18).
Fresno County and City Chamber of Commerce
1981   "News release: public inebriate legislation," (October 13).
Furra, Leon
1981   Letter to The Honorable Jim Costa, et al.; Commission on Alcoholism, County of Los Angeles, (December 15).
Galliher, John F.
1980   "The study of the social origins of criminal law: an inventory of research findings." In Steven Spitzer (ed.), Research in Law and Sociology, Vol. 3. Greenwich, Conn: JAI Press.
Griffen, P.J. and S. Lambert
1980   "Decriminalization of public drunkenness." In Yedi Israel, et. al, Research Advances in Alcohol and Drug Problems, Vol. 4. Pp. 395-440. New York: Plenum Press.
Hall, Jerome
1952   Theft, Law and Society. 2nd ed. Indianapolis: Bobbs-Merrill.
Johnson v. Municipal Court, Oakland Piedmont Judicial Dist.
1977   70 Cal.App.3d 761.
Kurtz, Norman and Marilyn Regier
1975   "The uniform alcoholism and intoxication act: the compromising process of social policy formation," Journal of Studies on Alcohol. Vol. 36, no. 11 1421-1441.
Lang, Lilsa
1981   "Public inebriates: beyond decriminalization." Alcoholism (Jan.-Feb.) 15-18.
LeRoy Powell v. State of Texas
1968   392 U.S. 514.
Lockhart, Diane and Michael Desrys
1975   "Detoxification center evaluation report: Sacramento County, June 1973-April 1974." Sacramento: Office of Alcohol Program Management.
Los Angeles Times
1981   (November 29).
"Minutes"
1979   Public Inebriate Roundtable Discussion, Sacramento, (October 30).
Molotch, Harvey
1976   "The city as a growth machine: toward a political economy of place." American Journal of Sociology, Vol. 82, no. 2.
Monkkonen, Eric H.
1981   "A disorderly people? urban order in the nineteenth and twentieth centuries." Journal of American History, Vol. 68, no. 3(December). 539-559.

National Conference of Commissioners on Uniform State Laws
    1971   "Uniform alcoholism and intoxication treatment act." Chicago.
People v. McNaught
    1973   31 Cal.Appl.3d 605.
People v. Superior Court for County of Monterey
    1973   29 Cal.App.3d 397.
Perlman, Janice
    1976   The Myth of Marginality: Urban Politics in Rio de Janeiro. Berkeley: University of California Press.
Piven, Frances Fox and Richard A. Cloward
    1971   Regulating the Poor: the Functions of Public Welfare. New York: Vintage Books.
"Public health services and the public inebriate."
    1975   Alcohol Health and Research World (Winter).
"Public inebriety and skidrow: preliminary formulations toward an executive initiative."
    1980   (August 12).
Reynolds, Jack
    1977   "Baseline data report for the public inebriate demonstration projects in Sacramento and Humboldt counties." San Diego: University Research Corporation, (December 28).
Robinson v. *California*
    1962   370 U.S. 660.
Roizen, Ron and Constance Weisner "Fragmentation in alcoholism treatment services: an exploratory analysis." Report to Department of Health, Education and Welfare; Contract No. ADM 281-77-0025. Berkeley: Social Research Group, nd.
Roman, Paul M. and H. M. Trice
    1967   "Alcoholism and problem drinking as social roles: the effects of constructive coercion." Paper delivered before the Annual Meeting, Society or the Study of Social Problems, (August).
Room, Robin
    1976   "Drunkenness and the law: comment on 'the uniform alcoholism and intoxication tratment act,' " Journal of Studies on Alcohol, Vol. 37, no. 1(January):113-144.
Room, Robin
    1978   "Governing images of alcohol and drug problems; the structure, sources and sequels of conceptualizations of intractable problems." Ph.D. dissertation. Berkeley: University of California.
San Francisco Blue Ribbon Committee on Public Inebriates
    1981   "Report to the mayor." (Octrober 22).
Santa Barbara News and Review
    1981   (February 12).
Santa Barbara News and Review
    1981   (August 6).
Scrimgeour, Gary L. and James A. Palmer
    1976   "Guidance manual for implementation of the uniform alcoholism and intoxication act." Bloomington, Indiana: Institute for Research in Public Safety.
Smart, Reginald G.
    1974   "Employed alcoholics treated voluntarily and under constructive coercion," Quarterly Journal of Studies on Alcohol Vol. 35: 196-209.
Speiglman, Richard
    1976   "Building the walls inside: medicine, corrections, and the state apparatus for repression." D. Crim. dissertation. Berkeley: University of California.
Speiglman, Richard
    1982   "Fresno drunk arrests." Berkeley: Alcohol Research Group.

Speiglman, Richard and Connie Weisner
1982   "Accommodation to coercion: changes in alcoholism treatment paradigms." Paper pre-
        pared for presentation at the Annual Meeting, Society for the Study of Social Problems,
        San Francisco, (September).
Speiglman, Richard, Connie Weisner, and James F. Mosher
1981   "Mental health, drugs, alcohol, and the criminal justice system; testimony to the Senate
        Committee on Health and Welfare, State of California." Berkeley: Alcohol Research
        Group, (December 14).
Stern, G.
1978   "The National Crime Commission's Report on public drunkenness—where do we go from
        here?" In Selected Papers from the 18th Annual Meeting of the North American Association
        of Alcoholism Programs. Washington, D.C.: NAAAP, 1967. Cited in Room.
Stevens, Greta B.
1981   "Decriminalization and beyond: public inebriety in Los Angeles county," Whittier Law
        Review, Vol. 3, no. 1.
Stockton, California, Mayor's Urban Blight Committee
1957   "Report on alcoholism" (June 24, 1955). Reprinted in California, State Alcoholic Re-
        habilitation Commission, Interim Report. Berkeley.
Sundance et al. v. Municipal Court of Los Angeles Judicial District et al.
1977   (December 5) Harry L. Hupp, Judge.
Tidmarsh, D. and S. M. Wood
1979   "Camberwell reception centre; summary of research findings and recommendations."
        London: Department of Health and Social Security, 1972. Cited in Archard.
United States, Congress
1968   "District of Columbia Alcoholic Rehabilitation Act of 1967," Public Law No. 90-452,
        82 Stat. 618.
United States, Congress
1970   "Comprehensive Alcohol Abuse and Alcoholism Prevention, Treatment, and Rehabili-
        tation Act," Public Law No. 91-616, 84 Stat. 1848.
United States, Congress.
1974   "Comprehensive Alcohol Abuse and Alcoholism Prevention, Treatment, and Rehabili-
        tation Act, Amendments of 1974," Public Law No. 93-282, 88 Stat. 125.
United States, Department of Commerce, Bureau of the Census
1971   "1970 census of population: general population characteristics, California," (October).
United States, Department of Commerce, Bureau of the Census
1981   "1980 census of population and housing: advance reports, California final population and
        housing unit counts," (March).
United States, Department of Commerce, Bureau of the Census
1981   "1980 census of population, race of population by states." Series PC 80-51-3. (July).
United States, National Institute on Alcohol Abuse and Alcoholism
1971   First Special Report to the United States Congress on Alcohol and Health from the Secretary
        of Health, Education and Welfare, DHEW publication number HSM 72-9099. Washington,
        D.C.: U.S. Gov't Printing Office.
United States, President's Commission on Crime in the District of Columbia, Report
1966   Washington, D.C.: U.S. Gov't. Printing Office.
United States, President's Commission on Law Enforcement and Administration of Justice
1967   Task Force Report: Drunkenness. Washington, D.C.: U.S. Gov't. Printing Office.
Wallace, Samuel E.
1968   "The road to skid row." Social Problems, Vol. 16: 92-105.
Ward, David A.
1982   "Introduction: use of legal and non-legal coercion in the prevention and treatment of drug
        abuse." Journal of Drug Issues Vol. 12, no. 1 (Winter).

PARENTS IN PRISON:
A COMPARATIVE ANALYSIS OF THE EFFECTS OF INCARCERATION ON THE FAMILIES OF MEN AND WOMEN

Linda Abram Koban

Women account for less than 8% of the population of lockups, jails and prisons nationally (U.C.R., 1979). This fact has affected the lives of women incarcerated in many important ways. In jails and lockups women may be exposed to sexual harassment and are frequently prevented from taking advantage of the limited recreational or educational program opportunities provided. The effect continues through sentencing. In 1975 the average number of programs in the men's prisons was 10; in female instituions it was 2.7 (Simon, 1975). Despite the fact that the disparity of job training opportunities was dramatically exposed in 1974, a national study of women's correction programs in 1977 indicated no progress or reform (Glick and Neto, 1977). A government report issued in 1980 concluded categorically that women offenders are not provided the facilities, training, and services equivalent to those provided male offenders (General Accounting Office, 1980).

Because there are fewer female institutions, when a woman is committed, she

Research in Law, Deviance and Social Control, Volume 5, pages 171-183
Copyright © 1983 by JAI Press, Inc.
All rights of reproduction in any form reserved
ISBN: 0-89232-334-5

is likely to be sent much farther from her community than her male counterpart. No state operates more than one female penal institution and eight states do not have prisons for women. This often means that women are sent great distances from home and therefore experience greater difficulty in keeping track of possessions and family.

An increasing number of studies (Ward and Kassebaum, 1965; Baunach, 1978) are documenting the incarcerated woman's traumatic adjustment to being deprived of her maternal role and her children's higher incidence of problems in school and contacts with law enforcement. In a study of inmate mothers at the California Institute for Women, Zalba (1964) focused on the obstacles to establishing effective community cooperation and coordination among agencies which deal with inmate mothers and their children. Interviews were conducted with 124 inmate mothers. A significant finding in the study was the inmate mothers' dissatisfaction with the care for children provided by others; a large percentage of the mothers (61%) indicated that they planned to reunite with their children immediately after release or after an adjustment period. However, 47% of the children had not seen their mother since her incarceration, and 32% of those children who had lived with their mother prior to her incarceration had not visited her at the institution. The authors felt that in light of the minimal contact throughout incarceration, the women may have been fostering unrealistic expectations about reuniting with their children. This behavior, the authors said, could lead to unforeseeable difficulties in coping and adjustment and could seriously jeopardize the mothers' rehabilitation potential while on parole (Zalba, 1964:119).

Subsequent studies reinforced the conclusion that the maternal role was closely tied to self-esteem and that "recognition and enhancement of the maternal role in correctional policies would probably tend to promote rehabilitation as well as contribute to family solidarity (Bonfanti et al., 1974; Lundberg et al., 1975). Though Lundberg et al. found that maintaining the mother-child relationship during incarceration played a significant role in minimizing the impact of the separation, the authors described institutional obstacles to the maintenance of contact. They recommended investigation of alternatives to the current system such as nursery care within the prison.

McGowan and Blumenthal (1978) conducted a study designed to document the special problems confronting inmate mothers and their children. Data from 74 facilities and 9379 confined women were obtained from a national mail survey. The authors suggested that this represented slightly more than one-half of all incarcerated women in any given day. The findings indicated that about two-thirds of the sampled women were mothers and that about three-fourths of the children had lived with their mothers prior to her arrest. About 85% of the inmate mothers maintained some contact with their children during incarceration, and about 78.9% of the inmate mothers reported that they planned to live with their children after release. More than half of the mothers expressed favorable feelings about their child's present living situation, but one-third noted serious concerns.

Mothers were generally more satisfied if children lived with grandparents than with anyone else including the father or other relatives. Most concern was expressed when children were in foster care. The authors noted generally that the inmate mothers suffered anguish and anxiety about the conditions under which the children were living and about their future ability to reestablish an intimate and stable relationship with them. They concluded (1978:71) that "there is a strong likelihood that the incarceration of a mother is related to long-term severance of the family unit."

This study of female offenders and their families conducted in Kentucky started with the assumptions that being stripped of the role of mother was one of the most traumatic factors in a woman's adjustment to institutionalization and that a female inmate's failure to maintain contact with her children would negatively affect her chances for rehabilitation and reunification with her family.[1] It addressed the issue of whether women were uniquely affected by the disruption of the family or whether incarcerated men and their children suffered equally.

There are two women's facilities in Kentucky: Kentucky Correctional Institute for Women (KCIW), a medium-security institution with an average population of 95, and Daniel Boone Career Development Center (Boone), a minimum-security facility with an average population of 35. Both prisons are in isolated rural settings. Neither is served by public transportation. All of the women in the Kentucky prison system were contacted, and 85% agreed to be interviewed. An equal number of men were selected from two men's prisons comparable to the women's in location and security classification. An attempt was made to control male participants for their comparability to the female population in offense, age, race and length of time served.

Several of the questions posed to men and women directly addressed their satisfaction with the children's placement and their feelings about whether the children were happy and well cared for. The majority of the questions focused on more objective indicators of the stability of the relationship, such as the prisoner's marital status; the placement of children prior to the parent's arrest and incarceration; the frequency of visits by children; the frequency of contact with the caretaker; and the inmate's plan to reunite with his/her family upon release. In assessing the effect of external factors on the disruption of inmate families we collected information on the geographic distance between the incarcerated parent and his/her children, and on institutional, family, and social agency obstacles to visitation and telephone, or mail contact.

Women in prison in Kentucky, at a median age of 29, were older than the average male inmate, who was 25. A relatively small percentage of both men and women reported intact marriages. More women than men had been married, but more men were married during incarceration (see Table 1 below).

It is not surprising in light of these differences in age and marital status that women inmates were more likely to be parents and to have more children than male inmates. Seventy-six percent of the women and 56% of the men surveyed

Table 1.   Marital Status by Prisoners' Sex (percentages)

	Sex	
Marital Status	*Female*	*Male*
Single	25.3	47.7
Married	16.8	21.6
Divorced	323.6	23.5
Separated	13.7	6.3
Widowed	11.6	0.9
(Total n)	(95)	(111)

were parents. The female residents had an average of 2.1 children; the males, an average of 1.3 children.

A far greater number of female inmates lived with their children prior to arrest and incarceration than did male inmates. This is consistent with recent findings by Baunach (1978) and McGowan and Blumenthal (1978) that most women lived with their children prior to sentencing (see Table 2).

The majority of male prisoners reported that their children had lived with their mothers prior to the resident's sentencing.

Responses about the current placement of children revealed a large discrepancy between men and women (see Table 3). The men's children were more likely to be with the child's mother, whereas women were more likely to resort to placements in and beyond the extended family, with roughly a third of their children going to the father, a third to a grandparent and a third to friends, relatives or foster placements.

Four women reported having children in foster homes. Three out of the four expressed despair and frustration in the arrangements.

- One resident stated that originally her child was with the resident's sister. She spoke with the child three or four times a month and was visited by

Table 2.   Preincarceration Placement of Children by
Prisoners' Sex (percentages)

	Sex	
Preincarceration Placement	*Female*	*Male*
With resident	74.3	24.5
With parent	7.1	60.7
Other	18.6	14.8
(Total n)	(70)	(61)

Table 3. Current Placement of Children by
Prisoner's Sex (percentages)

	Sex	
Current Placement	*Female*	*Male*
With parent	28.6	87.1
With grandparent	34.3	8.1
Other	37.1	4.8
(Total n)	(70)	(62)

her twice a month. The resident was not informed for a week and a half that the child had been placed in a foster home. Now she has no contact at all with the child or the foster parents.

- One resident whose teenage daughter was placed in a foster home with five other foster children accused the foster parents, who never had children of their own, of doing it for the money. She said her daughter is 'doing drugs and not going to school regularly.' The foster parents had the phone number changed so that she could not call.

- A resident whose child is in a foster placement stated that she did not know the phone number or address of the home. The child's grandmother visited him in the home and told the resident that the foster parents wanted to adopt him. The resident said she gave up custody involuntarily and hoped to be reunited with the child.

These limited data tend to support the conclusion that the imprisonment of a woman is more disruptive to her family than the incarceration of a man. Presumably, 61% of the men's children remained with their mother in an environment basically unaffected by incarceration, whereas only 26% of the women's children had the chance to remain in a stable household with a continuous, primary caretaker.

Seventy-two percent of the men and 62% of the women claimed responsibility for the placement decision. However, women reacted positively to the placement only 38% of the time, whereas 63% of the men expressed satisfaction. This is consistent with the pattern already noted. In the case of most men's children, the change brought about by a parent's incarceration was less drastic. The men's children usually remained with their mother. Only 31% of the men as compared to 58% of the women retained custody. This reluctance to relinquish legal custody is indicative of the conflict experienced by women due to separation from their children. In contrast, the men's willingness to surrender custody could be predicted from their relative failure to assume principal responsibility prior to incarceration. These men may not suffer the reduction in rehabilitation potential

Table 4.   Children's Happiness by Prisoners' Sex (percentages)

Believe That	Sex	
Children Are Happy	Female	Male
Yes	72.7	92.9
No	27.3	7.1
(Total n)	(66)	(56)

which was linked in earlier studies with the conflict and anxiety experienced by female offenders over their parental roles.

A significantly greater percentage of men than women thought that their children were happy, although a large number of women vouched for their children's well-being (see Table 4).

Women tended to think their children were happiest when they were with a grandparent; men thought their children were happiest with the child's mother.

- One resident whose child was with her sister said that the child was fed and clothed but expressed concern that her sister took drugs and was giving them to the child. She said her sister spent the child's public assistance checks on drugs.
- A resident whose child is with her brother stated that she lost weight because her sister-in-law is Muslim and is on a special diet.
- One resident who voiced the sentiments of many inmate mothers stated simply that she felt her children weren't happy because they had never been away from her.

Interviews with male and female residents in Kentucky showed that a sizeable percentage of men were more likely to have telephone or mail contact with their children or caretakers on a weekly basis. More women were in contact once a month. Nearly half of the men but only 21% of the women had contact less than once a month. There was no drop-off in caretaker contact with men or women at the end of one year; therefore, the disadvantage to women regarding consistent contact with caretakers remained constant over the course of incarceration. When asked if they had problems getting through to their children, 25% of the women said they frequently had problems but only 3% of the men had frequent problems. Some women stated during the interview that the caretakers discouraged the residents from having contact with the children. This was most often cited as a problem when the child was placed with an ex-spouse or a former spouse's family.

- One resident reported: 'Their father took the kids to try to hurt me. He's moved again and wouldn't communicate about the kids. He took them because he didn't want to pay child support. My husband's parents never even get to see the children now. My oldest daughter was in ballet and the Brownies and had to change to another school. My mother-in-law says this school is condemned and the neighborhood is bad.'

In addition to encountering obstacles to maintaining contact generated by relationships with caretakers, there were problems attributable to facility policies. Residents cannot directly receive calls, and messages are often not relayed for weeks.

- One resident's 'in-laws found my husband with another woman and took the child away. I didn't hear about it until the day before my parole hearing so I had no plans to present at the hearing.'
- A resident who was placed on 'restriction' over the Christmas holidays wasn't allowed to call her daughter. The child's grandmother told the resident that her daughter had cried all day. The resident said, 'I'm afraid she'll think that I don't care.'

At KCIW, outgoing phone calls are strictly allocated and range from zero (resident in segregation) to three a week (residents in upper levels).[2] They are limited to between 6:00 P.M. and 9:00 P.M. Many women stated that their young children were asleep by the time they could get to the phone. Others lived so far from the prison that the grandparent or relative caring for the child could not afford to accept a collect call. Caretakers in rural areas of the state often did not have telephones.

- One resident at KCIW claimed that she received legal notice of a hearing in which her ex-husband was going to attempt to gain custody of their child. This resident could not reach her lawyer during the evening hours allotted for phone calls, so she pleaded with her caseworker to call the lawyer's office during the day and request that he represent her at the hearing. The caseworker promised to call the lawyer, but the following week after the hearing date had passed she apologized for 'forgetting.'

When asked if they were consulted if there was some problem or emergency with the children, 72% of the women expected to be consulted frequently or occasionally. Only 52% of the men expected to participate in decision making. This reflects the fact that more men were likely to have relinquished their role as principal decision maker prior to incarceration and indicates another way in which institutionalization places disproportionate pressure on women.

During incarceration, the level of an inmate's contact with and involvement in the life of his/her child is presumably affected by their prior relationship but

Table 5.   Frequency of Visits by
Prisoners' Sex (percentages)

	Sex	
Frequency of Visits	*Female*	*Male*
Sometimes	66.2	45.9
Never	33.8	54.1
(Total n)	(68)	(61)

is demonstrably dependent on the quality of the resident's relationship with the caretaker and is complicated by facility policies. These conclusions are consistent with Zalba's (1964) assertion that some caretakers use the area of contact with the mothers as a means of expressing anger, hostility or disapproval of the mother's behavior. In contrast most male inmates' children were with their mothers before and after their father's incarceration. The relationship between prisoner and caretaker is established, as is the relationship between child and caretaker.

In contrast, the female resident's children could be with their father, their grandparent, placed with friends or relatives, or in foster homes. Frequently, women are not held in county jails and find themselves transferred directly, and without notice, from an arraignment to prison. Placement arrangements are, therefore, likely to be made hurriedly contributing to a difficult adjustment for the child and reduced understanding between the mother and the caretaker.

More women were visited by their children at least one time (see Table 5). However, men who were visited saw their children more often than women did, and while the frequency of visits to women decreased after one year it remained stable for men. Seventy percent of men's children were brought to the facility by their mothers, whereas only 19% of the women's children were brought by their fathers (see Table 6).

As has been seen repeatedly, women were disadvantaged by their dependency on an extended network of relatives, friends and social agencies for contact with their children while men could rely on the child's mother. This conclusion is supported by the responses of resident parents who were never visited by their children: 87% of the men claimed it was their decision that the children not come, whereas 54% of the women attributed the failure of their children to visit to the caretaker.

Internal facility visitation policies favored women, permitting them to spend more time with their children during visits (see Table 7). Lengthier visits for women are a result of parenting programs established at both of the women's prisons in Kentucky. These programs combine classroom instruction in parenting

Table 6. Who Brings the Children by Sex (percentages)

	Sex	
Who Brings the Children?	*Female*	*Male*
Parent	19.1	70.0
Grandparents	21.3	20.0
Friend or relative	31.9	6.7
Social worker	6.4	0
Other	21.3	3.3
(Total n)	(47)	(30)

with monthly extended visits with children—a six-hour Saturday visit at the medium-security prison and an overnight weekend visit at the minimum-security facility.

Most participants were enthusiastic about the program. Though extended visits were subject to cancellation because of bad weather or staff shortages, the main obstacle according to the women and the staff was arranging for transportation for the children. The women were imprisoned an average of 150 miles from their homes and were dependent on the caretaker bringing the child.[3] Some women indicated that often the caretakers were too old to drive long distances, worked on weekends, or could not afford a long trip with overnight accommodations. Several indicated that they had been promised by a child-care worker or a relative that transportation could be arranged for the children to visit, but at the last minute they were disappointed. Women at both facilities expressed anxiety about the regimentation of the visits themselves.

• A Boone resident said that, 'The visits are hard. The kids have to sit in one spot, even outside. We volunteered to make playground items, but they wouldn't let us.'

A furlough program at Boone allows eligible residents to return home for several days, every 90 days. Women participating in this program expressed

Table 7. Length of Visit by Prisoners' Sex (percentages)

	Sex	
Length of Visit	*Female*	*Male*
1 hour or less	14.0	29.0
Between 1 and 2 hours	25.6	48.4
Over 2 hours	60.4	22.6
(Total n)	(45)	(31)

Table 8.   Plan to Reunite by Prisoners' Sex (percentages)

Plan to Reunite with Children	Sex	
	Female	Male
Yes, immediately	51.5	47.4
Yes, after time	31.8	21.0
No	16.7	31.6
(Total n)	(66)	(57)

extreme satisfaction at the opportunity to relate to their children in a normal environment, free of restrictions imposed by staff and other inmates. The factors which most often determined the frequency of visits were the preincarceration placement of the child (if the child lived with the resident prior to incarceration, he/she was more likely to visit) and the distance from the facility, with increasing mileage having an inverse relation to frequency of visits.

The remote location of the women's prisons in Kentucky, as in most states, is a critical factor in undermining the parent-child relationship even in the presence of closer preincarceration ties and institutional policies allowing for extended visits.

We asked parents about their postrelease plans, whether they expected to reunite with their children, and if so, when. The most relevant factors in predicting whether a resident planned to reunite were the sex of the resident (more men were likely not to reunite or to reunite after a longer time); whether the resident was employed at the time of arrest; the length of time the resident had been incarcerated; the frequency of visits; and the number of children (the fewer the children, the more likely the family is to reunite). The most significant individual factor determining reuniting was the preimprisonment placement of the child. The parent that lived with his/her child prior to incarceration was more likely to reunite with the child. There was a slight increased probability that single women were more likely to reunite with their children than either married women or men.

The percentages of men and women who said they planned to reunite with their children immediately were similar (see Table 8). About 83.3% of the women stated that they planned to reunite eventually, a figure comparable to McGowan and Blumenthal's (1978) finding that 78.9% of inmate mothers surveyed planned to live with their children after release. McGown and Blumenthal interpreted these reponses as indicating that inmate mothers feel responsible for their children. However 68.4% of the men interviewed indicated that they planned to reunite with their children. Though less men than women planned to reunite, as would be expected from earlier data, the figure still seems inflated since only

Table 9. Siblings Currently Placed Together
by Prisoners' Sex (percentages)

	Sex	
Placement of Siblings	Female	Male
Together	66.0	83.3
(Total n)	(50)	(36)

24.5% of the men lived with their children prior to incarceration. Clearly, a substantial percentage of these men have unrealistic expectations about their future living arrangements.

Women spoke of reuniting, after an adjustment period when "I get myself together," or after "I get a job and an apartment." There was a noticeable absence of concrete details in female residents' discussions of their future plans.

Goffman (1961) suggested that total institutions, like prisons, separate persons from the larger world and from their usual status positions. In this sense, imprisoned mothers are "disculturated," or made incapable of engaging in aspects of their lives associated with their responsibilities as mothers. This disculturation could have serious psychological effects on incarcerated mothers, causing them to lose confidence in their ability to accept responsibility for their children or to fear they will lose their children's love. Though men are not immune from this form of alienation, the data suggest that the parental status position did not occupy as central a place in their lives prior to incarceration as it did in the lives of the female offenders surveyed. In this respect, women are penalized for their maternal indentification. Men and women may have equally unrealistic expectations about future family life, but women have a greater emotional investment in the outcome and are more vulnerable.

Despite their need and their determination to reunite, women are also more likely to face serious problems upon release. The women in Kentucky prisons were better educated but lower paid than the men in the system. The vocational training they received was inferior to training provided for men. There was no employment placement officer at either women's institution and only one transitional community program to alleviate the trauma of reentry into society.

Women are in less frequent contact with their children, a factor that tends to increase the difficulty in their adjusting to living together again. Baunach (1978) has documented the increase in problems at school and contacts with law enforcement among children of incarcerated mothers. Female offenders return more often to a splintered family than do men because the primary caretaker has changed and sibling groups have been divided (see Table 9).

Two conclusions can be drawn from the information collected in Kentucky. First, female offenders had closer relationships with their children prior to their incarceration. This is evidenced by the fact that most women were living with their children and most men were not; that most women retained legal custody; that fewer women than men made the decision not to have their children visit; that women are more likely to be visited at least once; and that more women planned to reunite with their children after release.

The second conclusion is that women's relationships with their children and the family structure are more stressed by incarceration than are men's families. This is shown by the fact that men's children usually remain with their mothers; that men think their children are happier; that more men than women have frequent contact with their children; that fewer men have problems getting through to their children; that men can depend on the child's mother to bring the children for a visit; that men's children are less often separated from their siblings; and that men are usually not incarcerated as far from their home communities as women are.

The disproportionate concern about women in prison and their families is valid because the evidence suggests that the cost to the female inmate's family and to society is greater. The movement in Kentucky and across the country to institute programs for extended visitation, furloughs and more community-based treatment centers is rational and necessary. Women show greater commitment to and responsibility for their families prior to institutionalization. This commitment does not diminish with incarceration, as was illustrated here and in previous studies. But men have the advantage of an established support system for the family they leave behind. Despite the appearance of liberal parenting programming in Kentucky, women are as clearly discriminated against in their attempt to maintain family contact while in prison as they are by inadequate vocational training, employment counseling and community reentry resources.

NOTES

1. Women in Kentucky prisons are demographically comparable to female offenders surveyed in national studies. Glick and Neto (1977) surveyed women in 14 states and found the median age of a convicted female felon was 27 and most were under 30. In Kentucky the median age of an incarcerated female was 29.4 years. The Glick and Neto study showed that 19.9% of female offenders were married during incarceration; in Kentucky 16.8% were married. Ninety-three percent of women in Kentucky had worked in the past, and 42% were working at time of arrest. In the national study 91.5% of the women had employment histories and 45.4% were working when arrested. The number of mothers in Kentucky prisons and the percentage of mothers living with their children in Kentucky was remarkably similar to national results. In the national sample 74.4% of female offenders were mothers and 74.4% of the mothers lived with their children prior to arrest. In Kentucky 75.5% of women residents were mothers and 71.4% lived with their children before they were incarcerated.

2. KCIW operates on a level system. New admissions enter the facilities with no privileges and can accumulate privileges by working their way up through five levels.

3. Men were an average of 125 miles from home.

REFERENCES

Baunach, P.
  1978 The Separating of Inmate Mothers from their children. Washington, D.C.: National Institute of Law Enforcement and Criminal Justice (Grant No. 8-0754-5).
Bonfanti, M.A., S.S. Felder, M.L. Vincent and N.J. Vincent
  1974 "Enactment and perception of maternal role of incarcerated mothers." Unpublished paper. Baton Rouge: Louisiana State University.
General Accounting Office
  1980 Women in Prison: Inequitable Treatment Requires Treatment. Washington, D.C.
Glick, R. and V. Neto
  1977 National Study of Women's Correctional Programs. Washington, D.C.: National Institute of Law Enforcement and Criminal Justice.
Goffman, E.
  1961 Asylums. Chicago. Aldine.
Lundberg, D., A. Skeckley and T. Voelkor
  1975 "An exploration of the feelings and attitudes of women separated from their children due to incarceration." Unpublished paper. Portland: Portland University.
McGowan, B.G. and K.C. Blumenthal
  1978 Why Punish Children? Washington, D.C.: National Council on Crime and Delinquency.
Simon, R.
  1975 Women and Crime. Washington, D.C.: National Institute of Mental Health, Center for Crime and Delinquency
Uniform Crime Reports
  1979 "Crime in the United States." Washington, D.C.: U.S. Department of Justice, Federal Bureau of Investigation (Released 9/24/80).
Ward, D. and G. Kassebaum
  1965 Women's Prisons. Chicago: Aldine.
Zalba, S.
  1964 Women Prisoners and Their Families. Sacramento: California Department of Social Welfare and Department of Corrections.

PART III

ISSUES IN LAW, DEVIANCE AND SOCIAL THEORY

RETHINKING DEVIANCE:

TOWARD A SOCIOLOGY OF CENSURES

Colin Sumner

I. INTRODUCTION

Students still ask "Whatever happened to the theoretical debate about deviance in the early seventies?" (see Hirst, 1975; Taylor et al., 1973, 1975; Pearson, 1975; and Sumner, 1976). It is a very good question since recent Marxist work in this area is clearly outside the old deviancy theory framework, yet there has been little attempt in those studies to reconceptualize "deviant behavior" (e.g. Thompson, 1975; Glasgow Media Group, 1976; Hall et al., 1978; Corrigan, 1979; see also Sumner, 1981a). Perhaps the revulsion against theoretics and theoretical wrangling, the return of empirical research, the new popularity of historical work and the general air of hard-nosed realism in the late 1970s and early 1980s have all contributed to the demise of theoretical dynamics in this field. Deviance is certainly no longer at the forefront of debates in sociology:

Research in Law, Deviance and Social Control, Volume 5, pages 187-204
Copyright © 1983 by JAI Press, Inc.
All rights of reproduction in any form reserved
ISBN: 0-89232-334-5

some Leninist comrades would see it as one of those pretheoretical discourses that are only of value in teaching first year undergraduates.

Of course, Marxist scholarship is little concerned to rescue the sociology of deviance and has its own imperatives. It could hardly be expected to doff its forelock to the sociology of deviance. Marxists studying crime and morality will today rarely be in criminology centers or even conceive of their work as sociology or criminology. Their theoretical and political concerns go beyond disciplinary insularity and liberal reformism.

On the other hand, it has never been a Marxist view that better concepts will emerge if researchers simply immerse themselves in historiography. Facts about the past are no better than contemporary ones at speaking for themselves. And good historians are more aware of this than ever. Theory must always be integral to Marxist analysis. Of course, this does not mean that we want to return to that impossibly idealist search for a general theory applicable to all times and places. In Marxism, concepts are mostly historically specific and there are only a few universal principles of approach. However, there are general concepts in Marxist theory and there is an abiding concern to supersede alternative or past interpretations. This essay is thus seen as a minor contribution to the development of a Marxian conception of what used to be called deviance. It is premised on the view that empirical research, however radical its concerns, is not enough on its own and that good concepts are vital in discovering, shaping and reflecting good information.

In trying to develop my earlier observations on the subject of Marxism and deviancy theory (see Sumner, 1976, 1981a, 1982), I shall argue that, in modern Marxist work, the categories of deviance are treated as social censures, which generally speaking can only be said to have a loose and selective proximity to their supposed empirical referents. Categories such as militants, muggers, extremists, criminals, thieves, prostitutes, perverts, nutters, slags, bastards, villains, freaks, rioters, loonies and scroungers (believe it or not) are not adequate behavioral categories. Apart from being plainly culturally and historically specific, they can be seen as negative notions within dominant ideological formations. They make no sense at all outside the sectional ideologies which constitute them and the economic, political and cultural contexts which generate, sustain and precipitate their use. In short, deviance is not best defined as a set of distinguishable behaviors offending collective norms but as a series of flexible ideological terms of abuse or disapproval which are used with varying regularity and openness in the practical networks of domination. Censures are key features of the discourses of the dominant—weapons employed in the policing of what they specify as deviance and dissent. Although often presented in legal, technical or universal forms (i.e., as legitimate descriptions), they are organized slanders in what is essentially a political or moral conflict. Clearly, then, it is vital to study the institutional sanctification, development and use of these censures in the networks of state "tutelage" (Donzelot, 1979) and "discipline" (Foucault, 1977), their practical application in particular cases by the state's agencies of moral and political hygiene, and, of course, the kinds of social practice to which the censures are applied. But first let us specify the problems with the concept of deviance and existing efforts to overhaul it.

II. THE CONCEPT OF DEVIANCE IN SOCIOLOGY

Although ultimately rooted in the Durkheimian dream of a social order with fully matching normative consensus and division of labor, the concept of deviant behavior is first and most plainly manifested in Parson's work (see, e.g., 1951). Here deviance was non-conformity with others' expectations in a given social system. Plainly, such a notion does not *of itself* negatively portray the act of deviation nor demand a focus on deviant action. Logically, it does not even require us to think of deviance as an action; it surely posits, at root, that deviance is an outcome of a relation between people in conflict. Yet the subsequent history of deviancy sociology has on the whole tended to focus on "deviant behavior" as though it was a coherent behavioral category, and to portray it negatively. Nonconformity soon became "failure to conform" (Bredemeier and Stephenson, 1970:123), and the search was on for the social strains, personality weaknesses and interactional milieus which supposedly induced that "failure" and the "careers" of "failure" found in the urban and cultural ghettoes of the new welfare states. The "expectations" of the dominant "culture," which in the original formulation are defined as vital constituents of social deviance, were taken for granted (as a consensual natural evolution) and forgotten: could they also be accounted for as the unfortunate outcomes of "social strain" or of the deficiencies of conscience in opinion leaders, or of the "moral" (sic) careers of politican-legislators? Deviancy sociology soon became the sociology of deviant behavior, and even today it has still not become a sociology of dominant culture. Its various theoretical possibilities have been very partially exploited, which naturally suggests that ideology has played its customary part.

The sociology of deviant behavior was framed in a cybernetic social theory and helped in a small way to legitimize the postwar state's development of forms of psychotherapy and intervention in the working-class family. To this extent it is an objectionable analytic framework. Following Habermas (1971), we can see it as a clear example of the modern technocratic rationality—as instrumentalist reason which detaches action from its moral and political context and reframes it within the behavioristic categories and systems analysis of supposedly scientific discourse:

> The personalization of what is public is thus the cement in the cracks of a relatively well-integrated society, which forces suspended conflicts into areas of social psychology. There they are absorbed in categories of deviant behavior: as private conflicts, illness and crime. These containers now appear to be overflowing (Habermas, 1971:42-43).

Once divorced from the normative and political conjuncture that give it meaning "deviant behavior" was ready as an apparently neutral object of knowledge to serve in the power-laden practices of policing, tutelage and discipline as an agency in the process of domination: "Today the psychotechnic manipulation of behaviour can already liquidate the old fashioned detour through norms" (Habermas, 1971:118). The deviant was now identifiable directly, as an "inadequate," "undersocialized," or "inappropriately" socialized cultural rebel: properly "fitted up" after an identification parade where only the police were present, the rogues gallery of deviance was constructed in a way that took some knocking down. The fact that the concept of deviant behavior is still used by radicals today, if only for the lack of a better concept, is testimony to its endurance as well as its significance for the postwar age. It is my persuasion that the concept is so contestable in itself and so dangerous in its consequences that it should be abandoned once and for all—along with all the theoretical baggage that goes with it. As the Thatcher and Reagan regimes mark the demise of the postwar age of "welfare consensus" (the age of the "end of ideology" and the "one nation"), we should move into line and finally *unequivocally* abandon the problematic of deviant behavior which this period engendered.

Of course, it is not new to question behavioristic concepts of immorality. Since Durkheim's day, some leading students of crime have rejected the reliance on the moral-political categories of crime and deviance to deliver a behavioral explicandum. Sometimes, as in Sellin's work, the emphasis was on the normative conflict in society which prevented the presentation of such reliance as a neutral scientific activity: "The unqualified acceptance of the legal definitions as the basic units or elements of criminological inquiry violates a fundamental criterion of science" (Sellin, 1938:23). And, sometimes, attention was simply drawn to the normative character of the object of enquiry: "In this respect crime is like all other social phenomena, and the possibility of criminal behaviour is similar to the possibility of a science of any other behavior. Social science has no stable unit, as it deals with phenomena involving group evaluations" (Sutherland and Cressey, 1974:20).

The simple observation that what is labeled crime and deviance reflects the political economy and culture of a society is also antithetical to treating deviance as behavior. Anthropologists (see Schapera, 1972; Robertson and Taylor, 1973) and internationalist scholars have not been silent on this. Lopez-Rey, for example, argues that criminology has relied too much on the statistics of government officials and has thus focused on "juvenile delinquent behavior" at the expense of the majority of crimes (including the most serious ones such as genocide). This recalls Paul Rock's observation that "the erratic history of criminology has been marked by the organised neglect of many, if not most, of the phenomena that constitute crime" (1977:392). Lopez-Rey complains that:

> Criminology still persists in styling itself a natural or naturalistic science by borrowing more and more concepts, methods and techniques from natural sciences. This ignores the fact that

natural science is unable to provide the socio-political approach required by the extent of crime. . .

Criminologists have frequently overlooked the fact that the explanation of conventional crime, even if successful, would never be valid for the whole of crime, the greater proportion of which is conveniently ignored not only by most of them but also by the vast majority of governments and agencies as well as political parties and politicians in developed and developing countries (Lopez-Rey, 1971:xii).

Consequently, he says, criminology has mistaken the essential character of its central topic: "Contemporary criminology regards crime as socio-economic or a psycho-psychiatric entity or a combination of both. *Actually, it is primarily a socio-political concept and only secondarily a causal event*" (Lopez-Rey, 1970:234; my emphasis). Foreshadowing my own argument, he implores us to see criminology as the study of the "socio-political concepts" and as part of the struggle for justice. Naturally, if crime is returned to its normative-political home, the liberal or radical politics that flow from this must be to reform or revolutionize the "socio-political concepts" and the institutions that apply them. Such conclusions seem virtually inevitable when we look at crime in the Third World (see Sumner, 1982). Mushanga illustrates my proposition well when he reverses normal usage and writes that the social censures of crime and deviance are selective, "interested" and often insulting moral-political categories: "Mass murders, massacres, genocide and general brutality and terrorism against civilians by those in power may be due to the fact that power is in the hands of vandals, hooligans, nitwits and anomic delinquents" (1976:18). But, it is not necessary to study the Third World to arrive at the harsh reality of the matter. Gordon Trasler, a leading British psychologist in the area of crime, stated in 1973 that:

It is not immediately obvious that criminal behaviour constitutes a viable field of scientific discourse. . . .[R]epeated attempts to show that offenders as a class can be sharply distinguished from the law-abiding in respect to intelligence, emotionality, extraversion, physique, and social origin have generally met with little success. . .[W]hat is and what is not criminal is defined by the laws of the state presently in force; consequently the meaning of the categories 'criminal' and 'crime' varies substantially between one society and another (p. 67).

So it is clear, that it is not a recent discovery of radical scholarship that no behavior or personality can be shown to be universally labeled deviant or criminal and that the labels of crime and deviance are irredeemably suffused with social ideology. More orthodox scholars have nevertheless persisted in studying deviant or criminal behavior separate from their definitive ideological concepts and political practices of application. One can only conclude that this apparently perverse persistence has political, ideological and maybe even financial roots. On the other hand, the hallmark of radical intellectual work in sociology has been its constant drive to demystify the categories of crime and deviance (see Sumner, 1981a).

As early as 1943, C. Wright Mills argued that what was defined in the literature

of social science as "deviant," "maladjusted" or "pathological" behavior, or
as a "social problem," was very much a product of the ideology of the definers.
Their definitions were constituted by the yardstick of their own ideals and norms,
which were usually those of "independent middle-class persons verbally living
out Protestant ideals in the small towns of America" (Mills, 1943:180). In effect,
he concluded that their definitions of social pathology actually amounted to
"propaganda" for their own distinctive, sectional morality. Edwin Lemert formulated the early position with some clarity:

> Generally speaking, these late nineteenth and early twentieth century sociologists grouped
> together under the heading of 'social pathology' those human actions which ran counter to
> ideals of residential stability, property ownership, sobriety, thrift, habituation to work, small
> business enterprises, sexual discretion, family solidarity, neighbourliness and discipline of
> the will. In effect, social problems were considered to be any forms of behavior violating
> the mores from which these ideals were projected (1951:1).

Since Lemert wrote that, however, many sociologists of deviance have persisted
in studying the exotic "subcultures" of "delinquents," "nuts, sluts and perverts" (to use Liazos's phrase) to find out, essentially, what is so nutty, slutty
or perverted about these people as if they (and their behaviors) are quite different
from the rest of the human race (see Liazos, 1972). On the other hand, many
other sociologists have turned their attention to the labels themselves and have
shown that they are best understood as moral or political categories representing
specific moral or political interests (e.g., Becker, 1963; Chambliss, 1964; Gusfield, 1967). This work, commonly known as that of the "labeling theorists"
(a misleading and imprecise label itself) has frequently been criticized for its
liberal, pluralist perspective which is limited to attributing the origin of the moral
categories to interest groups active on the political scene. Such a limit, it is
argued, results in superficial analysis of symbolic political infighting for legislation, or of merely stated moral beliefs, and a neglect of the more fundamental
social structures and institutions of our age. This criticism is more or less true;
however, it is equally problematic that the "labeling theorists" never specified
in detail the ideological constitution of the moral and criminal categories. In
consequence, the links between these categories and the social structure were
never fully explored; the relationships between moral/legal condemnation and
"interest" were only dealt with in an instrumentalist way. That is, the advantage
of a moral or legal campaign to its immediate protagonists were observed, but
little more than that.

The rise of radical approaches (conflict theory, Marxism and anarchism) to
crime and deviance in the late 1960s, and their continued growth in the 1970s,
did lead to a more profound analysis of criminal law which linked the interests
and ideologies of legislative groups to the basic structures of economy and
politics. Often using historical research, such scholars draw attention to the
constancy and armory of established political power and to its roots in economic

exploitation (see, e.g., Chambliss, 1974; Thompson, 1975; Quinney, 1977). However, this work has focused on criminal law and, like pluralist analysis, has tended to emphasize its material and instrumental functions. Work has been done on the mass-media portrayal of deviance (see Cohen and Young, 1973; Glasgow Media Group, 1976; Hall et al., 1978), but this also has not involved a formal reconceptualization of deviance. The moral roots of the criminal law in ideological categories (stereotypes) of deviance, and the concepts for grasping this, have been relatively neglected. Power and general economic functions have been at the fore; not surprisingly, since these are the areas that radical critics of "labeling theory" felt were neglected (see Gouldner, 1968; Liazos, 1972; Taylor et al., 1973; and Thio, 1973, for clear expressions of this).

In consequence, a common position emerged which is well defined in an important paper by Chambliss:

> The criminal law is...first and foremost a reflection of the interests and ideologies of the governing class.... [T]hose who control the economic and political resources of the society will inevitably see their interests and ideologies more often represented in the law than will others.... Nothing is inherently criminal, it is only the response that makes it so. If we are to explain crime, we must first explain the social forces that cause some acts to be defined as criminal while other acts are not (1974:37,38,39).

The danger in this view is that it has a tendency to reduce the origins of criminal law to class conflicts over material resources and to gloss the ideological character and composition of such laws: the origins and prehistory of the ideological categories in the law rarely get a look-in. Of course, it is vital that studies such as those of Thompson (1975) and Shivji (1982) should be done—to indicate the role of the criminal law as a crucial instrument of class power in the development of an economic system. But, logically, we also need to understand fully the forms of consciousness (or ideologies) which lie at the back of apparently general, universalistically expressed legislation in order to comprehend its precise social purposes and functions. Forms of thought, too, are powerful forces in human history. I reject Haberman's view (see, e.g, 1979) that law and morality are now at such a distance, because of the expediency and technological rationality of legislators in advanced capitalist states in crisis, that moral ideology is not a key component of modern law. Even legislators in such states attempt to formulate their interest according to ideas which have potential for gaining common assent—when they bother to use the law at all. It therefore cannot be precise enought to say that "it is the existence of structurally induced conflicts between groups in the society that determines the form and the content of the criminal law" (Chambliss, 1974:8). Such a formulation does not make clear the role of ideology in determining the content of the criminal law. Structure, interest and consciousness are rolled together to produce an all-too-neat picture: the relative autonomy of each of these aspects and their uneven interrelations are not brought out. The radical criminologists of the early 1970s, I suggest (see also Spitzer,

1980), tended to read off criminal law from the social structure as a fairly direct expression in political consciousness of a monolithic "dominant economic class interest" (with the notable exception of Carson's work; see, e.g., 1974, 1979, 1982).

This failure to take account of the distinctive and relatively autonomous dialectics of politics and ideology often left radical criminological analysis of law with an economistic and instrumentalist character (see, for example, Taylor et al., 1975; Quinney, 1977; Reiman, 1979). Such weakness was unfortunately repeated and compounded when we switch from criminal law to the more neglected area of deviance. Some writers romanticized deviation as generally political activity and thus turned the clock back by reaffirming that deviants were different kinds of people (for example, Taylor et al., 1973; see the critique in Sumner, 1976). Very few attempted to reformulate the concept of deviance in alternative theoretical terms-the tendency being to say "Deviance, yeah, right on" (see Pearson, 1975, for an excellent commentary on radical criminology and the cultural revolt of the late 1960s). Even recent perceptive Marxist commentaries present no clear alternative (see Werkentin et al., 1974; Greenberg, 1981).

The one outstanding attempt to retheorize deviance, by Spitzer (1975), unfortunately suffers much from this tendency to economism. For Spitzer, the "problematic quality" of deviant groups "ultimately" resides in their challenge to "class rule" (1975:640). "Problem populations" are said to present a threat or cost to capitalist relations of production, although he does include within this category people who challenge socialization practices and revered "forms of social organization." Such a formulation reduces problems of deviance to threats to the relations of production. A better formulation, I shall argue, is that violations of political and cultural rules can be socially censured as well as violations of economic rules. More importantly, Spitzer does not attempt to rethink the meaning of the concept of deviance, being happy to continue the view held by some interactionists that it refers to a status. This is not a tenable position, in my view, in that it conceals the fact that different censures have different implications for social status and that only the most severe censures automatically and totally reconstruct the recipient's social status. The very conception of deviance as status presupposes the importance of deviance for social status and, in effect, takes a consequence of deviance as its essence.

However, Spitzer does recognize that these deviant statuses are "social categories" and that:

Most fundamentally, deviance production involves the development of and changes in deviant categories and images. A critical theory must examine where these images and definitions came from, what they reflect about the structure of and priorities in specific class societies, and how they are related to class conflict (1975:640).

This is precisely the direction I wanted to follow—without reducing the origins of social censures to class relations. Relations of race and gender (for example) are indeed often coordinated with class relations but are not reducible to them.

III. SOCIAL CENSURES

The conception of social censures is simple. Years of research in sociology and criminology have shown that the categories of the criminal law and common morality are hopelessly inadequate as empirical descriptions of specific social behaviors. Whether we take their discursive definitions or their practical definitions in the course of law enforcement or moral stigmatization, it is clear that the definitions of deviant behavior exclude what should be included, include what should be excluded, and generally fail to attain an unambiguous, consistent and settled social meaning. This is apart from massive cross-cultural difference in the meaning and existence of categories of deviance, and apart from the frequent instances of resistance to or reinterpretation of labels. Therefore, these categories cannot be treated as observational terms with unproblematic, empirical reference. As Thompson said, they are moral categories which, if relied upon as descriptive, will automatically undermine scientific enquiry (1975:193-94; see also Sumner, 1981a). In the words of Hall et al.:

'crime' is differently *defined* (in both official and lay ideologies) at different periods; and this reflects, not only changing attitudes amongst different sectors of the population to crime, as well as real historical changes in the social organisation of criminal activity, but also the shifting *application* of the category itself, by the governing classes, to different groups and activities in the course of—and sometimes for the purpose of preparing the ground for—the exercise of legal restraint and political control (1978:189; emphasis in original).

Given the impossiblity of using the social categories of crime and deviance as scientific categories with a definable, constant and consistent behavioral references, it makes most sense to treat them as elements of highly contextualized moral and political discourses, that is, as *negative ideological categories with specific historical, material applications*. These negative categories of moral ideology are *censures* [for a fuller technical definition of ideology see Sumner (1976, 1979), where ideologies are clearly located as reflections of social relations and not simply group interest; see also the critique of the interactionists' conception of labels in Werkentin et al. (1974).]

Censures are used for a variety of purposes and in a variety of contexts. Their meaning is usually fairly flexible. They are "practical" not scientific (see also Becker, 1963). Their general function is to denounce and control, not to explain. Their typical consequence is not an adequate account of a social conflict but rather the distinguishing of "offenders" from "nonoffenders." They mark off the deviant, the pathological, the dangerous and the criminal from the normal and the good. As such, they are clearly moral and political in character. Since they delineate worth and correctness, they simultaneously form a legitimation or justification for repressive action against the offender and for attempts to educate the recipient into the desired habits and way of life. Their appeal to general moral principles gives them inherent political potential for mobilizing the forces of law and order and moral purity against labeled offenders. Nuts, sluts, perverts, prostitutes, slags, psychopaths, villians, freaks, wreckers, troublemakers, mindless militants, muggers, rioters, squatters and scroungers are all censures with such potential. The capacity of such censures for producing in-justice or oppression is always present, since they are self-legitimating expressions of a desire to suppress.

In societies which are substantially divided by class in terms of wealth, power and ideology, it is inevitable that the class which dominates the economy, owns the means of mass communication and controls the reins of political power will find its censures preeminent in the legal and moral discourses of our society. But this will also be true of the dominant gender and the dominant race. Enunciated in the mass media, often enforced in the courts and other policing institutions, and materially rooted in the dominant social relations of the epoch, such censures must soon take on a more generalized character as other people internalize them. And if the subordinate groups do not "learn," we can expect the dominant agencies of control to destroy, colonize or police their cultures until resistance is weakened. Their ideological or cultural struggle is a real and very concrete process.

It is vitally important to realize that, as ideological categories, moral/legal censures are not behavioral categories and therefore cannot be used descriptively in a scientific way. However, it is also very important to recognize that all censures contain two elements which constitute their *plausibility* and *legitimacy*:

1.   They do relate to real people, and real social relations, albeit superficially, selectively and partially.
2.   They do contain a reliance on the widely accepted general moral principles of an epoch, e.g., condemning violence, exploitation, and idleness, albeit in a superficial, selective and partial way.

In other words, these complex ideological formations we are calling censures are not *just* labels; the word *label* implies no real reference point or justifiability. They are loaded with implied interpretations of real phenomena, models of human nature, and the weight of political self-interest. Thus conceived they cannot be fully understood without reference to (a) the ideological discourse and social relations which support and constitute them; (b) the phenomena they interpret and classify; and (c) the historical conjucture within which they are applied.

The concept of social censures thus defined breaks from the interactionists' tendency to dislocate deviant labels from the wider social structure while retaining their sense of the importance of specific agencies ("moral entrepreneurs") in mobilizing particular campaigns. This break is primarily achieved through the modern Marxist *theory of ideology* which sees dominant social ideologies as reflections of dominant social relations as experienced by dominant social groups standing in conflict with their subordinate opposition. This is decisive: what was conceived of as deviance can only be progressively retheorized through the developed Marxist theory of ideology. Such a movement also takes the argument beyond instrumentalist (conflict theory or Marxist) approaches, because the modern Marxist analysis of ideology posits many qualifications to the orthodoxy of economism and class reductionism, as well to the concept of ideology itself (see Hall et al., 1978; Laclau, 1977; Johnson, 1979; and Sumner, 1979:10-56, 207-38, 286-97). While it tries to avoid lapsing into "culturalism" (see Johnson, 1979), this analysis insists that the state is a site of considerable struggle; that capitalist social relations can involve complex overlaps of and divisions between class, race, gender, age and nationality; that ideologies (as reflections of these social relations) can thus be extremely complex forms; that in advanced capitalism the high development of the industries and institutions of ideological practice can institutionalize ideologies to the point where they become major, relatively autonomous forces of social development; and, finally, that all formulations about the contemporary role of dominant ideology should be historically specific. And in terms of the concept of ideology itself, broadly speaking (again), the analysis holds that, on the negative side, it is not to be equated necessarily with the false, the bourgeois, the political, the systematic or the economic reflex, but rather that, on the positive side, it can be enlightening, revolutionary, practical and sustained in sites of oppositional culture. In short, while the dominant symbols of an epoch will still stand for its fundamental structural features and will mobilize support for them, the modern analysis of ideology recognizes that most symbols or signs can be mobilized in many ways and that most aspects of social life have acquired surplus significance, becoming emblems of one political discourse or another. What makes this a distinctively Marxist position is the retention of the insistence that the dialectics of social ideologies remain dominated by the dynamics of class formation, struggle, alliance and demise which reflect the development of the dominant mode of production.

It follows from this theory of ideology that the content of specific ideological formations finds its unity in the target of the ideological discourse which is employing them: a thesis drawn from Laclau's broader formulations (1977:92-111). The targeted character of ideological discourses brings together various symbolic components into an ideological formation, despite their occasional inconsistency and varied historical origin and use. Social censures, as negative ideological formations, are thus highly targeted despite the frequent universality or indeterminateness of their form. In Marxist theory, then, these censures can be explained and characterized by their location in the ideological discourses involved in and generated by the historical struggles between classes, genders, nations etc. Therefore, in research, our starting point must be to unearth the social relations material to the genesis of the conflicts of interest and mores which are the cradle of the censorious ideological discourses.

The theory of ideology adopted above does not of course subsume form under content. The form of the social censure has its own distinctive historical character. At this stage my thoughts are tentative, but I would suggest that the general form of censures as moral categories is not to be taken for granted but seen as a result of the historical divergence of class (and other social group) moralities and the development of dominant group agencies whose task it is to engage in moral and political surveillance of the subordinate orders. The emergence of moral categories from mere social process and then the increase in the number of categories seem to be milestones in the development of social differentiation accentuated by the specific, contradictory character of modern capitalist hegemony which works to collectivize and integrate under its aegis through the mechanisms of individualization, classification, marginalization and stratification.

IV. SOME EXAMPLES

Maggie Sumner's research (1980) on the censure of prostitution in Victorian England provides a good illustration of the value and character of the concept of censure. Her analysis demonstrates that prostitution refers to what women defined as prostitutes represent, rather than to a specific social practice. These women were observed and dealt with as signs—of various awful social possibilities concerning work, public order and sexuality. Various texts by doctors, priests and legislators reveal that the Victorian middle class had nothing like a precise definition of prostitution. Their writings refer to delivering herself up "to a life of impurity and licentiousness," being "indiscriminate in the selection of her lovers," "using his person other than for procreation," "Illicit intercourse" (meaning "the voluntary surrender of her virture"), existing professionally "by the fruits of her lewd conduct," and being "a kept woman" (see M. Sumner, 1980:Ch.3). Whatever it was exactly, prostitution as far as the police were concerned was a way of earning a living: in the practice of enforcing the censure, clandestines (part-timers) did not count (ibid., pp. 117-18). The clearest definition came from one Mr. Thomas, secretary of the London Female Preventive and Reformatory Institution, who submitted to the 1871 Royal Commission on the Administration and Operation of the Contagious Deseases Act that "prostitution is prostitution."

The kind of woman referred to as a prostitute is characterized by Lord Acion:

> What is a prostitute? She is a woman who gives for money that which she ought to give only for love, who ministers to passion and lust alone, to the exclusion and extinction of all the higher qualities derived from the intercourse of the sexes. She is a woman with half the

woman gone, and that half containing all that elevates her nature, leaving her a mere instrument of impurity (Acion, quoted in M. Sumner 1980:129).

This "sad burlesque of a woman" (prostitutes are nearly always defined as female) was usually identified or sterotyped in middle-class discourse (i.e., *targeted*, in the sense defined above) as follows: She was working class, either a laborer's daughter or a servant, and had distinct "mannerisms." Her appearance was shameless, being dirty and dressed in scruffy, tawdry garments. She cursed, was ignorant of religion, drank heavily and was frequently seen in public houses or in the streets of poor districts. She was a bad parent, lacked maternal instincts and was often infertile. And, of course she was a nymphomaniac, tending to abort during her third month of pregnancy and having a completely different menstrual cycle to other women. Prostitution was what she represented. She was the living symbol: the material proof and target of the ideological censure of prostitution. And, as David Matza might put it, she was fruitfully employed as the symbolic opposite of Leviathan's collective representation of bourgeois-Protestant sexuality.

Maggie Sumner concluded that:

> The examination of the nineteenth century material. . .makes it abundantly clear that 'prostitution' is not just a simple observational category referring to the sale of sexuality: such a sale is only prostitution when it is conducted publicly in the streets, when vendors actively seek purchasers with whom they may have no other relationship, are dressed in particular types of clothing, have no other jobs, and so forth (1980:277-78).

Although the content of the censure was clearly in part mythical, it also clearly contains references to many real aspects of working-class culture (compare Friedrich Engel's 1844 decription of English workers). However, equally plainly, this was no neutral moral symbol free of class prejudice or gender stereotypes. Nor was it free of political interest. It was a censure that reflected the desire and the need to keep "public order" in the urban areas, that is, to control and prevent the emergence of working-class resistance to the developing bourgeois society. Maggie Sumner argues that the censure (and the interests behind it) is expressed at the intersection of three Victorian discourses. The prostitute was represented as (1) a fallen woman, (2) a fallen worker and (3) a dangerous citizen. She offended the ideal image of bourgeois womanhood, the ideology of the industrious worker, and the ideal of the law-abiding, privatized, subordinate citizen. As such, she offended three ideological conceptions which were direct and active reflections of the dominant social relations of British capitalism during a particular phase of industrialization:

> These complex, composite cultural forms, containing the ideology of the dominant classes and a selective sprinkling of reality, continue to block clear-headed enquiry.... The first step of any intellectually rigorous enquiry into matters of crime and deviance must be to suspend a commonsensical acceptance of these categories and to investigate the social relationships,

ideologies and contexts which combine to form them and give specific historical meaning
(Sumner, 1981a:279).

The ideological character of censures is nowhere clearer than in the history
of colonialism. Today, Zimbabwe's landless poor try to reclaim their land often
by simply repossessing it, only to find white settler farmers denouncing them
as squatters and calling for the enforcement of the law. Of course, as many have
pointed out, in fact the white farmers are the squatters. Similarly, the violence
of military conquests could be legitimized as part of the "civilizing mission"
while the violence of nationalist revolt was, and is, denounced as "terrorism."
Refusal to leave the land to move from subsistence farming to wage labor in the
colonists' mines and plantations was met with the violence of a militaristic police
and the persuasiveness of penal tax legislation (see Van Onselen, 1976; Fitzpatrick, 1980; Shivji, 1982). Once converted to the horrors of wage slavery in
brutal, unhygienic and ill-paid working conditions, workers often did not work
well—only to find themselves heavily censured as loafers and deserters (Shivji,
1982). Traditional mores suffered no better than the economy supporting them:
in the drive to capitalist agriculture, indigenous farmers found their supporting
land tenure practices and agricultural techniques censured as criminal offenses
against the Western colonial ideology of appropriate agriculture (see Sweet,
1982). And when the local people resisted the colonists through secret societies,
cults, syncretic religions, trade unions and nationalist movements they were
further censured and suppressed, often in the name of Western religion and
ethnic superiority.

Colonial censures may be stark examples, but their parallels in our own history
are not hard to find. Besides, the complex ideological masking of contemporary
Western capitalism is a facade which frequently slips. What the colonial episodes
reveal with clarity are the sectional and often amoral character of moral censures,
and their class connections with the practical dynamics of economic life. They
compel us to begin the political economy of morality.

Similar tales from close to home are not difficult to find. Corrigan's recent
study (1979) showed that, in a period of high unemployment, schoolteachers'
censures of pupils as lazy, slow or rebellious look strikingly ideological, in the
service of keeping order in the school and appropriately filtering and certificating
the future labor force, when the school is seen as most working-class pupils see
it, as an alien, oppressive culture compelling them to do many useless subjects
for no obvious purpose. *Policing the Crisis* (by Hall et al., 1978) suggests that
the press and police censure of "the mugging wave" looks highly ideological
in the light of the lack of evidence for it, the variety of acts brought under the
label, and the continual police pressure on blacks from poor areas. Finally, *Bad
News* (Glasgow Media Group, 1976) documents the way the intensive censure
of industrial "militancy" is constructed by television news out of evidence which
could indicate that the real militancy is that of industrialists and government in

adopting policies of severe wage restraint, masked of course in ideology as "the social contract."

V. CONCLUSION

> Delinquency, with the secret agents that it procures, but also with the generalized policing that it authorizes, constitutes a means of perpetual surveillance of the population: an apparatus that makes it possible to supervise, through the delinquents themselves, the whole social field. Delinquency functions as a political observatory.... This production of delinquency and its investment by the penal apparatus must be taken for what they are; not results acquired once and for all, but tactics that shift according to how closely they reach their target (Foucault, 1977:271, 285).

Social censures combine with forms of power and economy to provide the distinct features of specific practices of domination and "social control." These ideologies help to explain and to mystify the routine targeting of the practices of surveillance and control: explain, because their surrounding discourse tells us something about the specific complaint; and mystify, because censures are often expressed in universalistic language which appeals to general moral principles. Targeted law enforcement practices have been described by interactionists and ethnomethodologists, but their theoretical approach left them as unexplained biases: it presented them as merely incidental or organizational. Such accounts never came to terms with the fact that these prejudices and targets are lodged in broader ideological formations/discourses related to dominant interests and prevalent social structures.

The concept of social censure registers several key features of modern practices of social control; their political character; their reliance on fixed categories; and their formal, bureaucratic character. It also clearly conveys the sense of control from above—unlike "deviance," which implies abnormal individual psychology and action. "Deviance" is in itself a concept silent on the political activity involved in control. It suggests that a norm has been broken, but little more. As a description of a whole branch of sociology, however, it is more dangerous in suggesting that there are a set of definable behaviors in breach of a normative consensus. On the other hand, a sociology of social censures, almost by definition, throws its emphasis on the social relationships which generate opposing ideas and interests and on the political conflicts which precipitate their condensation in censure and its subsequent implementation in practices of penalty and tutelage. Thus, its immediate strategic political implications relate to the struggles for justice and rights. The critique of social censures in the short run demands protection against their arbitrary and unreasonable application, and in the long run their transformation in line with the ideas of another political force. The full recognition of the political and ideological character of "deviance" must lead to a politics of defensive *and* prefigurative rights struggles (see Sumner, 1981b), and that is precisely the direction in which Marxist criminology in contemporary Britain is going. Abandoning deviancy theory has coincided with the growth of a new classicist criminology—that of enlightened socialism.

ACKNOWLEDGMENTS

The article is a revised version of a paper called "Abandoning Deviancy Theory' given to the American Society of Criminology conference on "The Future of Criminology" in Washington, D.C., in November 1981. John Clarke, Caryn Horwitz, Steven Spitzer and Alan Hunt gave me several useful comments and much encouragement at that conference; and the enthusiasm of successive generations of students at Cambridge University has persuaded me to persist with my ideas.

REFERENCES

Becker, H.
  1963   Outsiders, New York: Free Press.
Bredemeier, H. and Stephenson, R. M.
  1970   The analysis of social systems. London: Holt Rinehart and Winston.
Carlson, W. G.
  1974   "Symbolic and instrumental dimensions of early factor legislation," In: Hood, R. (ed.)
          Crime criminology and public policy, London: Heinemann. 1974.
Carson, W. G.
  1979   "The conventionalization of early factory crime," Int. Jo. of Sociol. of Law, 7:37-60.
Carson, W. G.
  1982   The other price of Britain's oil. Oxford: Martin Robertson.
Chambliss, W. J.
  1964   "A sociological analysis of the law of vagrancy." Social Problems 12:67-77.
Chambliss, W. J.
  1974   "The state the law and the definition of behavior as criminal or delinquent." In: Glaser,
          D. (ed.), Handbook of Criminology. Chicago: Rand McNally.
Cohen, S. and Young, J. (eds.)
  1973   The manufacture of news. London: Constable.
Corrigan, P.
  1979   Schooling the smash street kinds. London: Macmillan.
Donzelot, J.
  1979   The policing of families. London: Hutchinson.
Glasgow Media Group
  1976   Bad news. London: Routlege.
Gouldner, A. W.
  1968   "The sociologist as partisan." The American Sociologist (May) 103-116.
Foucault, M.
  1977   Discipline and punish. London: Allen Lane.
Fitzpatrick, P.
  1980   Law and state in Papua New Guinea. London: Academic Press.
Greenberg, D. (ed)
  1981   Crime and capitalism. Palo Alto: Mayfield.

Gusfield, J.
 1967   "Moral passage." Social Problems, 15: 175-188.
Habermas, J.
 1971   Toward a rational society. London: Heinemann.
Habermas, J.
 1979   Communication and the evolution of society. London: Heinemann.
Hall, S., Critcher, C., Jefferson, T., Clarke, J. and Roberts, B.
 1978   Policing the crisis. London: Macmillan.
Hirst, P.Q.
 1975   "Marx and Engels on law, crime and morality." In: Taylor, I., Walton, P. and Young,
         J. (eds.), Critical criminology. London: Routledge.
Johnson, R.
 1979   "Histories of culture/theories of ideology." In: Barrett, M., Corrigan, P., Kuhn, A. and
         Wolff, J. (eds.) Ideology and cultural production. London: Croom Helm.
Laclau, E.
 1977   Politics and ideology in Marxist theory. London: New Left Books.
Lemert, E.
 1951   Social pathology. London: McGraw-Hill.
Liazos, A.
 1972   "Nuts, sluts and perverts." Social Problems, 20:103-20.
Lopez-Rey, M.
 1971   Crime. London: Routledge.
Mills, C. W.
 1943   "The professional ideology of social patholotists." American Journal of Sociology, 49
         (2):165-180.
Mushanga, T. M.
 1976   Crime and deviance. Kampala: E. Africa Lit. Bureau.
Parsons, T.
 1951   The social system. London: Routledge.
Pearson, G.
 1975   The deviant imagination. London: Macmillan.
Quinney, R.
 1977   Class, state and crime. New York: David and McKay.
Reiman, G
 1979   The rich get richer and the poor get prison. New York: Wiley.
Robertson, R. and Taylor, L.
 1973   Deviance and socio-legal control. London: Martin Robertson.
Rock, P.
 1977   Review Symposium. Brit. Jo. of Crim. 390-4.
Schapera, I.
 1972   "Some anthropological concepts of 'crime'." B.J.S., 23(4):381-394.
Sellin, T.
 1938   Culture, conflict and crime. New York: S.S.R.C.
Shivji, I.
 1982   "Semi-proletarian labour and the use of penal sanctions in the labour law of colonial
         Tanganyika (1920-38)." In: Sumner, C.S. infra.
Spitzer, S.
 1975   "Toward a Marxian theory of deviance." Social Problems, 22: 638-51.
Spitzer, S.
 1980   " 'Left-wing' criminology -an infantile disorder?." In: Inciardi, J.A. (ed.) Radical cri-
         minology. Beverly Hills: Sage.

Sumner, C.S.
    1976 "Marxism and deviancy theory." In: Wiles, P. (ed.), Sociology of crime and delinquency
          in Britain, Vol. 2: The New criminologies. London: Martin Robertson.
Sumner, C.S.
    1979 Reading ideologies. London: Academic Press.
Sumner, C.S.
    1981a "Race, crime and hegemony." Contemporary Crises, 5(3):277-91.
Sumner, C.S.
    1981b "The rule of law and civil rights in contemporary Marxist theory." Kapitalistate. 9:63-
           91.
Sumner, C.S. (ed)
    1982 Crime, justice and underdevelopment. London: Heinemann.
Sumner, M.
    1980 Prostitution and images of women: a critique of the Victorian censure of prostitution.
          Unpublished M. Sc. thesis, University College of Wales, Aberystwyth.
Sutherland, E.H. and Cressey, D.R.
    1974 Criminology. Philadelphia: Lippincott.
Sweet, L.
    1982 "Inventing crime: British colonial land policy in Tanganyika." In: Sumner, C.S. infra.
Taylor, I., Walton, P. and Young J.
    1973 The new criminology. London: Routledge.
Taylor, I., Walton, P. and Young, J. (eds)
    1975 Critical criminology. London: Routledge.
Thio, A.
    1973 "Class bias in the sociology of deviance." American Sociologist 8: 1-12.
Thompson, E.P.
    1975 Whigs and Hunters. London: Allen Lane.
Trasler, G.
    1973 "Criminal behavior." In: Eysenck, H.J. (ed) Handbook of abnormal psychology. London:
          Pitman.
Van Onselen, C.
    1976 Chibaro. London: Pluto Press.
Werkentin, F., Hofferkert, M. and Baurmann, M.
    1974 "Criminology as police science: or how old is the new criminology." Crime and social
          justice 2:24-40.

A POLITICS WITHOUT A STATE:
THE CONCEPTS OF "STATE" AND "SOCIAL CONTROL" FROM EUROPEAN TO AMERICAN SOCIAL SCIENCE

Dario Melossi

General, your tank is a powerful vehicle.
It smashes down forests and crushes a hundred men.
But it has one defect:
It needs a driver.

General, your bomber is powerful.
It flies faster than a storm and carries more than an elephant.
But it has one defect:
It needs a mechanic.

General, man is very useful.
He can fly and he can kill.
But he has one defect:
He can think.

—Brecht (1938:289)

Research in Law, Deviance and Social Control, Volume 5, pages 205-222
Copyright © 1983 by JAI Press, Inc.
All rights of reproduction in any form reserved
ISBN: 0-89232-334-5

"State" and "social control" are words which are widely used in the present language of everyday life and in the "scientific" language of the social sciences. Yet, in both cases their semantic area is so broad and so poorly defined that they end up playing a role of catchword phrases, used to any end. Such vagueness, in fact, is instrumental in allowing the speakers to play the most varied ideological games with these words. I think it is important to show that both concepts of "state" and "social control" are related to that highly sensitive area of social reality which is represented by the question of social and ethical cohesion. The problem of their definition is not merely nominalistic but concerns central issues in the continuous struggle for the construction and deconstruction of meanings which takes place in the political and cultural spheres of social activity.

The analysis which follows is preliminary to a larger study which seeks to verify two central hypotheses. The first is that the principle of social and ethical cohesion shifted, in the transition of social science from nineteenth century Europe to twentieth century America, from a concept in which it was seen as embodied in "the state" to one in which it was seen as an outcome of processes of "social control." The second hypothesis is that such a change can be explained only in the context of a broader social change which deeply affected the cultural, political and economic representations of reality from one situation to the next.

The prevailing contemporary concept of the state arose with the development of political thought between the seventeenth and the nineteenth century. The theory of sovereignty in the absolute monarchies, the theory of English liberalism and the theory of German idealism stand at the roots of intellectual discourse about the state, for the outcome of the political revolutions in this period shaped the legal and administrative character of what we still define as states. Much of the current debate about what the state is or ought to be seems to reflect an oscillation between the laissez-faire theory of liberalism and the "ethical" theory of Hegel.

According to Adam Smith's theory of the "Invisible Hand" (1776) there is no need for "outside" intervention into the workings of civil society because the latter is well equipped to function smoothly by itself. There is no Hobbesian problem of order because the apparent anarchy of conflict produces the best of the possible worlds. The only function of the state should be that of guaranteeing the self-development of civil society. But Smith's civil society was a society of merchants and manufacturers. It existed, if at all, only during a very short, ephemeral—perhaps only ideal-typical—situation in history when the new-born capitalist society had defeated the ancien régime and not yet confronted the rise of its own offspring, the proletariat. Viewed less ideally than it was conceived by Smith, this civil society had to fight the remnants of the old equilibrium of power: the Church, the aristocracy, the complex system of guilds and state monopolies in the economy of Absolutism. It also had to fight the outcome of the capitalist transformations: impoverished peasants turned into vagabonds, handcraftsmen refusing to work as daily labor, the resulting urban mobs, and other niceties of the industrial revolution. The state became necessary for management of this lack of unity, this anarchy, these conflicts which increasingly seemed unresolvable.

If during the Englightenment, then, the state was seen as a hostile force— outside the civil society and disruptive of it—which was to be negated by the full development of social interaction among individuals, this was not the case at the beginning of the new century. At first, the development of the state was paradoxically inherent in the antistatist concept of liberalism. This because the description of society as an association of free, rational producers who exchange the products of their labor and of their capital as each pursues his own maximum utility—and thus pursues the maximum utility of society according to the principle of the Invisible Hand—is, in fact, a *normative* description. That is, it is a description which, if it is to be accurate, must be imposed upon reality. The main agent of this imposition is the state. First in Europe, then in North America, political power was captured by groups representing or anyway sensitive to the capitalist "bourgeois" perspective. The "role of the state" in this period (which, as already noted, was perhaps more an "ideal-typical" than a "real" period) was that of freeing capitalist development from the "resistances" to development of "the factors of production." The shaping of men's bodies and minds in Bentham's *Panopticon* (1787) is one of the most straightforward examples of this very interventionist way of enforcing a laissez-faire ideology.

In Hegel's philosophy, the state responds to the necessity of overcoming the anarchy of civil society while at the same time preserving the principle of liberty which is the essence of such anarchy. This liberty is to be found in that higher sphere which is the *ethical* reality of the state (Hegel, 1821; Marcuse, 1960). As Cacciari puts it (1978), the Hegelian state tries to escape the dilemma posed by the Hobbesian and the Enlightenment solutions—it is not merely an agency for repression of freedom, and yet it is not merely an agency for guaranteeing such freedom either. How Hegel's state can accomplish these seemingly contradictory things is the mystery of both the poverty of Hegel's political philosophy and its greatness.

In classical political economy, civil society experiences the state only as *law*, i.e., only as the legal guarantor of the "natural rights" of the citizen/bourgeois. The state is nothing but a legal framework for safeguarding the workings of the Invisible Hand. The latter works according to "natural laws." It is the duty of the state to translate these "natural norms" into legal norms and then to enforce them. But between the time of Adam Smith's *Wealth of Nations* and the time of Hegel's *Philosophy of Right*, there lies the French political and social revolution and the English Industrial Revolution. In this critical period in European history and culture, law no longer was merely to reflect the workings of the market. It was to express the freedom of civil society and yet, at the same time, to overcome the contradictions which divided the latter. To achieve these goals, law was not to be a sheer expression of civil society. It was to be an expression of a higher ethical entity: the state.

To Hegel "the mystery of the state is the logic of *Aufhebung*" (Cacciari, 1978:17; my translation). Cacciari unveils this mystery by noting that either the civil society will function in an organicist manner, able to self-contain its own contradictions (as in the classical political economy model) or else the state, an entity different from the civil society and yet springing from within it, will "overcome and preserve" (*Aufheben*) these contradictions. In other words, either the state is an entity which is the outcome of the *Aufhebung* process, or the state is not, and if it is not, then it has no reality, because it can do nothing but stay within the contradictions of civil society (but this is not what the state, according to Hegel, by definition is). My suggestion is that Hegel was then defining, in his *Philosophy of Right*, a lasting concept of the state, of which our contemporary usage is still informed: the state was (and is) a specific, historically determined, way of responding to the problem of social cohesion and unity. Its "life and death" was to be the life and death of such response.

According to Hegel's *Philosophy of Right* the "ethical roots" of the state are to be found in marriage and in "the corporation" (the ancient guild). But marriage and corporations, as institutions, imply a "reduction" of the richness of those "natural" realities that they are supposed to overcome-and-preserve by *Aufhebung*—love and the "system of needs" of civil society. The contradiction between Goethe's *Wahlverwandschaften* and the institution of the family, just as that between creation of "an excess of wealth" and a corresponding "penurious rabble" (Hegel,1821:paragraph 245), cannot be rationally resolved by a superior reality—the state. The legal recognition that the state confers upon marriage, the family and the corporation must exclude those contradictions. What is missing from the ethical unity represented by Hegel's state, then, is a world which is not defined by work and by property. According to Hegel, work is the foundation for the acquisition and transformation of objects, and the foundation for individual property rights. Private property is the realization of the subect's free will. It is the cornerstone of the subject's autonomy and independence. But this is a characterization only of those adult men who have the property of their skills, thus making them eligible for membership in corporations. Women do not possess the acquisitive will and their natural place is the family (1821:paragraph 166). The out-of-work "rabble" is to be "policed" (paragraphs 244, 245). Those day laborers who do not have the property of a skill and who cannot then be admitted to a corporation are also to be policed (paragraph 252). The legal and political sytem which is sanctioned by the state thus has its roots in the institution of property. The full realization of "the will" corresponds to a full titolarity of legal and political rights.

The argument that propertyless persons do not have a will "of their own" and that they therefore must be excluded from the suffrage was quite common in Hegel's times. Blackstone (1765:165) wrote, "these people are in so mean a situation that they are esteemed to have no will of their own.'' As long as this ''lack of will'' could be considered an empirical fact, the idea of the state as an institution which overcomes and preserves the ''anarchy'' of civil society into a superior sphere of ethical unity could maintain some credibility. Hegel's state is this unity. But a conception of such a unity is possible only if that substantial part of empirical society which is not defined by work/property is ignored. The history following Hegel's great construction, as well as the history of the constitutional monarchies of his time, is a history of how people without work and without property first discovered and then expressed their ''will'' by organizing, and of how this organizing prompted the extension of the political system in the direction of democracy, i.e., toward an effort to represent them and their needs ''at the level of the state.'' In this development, the unity which was coherently conceived in Hegel's system was lost. Democracy can only be the image of civil society reflected in the political system. Its nature is conflict, not unity. It is, then, the very negation of ''the state.''

Marx's essay *On the Jewish Question* (1844) makes this point clear. According to his exposition, the democratic state brings the oppositon of man/bourgeois and citizen to perfection. Marx here shares with Hegel the idea that the development of freedom leads to a ''a state'' where the contradictions of the civil society will be overcome. But for Hegel this state is the ''political state,'' while for Marx it is ''communism.'' To Marx, the opposition of the state to civil society is the opposition of the citizen to the bourgeois. The more perfect the democratic form [as ''in certain states of North America,'' compared to Hegel's Prussian state (Marx, 1843:297)], the sharper the distinction between the egoism of the bourgeois within civil society and the ''abstract communality'' of the citizen. Why was this communality considered abstract by Marx? Because he saw the chains of slavery as social and economic. The ''political state'' emancipated itself from political slavery (as in feudalism) but at the same time set free the most powerful forces of social and economic domination. Only when these forces are eliminated, he maintained, will a real state of freedom be reached. The new reign of freedom will coincide with suppression of *both* the civil society and the political state as such. The root of the anarchy in civil society, and hence of the state, is the institution of private property. As it is abolished, the need for two separate concepts of civil society and the state will be abolished too.

From these fundamentals, Marx went on to deduce the extinction of the state, as communism developed. The state, he said, is needed by the civil society only because of the internal conflicts within it. But these conflicts are rooted in the institution of private property, or, more precisely, the institution of private property is the state's legal sanctioning of the anarchy de facto ruling within the civil society. Abolition of this anarchy, abolition of the institution of private property and abolition of the state are one and the same thing. From this point onward in history, Hegel's state, as any ''bourgeois state,'' was to be regarded, in the Marxist tradition of political thought, as something which claims to be what it is not—a "board of directors" of the bourgeoisie hidden under the sheepskin of a "general will" or of a "superior ethical reality." But the core of Hegel's teaching lives on in the struggle of the proletariat, in that image of abolishing private property and developing "the state" which will be "communism," and in the idea that Hegel's state will be incarnated as the withering away of any state.

After Marx's (and the organized proletariat's) criticism of Hegel's concept of the state, does the term retain any meaning? Marx showed that, if the "ethical" and "free" character of the state was to manifest itself, the state would have to annihilate those contradictions in civil society that Hegel's philosophy had been unable to really "overcome," i.e., the world "outside" private property. But such an annihiliation would make the very reason of existence of Hegel's concept of the state purposeless. The state would no longer be an entity for "overcoming and preserving" the contradictions in civil society because these contradictions would have been eliminated. For Marx, then, it must be recognized that the state, as such, has no ethical, transcendent character. But in such a character resided, according to Hegel, the very nature of the state.

As has been noted (Zeitlin, 1968), much of the early European sociological theories constituted an attempt at "responding" to Marx's critique of the existing state of affairs. After Marx's critique of Hegel's concept of the ethical state, it became impossible to conceive the state as a medium for social cohesion. At the same time, the rise of organized conflict among the classes unveiled (to use Marx's expression) "the state" of the late nineteenth century as a partisan instrument of the interests of the ruling class. On the other hand, if one rejected Marx's analysis, the search for other foundations of social cohesion became necessary. Two directions seemed to be open. One toward the idea of a collective and superindividual ethical feeling which held the social fabric together, even if such feeling was often conceived, for instance in Toennies' and Durkheim's theories, as being deeply shaken by the rise of industrialism. A second direction substantially accepted Marx's diagnosis of capitalism as a social form ridden with inequalities and harsh class conflicts but drew different consequences from such analysis. This was the position held by Max Weber and Hans Kelsen.

In twelve famous pages of his *General Theory of Law and State* (1946:181-92), Kelsen tried to demonstrate that "there is no sociological concept of the State different from the concept of the legal order; and that means, that we can describe the social reality without using the term 'State' (1946;192)." The heart of the matter is for Kelsen the question of "unity":

The assertion that the State is not merely a juristic but a sociological entity, a social reality existing independently of its legal order, can be substantiated only by showing that the individuals belonging to the same State form a unity and that this unity is not constituted by the legal order but by an element which has nothing to do with law. However, such an element constituting the 'one in the many' cannot be found (1946:183).

Kelsen goes to analyze the four principal answers which have been given to this question of the unity. These have held that a unity independent of the legal order exists in "interaction," or in "organic character," or in "common will or interest," or in "domination." For all these, Kelsen notes, the concept of the state is not a resultant of the various "principles of unity" but is, on the contrary, a presupposition which is founded on the existence of a "legal order." In other words, each of the four sociological concepts of unity rely on some implicit concept of the state as legal order and therefore do not lead to a sociological definition of the state which is independent of the legal one. According to Kelsen, a sociological theory of the state which deals with the state as something different from the legal order is "an animistic interpretation," a "hypostatized personification" of the law. The state is, for such a theory, "the god of the law" (1946:191).

We speak of "the state" *as if* it were a person. But the reason why we do so is exactly what has to be explained from the standpoint of a "sociology of the state." Kelsen recalls Max Weber's "interpretive sociology"[1] and then notes that when we speak sociologically of the state we are speaking at once of a fact, the legal order, and of an interpretation of it, namely, that it is *valid*. "This interpretation is made both by the rulers and the ruled and by the sociologist himself who is studying their behavior" (Kelsen, 1946:188). Put another way, human actors "orient" their behaviors toward the legal order and call it "the state." A consequence of these Kelsen's positions is then that a sociology which strives to understand what the state is, cannot define the state independently from the legal order. The legal order is the object studied by legal theorists. The objective of sociologists, on the contrary, must be the identification of the process by which the actors abide by the legal order and call it "the state." The object and the goal of sociology of the state do not seem very different, then, from that, e.g., of a sociology of religion. It could be even described as a branch of the latter. The great political relevance of this discussion by Kelsen is apparent in a passage where his words remind us of Brecht's poem quoted at the start of this paper.

Speaking of the power of the State, one usually thinks of prisons and electric chairs, machine guns and cannons. But one should not forget that these are all dead things which become instruments of power only when used by human beings, and that human beings are generally moved to use them for a given purpose only by commands they regard as norms. The phenomenon of political power manifests itself in the fact that the norms regulating the use of these instruments becomes efficacious. 'Power' is not prisons and electric chairs, machine guns and cannons: 'power' is not any kind of substance or entity hidden behind the social order. Political power is the efficacy of the coercive order recognized as law (1946:190-91).

Rudolf Metall, Kelsen's "official" biographer, tells us that on November 30, 1921, invited by Freud, Kelsen lectured on the concept of the state and Freud's mass psychology at the Viennese Psychoanalytic Society. Not only Freud, but also Siegfried Bernfeld, Paul Federn, Otto Rank, Theodor Reik and Herbert Silberer took part in the discussion which followed Kelsen's presentation (Metall, 1969:41). Later Kelsen published in *Imago*, the journal of the Freudian group, an enlarged and revised version of that paper (Kelsen, 1922b), which was then published in English in 1924. Kelsen's interest for psychoanalysis in those years is also present in one of his major works, *Der soziologische und der juristische Staatsbegriff* (1922a; 19-33) and in another article (1922/23). The article published in *Imago* is an essay in the "sociology of the state" as defined above. That is, it does not try to answer the question: "What is the state?" Instead it addresses the question: "Where does the idea of the state as something different from the legal order come from?" For Kelsen, the latter question is the only correct one from a sociological perspective. It is not reasonable to pose the first question because, due to the fact that the term "state" does not refer to any empirical reality different from the legal order, its answer must be tautological.

Kelsen starts with a discussion of ideas about the "specific nature" of the state (1922b:1). The problem is to determine whether there is any social bond, different from citizenship, i.e., different from a legal norm, which ties individuals together in a state. Kelsen finds no such bond, and he directs a polemic against any concept of a "supraindividual" bond, as it is expressed, for instance, in the concept of *Volksgeist*: "there is a distinct tendency to declare this folk-spirit to be a psychic reality differing from the individual psyche, whereby this conception of the folk-spirit (*Volksgeist*) acquires the metaphysical character of Hegel's objective spirit" (1922b:7). Kelsen goes on to argue that a "community of feeling or will" cannot be explained by reciprocal interaction. It must be explained "by a common influence upon them from without, that is to say, by a third party" (1922b:8). This actually is a comment on Freud's work, *Group Psychology and the Analysis of the Ego* (1921), the discussion of which takes the major part of Kelsen's article. Freud's book was devoted to discussing a number of essays, published at the turn of the century, which had attempted to explain "crowd" or "group" behavior, from Sighele (1894) and Le Bon (1895) to Tarde (1890), Moede (1915), Trotter (1916) and McDougall (1920).

After criticizing these works, which relied on explanatory mechanisms such as imitation and suggestion, Freud presented a "group psychology" explanation that was informed by the fundamentals of his psychoanalytic theory. The psychic bond among the members of the group is to be explained, according to Freud, by the libidinal relation of individual members with the leader of the group. According to Freud, the leader is an image of the member's ego-ideal (ultimately shaped on a father's image). In proposing this explanation, Freud roots the bond holding society together in the individuals' own psyches, escaping the fallacy of hypostatizing some supraindividual kind of relationship (thought by Kelsen as entirely "metaphysical"). Instances of groups formed around a leader are, according to Freud, the church and the army (1921:25-31). But these are highly organized and "artificial" groups, as opposed, say, to "crowd" behavior groups, and they represent a "transitional stage" toward another kind of group, the "leaderless group" where "an idea, an abstraction, may...take the place of the leader" (Freud, 1921:32). In commenting on Freud's ideas, Kelsen denies that what Freud calls "artificial groups" are "groups" at all. According to Kelsen, they are "institutions" and are based not on a psychological bond but on a normative structure, just as in the institution of "the state" (Kelsen, 1922b:22,23). The "artificial" groups that Freud assigns to the category of "leader groups" should be regarded as "leaderless groups," i.e., as groups which are psychologically organized by a "guiding idea," an ideology. The concept of the state is one of these guiding ideas.

But this guiding idea is exactly the target of Kelsen's attacks. The methodological criticism joins with a more substantive, political one. In the conclusive pages of his essay, Kelsen notes the parallelism between Freud's theory and his own idea that "the state" is "the god of the law." The only reality of the state is in the psychological process by which the state appears as a metaphysical substance hidden "behind the law, as the 'bearer' of the law" (1922b:36a). Kelsen's position is but a specific case of a more general critique of knowledge on which many Viennese contemporaries of Kelsen were working (see Janik and Toulmin, 1973). For example, he cites Fritz Mauthner's *Sprachkritik* (1901-1903), a critical examination of our "substantivistic" way of speaking/thinking, which was influential, e.g., on the development of Ludwig Wittgenstein's thought (Janik and Toulmin, 1973:121-32). Kelsen concludes that if we free ourselves of the concept of the state, as we freed ourselves from other "pseudoconcepts" like the "soul" in psychology or "force" in physics, than there will be "a politics without a state" (1922b:36). Or, in other words, as he was writing in an almost contemporaneous essay: "This *purely legal theory* of the state, which gets rid of the idea of a state distinct from law, is a *stateless theory of the state*" (Kelsen 1922/23:81; his emphasis).

A connection is easily made between the scientific thrust of Kelsen's critique of the idea of the state and his political thrust in the direction of a theory of democracy. A theory of democracy is the companion theory, at a more substantive level, of his methodology. Kelsen was to make clear this connection in an article published a few years later, expressing it, once again, with concepts that he borrowed from Freudian circles:

Democracy, on the whole, is a soil unfavourable to the ideal of a leader, because it does not favour the principle of authority as such. And so far as the archetype of all authority is the father, since that is the original experience of authority, democracy—in Idea, that is—is a fatherless society. It seeks, so far as possible, to be a leaderless association of equals. Its principle is coordination, its most primitive form, the matriarchal fraternity-relation. And thus, in a deeper sense than was ever intended, democracy dwells under the triple star of the French Revolution: liberty, equality, fraternity (Kelsen, 1933:105-106).

We have already noted that one of the members of that inner circle which was auditing Kelsen's lecture at the Viennese Psychoanalytic Society and took part in the following discussion was Paul Federn. Two years earlier, Federn had published, in *Der Oesterreichische Volkswirt*, a study on "The Psychology of Revolution" (1919) which carries as subtitle the expression *Die vaterlose Gesellschaft* (the fatherless society). Federn applies the main conceptual instruments of psychoanalysis, especially the ones developed by Freud in his seminal *Totem and Taboo* (1913), to his analysis of the "psychology" of the revolutions which were shaking Europe at the time, especially the Soviet and the Bavarian revolutions. A state organization based, as it was in those revolutions, on the power of workers' councils, is seen by Federn as a "society of brothers," giving birth to a traumatic conflict with the deeper structures of individuals' psychology. Without much recognition of this early contribution by Federn, (although Federn is cited in Freud, 1921:30), many years later Alexander Mitscherlich (1963) will delve, at too great but very successful length, into this concept of a "society without the father." Kelsen was probably impressed with this concept of a fatherless/leaderless society, which was circulating in psychoanalytic circles after the publication of *Totem and Taboo*. But on the valuation of such a political/ social psychological hypothesis, Kelsen's path departed radically from Freud's and Federn's. For them, a process of identification with the leader was necessary for the very existence of a social fabric. For Kelsen, democracy was the negation, at least "in Idea," of such a process. The very idea of the state is then intimately connected, according to Kelsen, with an authoritarian political thought. Whereas a "politics without a state" is a politics of democracy—no matter whether a "liberal" or a "socialist" democracy (see Kelsen 1933:101).

Kelsen's powerful critique of any "theological" position in politics leaves us with a coincidence of democracy and legal order. Law is just a set of rules, according to which it is possible to play the game of democracy. It does not aim at any "ethical" or "transcendent" character but merely at the highest degree of exactness and completion. The more exact and complete is the legal system, the better will it be able to express and "give form to" the political will. But how shall this political will be formed? Or better yet: on what ground will it rest? These are important questions because the very concept of the state had played the role in Hegel's philosophy, as we have seen, of vehicle and instrument for representing social cohesion. Once the metaphysical character of the state concept was exposed and criticized—as Kelsen was able to do very effectively—one was left with the original problem. How to account for that fundamental social unity on the ground of which a legal order can be enacted and enforced? Kelsen's democratic legal order was nothing but the reflection of the strains and conflicts which run through civil society. This was particularly true at the time when Kelsen was writing the essays which have been discussed here. Two decades of harsh and continued social strife both in Europe and North America had finally culminated in World War I and in the widespread revolutionary situation of the postwar period. If "the state" was nothing more than a legal order and could not in any way express a "higher" social and ethical equilibrium, the answer to the conflicts going on within the civil society had to be looked for inside the civil society itself. This was the direction toward which American social science had begun working during the same period.

In 1930 Freud wrote:

> the danger [lies in] a state of things which might be termed 'the psychological poverty of groups.' This danger is most threatening where the bonds of society are chiefly constituted by the identification of its members with one another, while individuals of the leader type do not acquire the importance that should fall to them in the formation of a group. The present cultural state of America would give us a good opportunity for studying the damage to civilization which is thus to be feared (p. 63).

According to Freud, the psychological situation of a land of immigrants, of people, that is, who left their "fathers" behind and who hoped to find a "brotherhood" in the New World (Federn 1919:598), was a situation of "poverty" and was a danger to "civilization." Undoubtedly, what Freud had in mind was the danger for that "social bond," represented in the father-son relationship, which according to him ran through the whole hierarchy of social "groups," from the family to the state. Indeed, a situation of leaderlessness and statelessness seemed quite compatible within the American experience. At the beginning of the century, a history of political tradition which had long been hostile to notions of "unity" and "centrality' in politics joined with the rise of pragmatism in social science to radically deny citizenship to the state concept in the American political vocabulary.

The effective government of a "democracy" had been from the beginning the central preoccupation of the American political system. And in a land without previous traditions, such effectiveness of government could not rely on traditional restraints. In a "Federalist Paper" that Charles Beard (1913) commented on at length, James Madison pointed to the necessity of a "republican" and not a purely "democratic" government. An "adequate control" of "factions" could not come from "moral or religious motives" (Madison, 1787:81). It had to be a product of that constitutional engineering which was to be expressed in the formula of "balance of powers." The fears of a "factionalism" that could have damaged the "vested interests" of the nation and of a centralization that could have limited the autonomy of the individual "states" to a greater extent than was deemed necessary, all worked against the construction of a too powerful central "state." As a matter of fact, such a unitary state in North America never existed as a concept, hampered by the need for a balance between the central federal government and the individual "states" members of the federation. This

traditional antistatist attitude found a new and stronger expression in the prag-
matists' political thought at the beginning of this century, with their emphasis
on "process" and "activity" and their distaste for anything which could represent "an arrest or crystallization" in the flow of political experience (Passerin
d'Entrèves, 1967:60, discussing Bentley, 1908).

In the pragmatist "revolt against formalism" which characterized the cultural
climate of the Progressive Era (White, 1947), political science and jurisprudence
found a poweiful ally in the newborn American sociological theory. The "re-
alistic" thrust of the two disciplines caused them to look for the foundation of
social order in sociological concepts, mainly in the concept of "social control."
Following the lead of antiformalist tendencies in European thought (Ihering's
Der Zweck im Recht was particularly influential), the "legal realists" and, in
different form, Roscoe Pound, rejected the autonomy of legal experience characteristic of natural law or normativistic theories and saw the law as one of the
instruments of social control (Pound, 1942). Pound, in particular, recognized
his debt to Ross's theory of social control (Ross, 1901; see Geis, 1964:273).

At first, within the more general Social Darwinist paradigm, the concept of
social control was shaded with organicist overtones. The nostalgia for the lost
Gemeinschaft seemed to prevail. But the subsequent developments of the Progressive Era compelled American social science to break away from any longing
for "the good old days" and to try to come to grip with the ruthless reality of
a genuine form of American capitalism and industrial urban society. The *city* in
fact represented an intellectual and practical set of issues on which the questions
of ethical cohesion and social organization had to be tackled by American social
science between the Progressive Era and the New Deal. Chicago was the best
example of such questions—a summation of the urban problems of the period
and a metaphor for the larger American society. "Social control" was defined,
by the sociologists of Chicago, as "the central problem of society" (Park and
Burgess, 1921:42). In the Chicago "laboratory," the sheer size and the trans-
parent nature of a capitalist development never before experienced in such a
massive fashion compelled American social scientists to make an effort to incorporate the results of European investigations but also, at the same time, to
search for new answers. The direction of this research was defined by the lack,
vis-à-vis the analogous European attempts, of the restraints posed by the persistence of precapitalist areas in economy and culture. The programs of ration-
alization and democratization which had been upheld by the most progressive
representatives of the European middle class found its own groundings, in Chicago, in the concept of social control. The disruptive tendency of a process of
mass democratization was then balanced, both in social theory and in the social
relations developing at the time, by the recognition of the necessity for policies
of social control which were able to avoid a situation of excessive strain in social
cohesion. In order to fully appreciate these developments, it is necessary to turn
to an analysis of the author who gave us the highest theoretical expression of

the concept of social control in the pragmatist and Chicago tradition, namely, George Herbert Mead.

In a 1925 article, Mead defined social control as depending "upon the degree to which the individuals in society are able to assume the attitudes of the others who are involved with them in common endeavor" (p. 291). To him, social control and self-consciousness coincide and are built around "an adequate social object." The problem of this "social object"

> is not that of becoming acquainted with the indefinite number of acts that are involved in social behavior, but that of so overcoming the distances in space and time, and the barriers of language and convention and social status, that we can converse with ourselves in the role of those who are involved with us in the common undertaking of life. . . . The task, however, is enormous enough, for it involves not simply breaking down passive barriers such as those of distance in space and time and vernacular, but those fixed attitudes of custom and status in which our selves are embedded. Any self is a social self, but it is restricted to the group whose roles it assumes, and it will never abandon this self until it finds itself entering into the larger society and maintaining itself there (1925:292).

In order to enter into the "larger society," in order to grasp the set of "social objects" which make up a person's universe, the person must take the role of a "generalized other," in a process which takes place by means of the vocal gesture, which is to say, *language* (Mead, 1934). Social integration is not to be sought in some "superindividual" entity or in "moral education" or in a "psychic bond." Social integration is warranted by the mastering of a common language. The process of language learning and language practicing, i.e., the process of communication, is "a principle of social organization" (1934:260) which makes any types of "cooperative activity" possible: "The process of communication is one which is more universal than that of the universal religion or universal economic process in that it is one that serves them both" (1934:259).

And yet, "back even of the process of discourse must lie cooperative activity" (*ibid.*). Language thus constitutes the mediator between the "self" and the "social." As a matter of fact, it *constitutes* them both. It is the creation and the creator of communication and interaction, so only in the abstract can we distinguish between the "individual" and the "social" perspectives (pp. 253-60). As the interaction takes place wholly among the "selves" and never in a "superindividual" fashion, "the individual" is not "sacrified" in this line of reasoning. A social control is the means by which self-control and self-criticism is exercised, but "self-criticism is essentially social criticism" (p. 255). The process of change and transformation can appear only in that social form which is the universal medium of interaction—language. Innovation can never be expressed in forms which are *entirely* new because, if there is to be a meaning for the innovator, there must be an at least potential response to his or her innovation. Innovation, then, is possible only in terms of conflict/change between different "universes" of discourse.

At this juncture, Mead's theory can be read as a theory of democracy. Democracy is a form of conflict and of compromise. As Weber would have said, disenchantement with any kind of synthetical *Aufhebung* is at the base of modern democratic societies, which are dominated by clashes of organized interests. But so that society is not destroyed by these conflicts, a fundamental line of social cohesion is found in the practice of social control at the level of language. Because the "legal order" is an "arena" of conflicts, a "politics without a state" is a politics of communication and language. If Kelsen, then, had shifted our attention from the state to "politics," Mead switched it from "politics" to the world of everyday life. The social world at large, i.e., the world of everyday life, is a world of "manufactured," so to speak, meanings. The definitions of these meanings "control" social behavior (Berger and Luckmann, 1966). Here we find the "content" of the "empty form" with which Kelsen had left us. The validity of the legal order finds its limits in its being "efficacious." Law can be an effective "mechanism of social control," as defined by Pound (1942) and by Parsons (1962), only insofar as such a mechanism is grounded in a situation where it is efficacious. But such efficacy—as Kelsen and Weber have shown-depends upon the orientation of those who are the enforcers and the receivers of the legal order. They orient their action toward a representation of the legal order as valid. But this orientation depends upon the struggle which goes on at the level of the symbolic construction of reality, a struggle which is decided by the successful implementation of strategies of social control. The more a society is permeated with conflicting interests, one could add, the more a situation of social cohesion is linked to the ability of a dominant perspective to exert control over the construction of social meanings. This could indeed be a more accurate "measure" of a situation of "democracy" than the traditional one based, as in Kelsen's work, on the existence of certain legal procedures and safeguards.

After the domination of a "systematic" approach in American social science between the 1940s and 1950s which, not considering the question of social and ethical cohesion as the central question, circumscribed the issue of social control to that of preventing and repressing deviance (Gibbs, 1982), a new sensitivity emerged toward this issue in recent years, in connection with the situation of conflict and change which shook most of the advanced industrial societies between the 1960s and 1970s. The convergence of a conflictual and an interactionist perspective brought forth many researchers in sociology of deviance, sociology of law, political sociology and sociology of language to deal with some of the issues I have touched upon (see, e.g., Rock and McIntosh, 1974; Hall et al., 1978; Fowler et al., 1979; Gitlin, 1980). Yet, what is almost always overlooked is the specific connection, which I tried to discuss here, between "the disruption of the notion of the state," as Passerin d'Entrèves called it (1967:59-65), and the development in sociology of a concept of "social control." It would be a definite advance for a "sociology of the state" trying to escape the traps of ideology to take Kelsen's critique of the state concept seriously, distinguishing what in the concept is a synonym for "legal order" and what is a mere phenomenon of speakers' (and sociologists') orientation toward certain social facts as possessing some kind of "state-quality," a social phenomenon which should be investigated on its own merits. Furthermore such a perspective would help by "freeing" many social objects which are now often described in terms of their being "part of the state," or a "function of the state," and so on, in the direction of a more autonomous focus of sociological concern. Especially in a situation like our present one, where the spreading of legal regulations tends to intermingle what we usually call "state" and "society" more and more, the adoption of a more skeptical attitude toward the concept of the state would reveal itself particularly useful. Last but not least, an interrogation as to what we really mean when we talk of "the state" and the substitution in our analysis of the individuation of specific strategies of social control for the state concept would help to show the heavy ideological character of much of our present discussion on "the god of the law" (see, e.g., Green, 1981). Both in social as well as in political theory we do not need to attack or defend "the state." What we really need is to know what we mean when we utter those words.

ACKNOWLEDGMENTS

This paper has been written during a period of study and research at the Department of Sociology of the University of California at Santa Barbara. I would like to thank, for their precious substantive and editorial comments, Donald R. Cressey, Richard Flacks, Charles Moore, Craig Reinermann and John Whalen, all from that Department. I would also like to thank, for the same reasons, Enrico Pattaro, from the School of Law of the University of Bologna. The paper was presented at the Tenth World Congress of Sociology, in Mexico City, 1982, in the session on "The Comparative Study of Social Control: Problems of Theory and Method."

NOTE

1. It lies within the scope of the broader research program, but not within the scope of the present paper, to discuss Max Weber's position on these issues. Max Weber was one of the major sociological figures to whom Hans Kelsen was considered to be very close (see Kelsen, 1922a:156-70). Especially on the specific question of the "state" concept, Weber's position is hardly far from Kelsen's. See, e.g., Weber's discussion of "social collectivities" in *Economy and Society* (1956:13-18) or, more descriptively, in a letter to Robert Liefmann: "If I am now a sociologist. . . .I am so essentially in order to put an end to the use of collective concepts. . .In the sociological sense, the state is nothing but the chance of certain kinds of specific actions taking place, the actions of certain individual persons. . . .The 'subjective' element in it is that the actions are oriented according to certain presuppositions. The 'objective' element is that we—the observers—make this judgement:

the chance exists that this action, orientated to these presuppositions, will ensue. If it does not exist, neither does 'the state''' (Weber, 1920).

REFERENCES

Beard, Charles A.
    1913   An Economic Interpretation of the Constitution of the United States. New York:Macmillan.
Bentham, Jeremy
    1787   "Panopticon." The Works of Jeremy Bentham, 4. New York:Russell and Russell, 1962.
Bentley, Arthur F.
    1908   The Process of Government. Chicago:University of Chicago Press.
Berger, Peter L. and Thomas Luckmann
    1966   The Social Construction of Reality. New York:Doubleday.
Blackstone, William
    1765   Commentaries on the Laws of England. New York:Oceana, 1966.
Brecht, Bertolt
    1938   Poems 1913-1956. New York:Methuen, 1976.
Cacciari, Massimo
    1978   Dialettica e critica del Politico. Milano:Feltrinelli.
Federn, Paul
    1919   "Zur psychologie der revolution:die vaterlose gesellschaft." Der Oesterreichische Volk-
            swirt 11:571-574, 595-598.
Fowler, Roger et al.
    1979   Language and Control. London:Routledge and Kegan Paul.
Freud, Sigmund
    1930   Civilization and its Discontents. New York:W.W. Norton, 1961.
    1921   Group Psychology and the Analysis of the Ego. New York:W.W. Norton, 1959.
    1913   Totem and Taboo. New York:W.W. Norton, 1952.
Geis, Gilbert
    1964   "Sociology and sociological jurisprudence:admixture of lore and law." Kentucky Law
            Journal 52:267-293.
Gibbs, Jack P.
    1982   "Law as a means of social control." In J.P. Gibbs (ed.), Social Control. Beverly Hills:SAGE.
Gitlin, Todd
    1980   The Whole World is Watching. Berkeley:University of California Press.
Green, Philip
    1981   "In defense of the state." Democracy 1:2:6-18, 3:52-69.
Hall, Stuart, Chas Critcher, Tony Jefferson, John Clarke and Brian Roberts
    1978   Policing the Crisis. New York:Holmes and Meier.
Hegel, Georg W.F.
    1821   Philosophy of Right. London:Oxford University Press, 1967.
Janik, Allan and Stephen Toulmin
    1973   Wittgenstein's Vienna. New York:Simon and Schuster.
Kelsen, Hans
    1946   General Theory of Law and State. New York:Russell and Russell, 1961.
    1933   "State-form and world-outlook." In H. Kelsen, Essays in Legal and Moral Philosophy.
            Dordrecht-Holland:D. Reidel. 1973. Pp. 95-113.
    1922/23 "God and the state." In H. Kelsen, Essays in Legal and Moral Philosophy. Dordrecht-
            Holland:D. Reidel. 1973. Pp. 60-82.
    1922a   Der soziologische und der juristische Staatsbegriff. Tübingen:Mohr.

1922b "The conception of the state and social psychology." The International Journal of Psychoanalysis 5:1-38, 1924.
LeBon, Gustave
1895 Psychologie des foules. Paris:Alcan.
Madison, James
1787 "Tenth federalist paper." In The Federalist Papers. New York:New American Library, 1961.
Marcuse, Herbert
1960 Reason and Revolution. Boston:Beacon Press.
Marx, Karl
1844 "Zur judenfrage." In K. Marx-F. Engels Werke 1:347-377. Berlin:Dietz Verlag, 1956.
1843 "Aus der kritik der hegelschen rechtsphilosophie. Kritik des hegelschen staatsrechts (261-313)." In K. Marx-F. Engels Werke 1:201-333. Berlin:Dietz Verlag, 1956.
Mauthner, Fritz
1901-1903 Beiträge zu einer Kritik der Sprache. Stuttgart:J.G. Cotta.
McDougall, William
1920 The Group Mind. Cambridge:The University Press.
Mead, George H.
1934 Mind, Self, and Society. Chicago: The University of Chicago Press.
1925 "The genesis of the self and social control." In G.H. Mead, Selected Writings. Indianapolis:Bobbs-Merrill Inc., 1964.
Metall, Rudolf A.
1969 Hans Kelsen. Wien:Verlag Franz Deuticke.
Mitscherlich, Alexander
1963 Society without the Father. New York:Harcourt, Brace and World, Inc. 1969.
Moede, W.
1915 "Die massen- und sozialpsychologie im kritischen überblick." Zeitschrift für pädagogische Psychologie 16:385.
Park, Robert E. and Ernest W. Burgess
1921 Introduction to the Science of Sociology. Chicago:The University of Chicago Press, 1969.
Parsons, Talcott
1962 "The law and social control." In W.M. Evan (ed.), Law and Sociology. Glencoe:The Free Press.
Passerin d'Entrèves, Alessandro
1967 The Notion of the State. Oxford:Clarendon Press.
Pound, Roscoe
1942 Social Control through Law. New Haven:Yale University Press.
Rock, Paul and Mary McIntosh (Eds.)
1974 Deviance and Social Control. London:Tavistock.
Ross, E.A.
1901 Social Control. New York:Macmillan.
Sighele, Scipio
1894 La folla delinquente. Torino:Bocca.
Smith, Adam
1776 The Wealth of Nations. London:J.M. Dent, 1961.
Tarde, Gabriel de
1890 Les lois de l'imitation. Paris:Alcan.
Trotter, Wilfred
1916 Instincts of the Herd in Peace and War. London:E. Benn.
Weber, Max
1956 Economy and Society. Berkeley:University of California Press, 1968.

1920 Letter written to Robert Liefmann on March 8, 1920 and found posthumously. In Wolfgang
      J. Mommsen's discussion of "Max Weber and power-politics." In O. Stammer (ed.),
      Max Weber and Sociology Today. New York:Harper and Row, 1971:115.
White, Morton
1947 Social Thought in America. The Revolt Against Formalism. Boston:Beacon Press.
Zeitlin, Irving M.
1968 Ideology and the Development of Sociological Theory. Englewood Cliffs N.J.:Prentice-
      Hall.

Research Annuals in
SOCIOLOGY

Advances in Early Education and Day Care
Series Editor: Sally Kilmer, *Bowling Green State University*

Advances in Health Economics and Health Services Research
(Volume 1 published as *Research in Health Economics*)
Series Editor: Richard M. Scheffler, *George Washington University*. Associate Series Editor: Louis F. Rossiter, *National Center for Health Services Research*

Advances in Special Education
Series Editor: Barbara K. Keogh, *University of California, Los Angeles*

Advances in Substance Abuse
Series Editor: Nancy K. Mello, *Harvard Medical School—McLean Hospital*

Comparative Social Research
Series Editor: Richard F. Tomasson, *The University of New Mexico*

Current Perspectives in Social Theory
Series Editors: Scott G. McNall and Gary N. Howe, *University of Kansas*

Knowledge and Society: Studies in the Sociology of Culture Past and Present
(Volumes 1-2 published as *Research in the Sociology of Knowledge, Sciences and Art*)
Series Editors: Robert Alun Jones, *University of Illinois* Henrika Kuklick, *University of Pennsylvania*

Perspectives in Organizational Sociology
Series Editor: Samuel B. Bacharach, *Cornell University*

Political Power and Social Theory
Series Editor: Maurice Zeitlin, *University of California, Los Angeles*

Research in Community and Mental Health
Series Editor: Roberta G. Simmons, *University of Minnesota*

Research in Economic Anthropology
Series Editor: George Dalton, *Northwestern University*

Research in Law, Deviance and Social Control
(Volumes 1-3 published as *Research in Law and Sociology*)
Series Editors: Rita J. Simon, *University of Illinois* and Steven Spitzer, *Suffolk University—Boston*

Research in Political Economy
Series Editor: Paul Zarembka, *State University of New York, Buffalo*

Research in Race and Ethnic Relations
Series Editors: Cora B. Marrett, *University of Wisconsin*, and Cheryl Leggon, *University of Chicago*

Research in Social Movements, Conflicts and Change
Series Editor: Louis Kriesberg, *Syracuse University*

Research in Social Problems and Public Policy
Series Editor: Michael Lewis, *University of Massachusetts*

Research in Social Stratification and Mobility
Series Editors: Donald J. Treiman, *National Academy of Sciences*, and Robert V. Robinson, *Indiana University*

Research in Sociology of Education and Socialization
Series Editor: Alan C. Kerckhoff, *Duke University*

Research in the Interweave of Social Roles
Series Editor: Helena Z. Lopata, *Loyola University of Chicago*

Research in the Sociology of Health Care
Series Editor: Julius A. Roth, *University of California, Davis*

Research in the Sociology of Work
Series Editors: Ida Harper Simpson, *Duke University*, and Richard L. Simpson, *University of North Carolina, Chapel Hill*

Studies in Communications
Series Editor: Thelma McCormack, *York University*

Studies in Symbolic Interaction
Series Editor: Norman K. Denzin, *University of Illinois*

Please inquire for detailed brochure on each series.

 **JAI PRESS INC.**